Liberal White Supremacy

Liberal White Supremacy

How Progressives Silence
Racial and Class Oppression

Angie Beeman

The University of Georgia Press

ATHENS

Sociology of Race and
Ethnicity web page

© 2022 by the University of Georgia Press
Athens, Georgia 30602
www.ugapress.org
All rights reserved
Designed by Kaelin Chappell Broaddus
Set in 10.5/13.5 Garamond Premier Pro Regular
by Kaelin Chappell Broaddus

Most University of Georgia Press titles are
available from popular e-book vendors.

Printed digitally

Library of Congress Cataloging-in-Publication Data

Names: Beeman, Angie, 1977– author.
Title: Liberal white supremacy : how progressives silence
    racial and class oppression / Angie Beeman.
Description: Athens : The University of Georgia Press,
    [2022] | Series: Sociology of race and ethnicity |
    Includes bibliographical references and index.
Identifiers: LCCN 2022003524 | ISBN 9780820362274
    (hardback) | ISBN 9780820362281 (paperback)
    | ISBN 9780820362298 (ebook)
Subjects: LCSH: Liberalism—United States. | Racism—
    United States. | Progressivism (United States politics)
    | Right and left (Political science)—United States. |
    Radicalism—United States. | United States—Race
    relations. | United States—Politics and government.
Classification: LCC JC574.2.U6 B445 2022 | DDC
    320.510973—dc23/eng/20220412
LC record available at https://lccn.loc.gov/2022003524

This book is dedicated to my children, Justice and Hope. And to my father, Larry Beeman, who felt pride rather than shame in working-class identity; who was the first person to teach me about John Brown's antiracism.

CONTENTS

ACKNOWLEDGMENTS

This book is the result of years of struggle, my own and those of the people I interviewed. Most importantly, I want to thank activists in the organizations I studied, and others, who work tirelessly against racism, class exploitation, transphobia, and patriarchy. So many people influenced the completion of this book through encouraging words, support through difficult times, and mentorship. I am grateful to one of my most influential mentors, Noel A. Cazenave, for encouraging me at every stage of my career to persist in the study of racism despite opposition. I continue to draw from Noel's examples of strength and courage as I battle racial hostility in my everyday life and what he calls "linguistic racial accommodation" in academia. I have been fortunate to have had many wonderful colleagues and advisers who have offered valuable feedback on my work at various stages of my academic career: Vilna Bashi, Mary Bernstein, Deanna Chang, Alex Heckert, Harvey Holtz, Herbert Hunter, Bandana Purkayastha, and Evelyn Simien. I want to especially thank my collaborators, accomplices, and coconspirators, Tsedale M. Melaku and Soribel Genao, my friend Pekah Wallace, and my colleagues Lizette Colón and Cecelia McCall, who offered me valuable advice on addressing racial hostility as I worked through this and other projects. I would like to thank Melanie E. L. Bush for inviting me to present previous drafts of this work at the Society for the Study of Social Problems panel on *The End of White World Supremacy*; the Association for Humanist Sociology, where I presented this work for the session on *Politics, Power and Resistance Movements*; and *Thinkolio*, a Brooklyn-based organization that provided me space to write and invited me to speak at various venues.

I want to sincerely thank David Embrick and David Brunsma for editing this important series and believing in my work. I am grateful for the feedback they and anonymous reviewers provided. Noel A. Cazenave, Catherine Mulder, and my research assistant, Kristine Riley, provided feedback on previous drafts of this book. Additionally, I want to acknowledge my current and former students, who inspire me and continue to remind me of the importance of this work, especially Jessica Hsiao and Chandra Waring, who is now a brilliant professor working on racial injustice. I consider both these wonderful women my dear friends. I also spent a great deal of uninterrupted writing time at Willow and Olivia Bakery, so I thank the owner, Gia, for our chats and the best coffee I have ever tasted.

I am especially grateful to my children, Hope and Justice, and my husband, who encouraged me through the many challenges reflected in this book and gave me the space and time I needed to think and write. Justice happily read chapters, offering me feedback, examples, articles, and songs that she thought expressed the ideas I was communicating. Hope, with her gentle and quiet demeanor, always knows more than she lets on, and when I am fortunate enough to hear her ideas, she puts everything into perspective. I am blessed to have such thoughtful, intelligent, and compassionate people in my life. Everything I write is touched by their insight.

Last but not least, I want to thank my parents, Larry Beeman and Kye Sun (Yi) Beeman. Through their struggles and those we endured together, I learned valuable lessons about racial and class inequality, and about feeling pride despite these struggles. An important theme in this book is silence; silence on oppression as a means of preventing significant social change and as a strategic response to surviving it. It is also about teasing out the ironies and contradictions of color-blind ideology, racism-evasiveness, and liberal white supremacy. Whether they realize it or not, my parents taught me a lot about how to engage these silences and analyze contradictions. I grew up in a predominantly "white," class-segregated community in western Pennsylvania. I wrote about some of these experiences in 2016 and connected them to the problems Hillary Clinton had relating to working-class people in "Why Doesn't Middle America Trust Hillary?" In my community, I dealt with both racist and classist bullying that took the form of physical and verbal attacks, including being called a "Chinese chink," even though I was Korean. One of the ways I learned to deal with racist attacks against me at a very young age was by engaging in stoic silence. I recall several instances where my racist attackers were impressed with my ability to stand still and absorb their punches without reaction.

As early as kindergarten, I endured both physical and verbal abuse from children who would punch me, kick me, or call me names, while others insisted on knowing "What are you?" My ethnicity was such a concern that my teacher once asked the class what I should mark as my ethnicity on the California Achievement Tests, the standardized testing we took every year. When I told my parents about these instances, they responded, "Tell them you're a human being." My father, being European American, did not know how to advise me on racist bullying, since he never really encountered it at the level I experienced it. My mother, having grown up in Korea and having immigrated to the United States in her twenties, did not deal with these kinds of questions as a child. She was also struggling to navigate her own experiences with everyday racism in the United States, her trauma, and her internalized oppression. Thus, color-blind humanism was the only suggestion my parents could provide.

At the same time that my parents advised me to dismiss the racism I was facing, I heard their anger against racist and classist behavior and watched my mother fight against people who wronged her. Despite the stereotype of Asian Americans as quiet, humble, and accommodating people, my mother was rarely silent against racist aggression and constantly argued with people who dismissed her, whether it be a store clerk, coworker, or friend. My father, who did not talk much about racism, clearly took a stand when he finally cut off contact with his mother, father, and other family members who disrespected his family.

Just as my mother was marked by her appearance and accent, my father was marked in a different way by his. Throughout my life, I have encountered classist behavior toward working-class and Appalachian people who do not conform to European American middle-class standards of perfect grammar and speech. My daughter has often noted that when I visit my hometown, she hears my "Appalachian accent" come out and realizes that I must have tried to unlearn it. Sounding intelligent is a classist attitude that both European Americans and people of color can adopt and use to silence and disregard working-class people. My father regularly used the word "hain't" instead of the more commonly used "ain't" or the more acceptable "is not, are not, or am not," but he was more intelligent than many of the people I have met in academia. His feedback on some of my written work was as good or better than what I received from people with advanced degrees. However, he refused to have a "proper" language forced upon him and never dismissed people who had less money or less formal education than he did.

The "politics of respectability" and civility (making an extra effort to dress nicely or to speak and behave in a dignified manner so as to gain acceptance into middle-class, white society) are both racialized and classed, as Evelyn Brooks Higginbotham discusses in *Righteous Discontent*. In either form, respectability politics are used to silence people who have something to say about inequality. I hope this book will offer insight into these manifestations of racism and class elitism, not only so that we can better understand these divides in politics and organizing, but also to recognize the experiences people of color and all working-class people face in their everyday lives.

Liberal White Supremacy

INTRODUCTION

A Divided Left

> Reformers and the democratically-oriented liberals are
> trapped by the limitations of the Democratic Party, but
> afraid of irrelevancy outside of it.
>
> —Students for a Democratic Society,
> "America and the New Era," 1963

> To the degree that White progressives think we have arrived,
> we will put our energy into making sure that others see us as
> having arrived.
>
> —Robin DiAngelo, *White Fragility*, 2018

In this book, I identify a fault line in American politics that is being played out on the local and national level. This fracture has to do with fundamental differences between liberals and radicals in their approaches to racism, class, capitalism, and social movement tactics that impact their ability to create significant social change in the areas they claim to care about most. Such divides were continually exemplified in divisions between more liberal Democratic presidential candidates, such as Joe Biden and Hillary Clinton, and more radical candidates, such as Bernie Sanders. These four key differences are also at the center of disagreements between Nancy Pelosi, Speaker of the U.S. House of Representatives, and Congresswomen Alexandria Ocasio-Cortez, Ilhan Omar, and Rashida Tlaib. Unlike Pelosi, Ocasio-Cortez more forcefully centers working-class issues, racism, and problems with capitalism.

Omar and Tlaib have openly criticized the Democratic Party for using women of color to present the illusion of diversity.[1] Likewise, I argue that liberals in communities throughout the United States use their support of candidates of color to deny their own personal racism. In this sense, Donald Trump and Barack Obama, ironically, serve the same psychological purpose for European American liberals. They simplify the world of racists into easy-to-compartmentalize, dichotomous groups of good and bad people. By loving Barack Obama and hating Donald Trump, liberals can prove that they belong on the good, nonracist side.[2]

Trump's persistent refusal to play along with liberal rhetoric of color-blindness and unity was a rude awakening for many progressives who were in a "post-racial" slumber during the presidency of Barack Obama. Many liberals became outraged and depressed after Trump's election and started forming organizations to deal with their frustrations.[3] In my own liberal community, nearly every street had a "Hate Has No Home Here" lawn sign to communicate liberal protest against Trump's anti-immigrant, racist policies. The problem with these liberals is that while they appear to care about racism, they fail to deal with their own prejudice against working-class people. Classist remarks about Trump voters as "deplorable," racist, and "rednecks" have become not only acceptable discourse but a signifier of how truly progressive one is. This classist behavior is an outgrowth of what I call "liberal white supremacy," the tendency of liberal European Americans to constantly place themselves in the superior moral position in a way that reinforces white supremacy and social injustice. To assert their moral superiority, they juxtapose themselves against "bad whites," who are usually working class and/or radically oriented but more recently have also included other middle-class European American liberals. Because critiques of color-blindness and white fragility are now in vogue, liberal European Americans will openly criticize other liberal European Americans whom they see as less intelligent or less "woke."[4] The purpose of this is not to become more "woke" themselves, but to remain superior vis-à-vis other European Americans.

Lawn signs, corporate and university statements supporting the Movement for Black Lives, and diversity committees present the facade that liberals care about racism without having to significantly alter the racial and economic status quo that privileges them. As Roderick Bush argues in *The End of World White Supremacy*, American liberalism "is torn between its egalitarian principles . . . and its desire for stability and social order."[5] At the same time, popular books such as *White Fragility* have inadvertently given permission to European American liberals to engage in the very behaviors these books warn against. It has made white fragile behavior acceptable. For instance, in one academic department, I observed a chairperson state that, according to the book, European Americans in the department would cry and become defensive in discussions on racism. Thus, he interpreted *White Fragility* as a guide for predicting and *excusing* how European American liberals were going to behave rather than as an analysis of what is wrong with white fragile behaviors and why these behaviors must stop. Ranita Ray has also found this phenomenon in what she calls "race-conscious racism," where European Americans will say something racist and then blame it on their implicit bias. Ray cautions her readers about the ways anti-racist training can be used to excuse racist behaviors.[6]

Progressives perceive these problems and divides between liberals and radicals, but few people have laid out, conceptually, what this split involves. I analyze two case studies that help clarify what these differences are and why they matter. This analysis will be useful, not only to academics, but to progressive organizations plagued by these divisions. In what follows, I address the scholarship relevant to my study and the concepts I develop.

Theories of Race and Racism

Systemic racism theory, particularly as conceptualized by Joe R. Feagin, is integral to understanding how modern-day racism works. Feagin's *Racist America: Roots, Current Realities and Future Reparations*; *Systemic Racism: A Theory of Oppression*; *The White Racial Frame: Centuries of Racial Framing and Counter-Framing*; and several of his other works challenge common understandings of racism as an individual-level problem. Systemic racism theory posits that racism is embedded within institutional practices that have historically marginalized people of color and can be reproduced without any intention of racial bigotry. Just as people of color face cumulative disadvantages from centuries of racial oppression, whether overt or covert, European Americans of all social classes accumulate privileges from whiteness, even if they hold no personal racial animus.

Noel A. Cazenave's *Conceptualizing Racism: Breaking the Chains of Racially Accommodative Language* corrects conceptual problems in systemic racism theory that is sometimes too abstract and lacking in an any analysis of human agency. Cazenave distinguishes between different levels and manifestations of racism and addresses ideologies of denial as "the hegemonic glue that holds systemic racism together."[7] His examination of Linguistic Racial Accommodation versus Linguistic Racial Confrontation and racism-evasiveness informs my analysis of how liberal and radical methods differ and the central role of ideology in upholding racism. Cazenave's problematization of "race," along with the in-depth historical analyses offered by Audrey Smedley, Theodore Allen, Noel Ignatiev, and David Roediger influence my understanding of the racial categories of "white" and "black."

Carter Wilson's important work *Racism: From Slavery to Advanced Capitalism* puts forth a systemic theory of racism that does not minimize the role of human actions in maintaining it. According to Wilson, economic and political elites, who benefit from an oppressive economic structure, actively create a racist culture to sustain racial and economic oppression. As a historical materialist, he conceptualizes different manifestations of racism that developed in different time periods, depending on the mode of production in place. For example, the system of slavery manifested dominative racism, which allowed for the total control of African Americans, whereas the era of de jure segregation manifested aversive racism.

Theories that focus on ideologies, such as color-blindness, are also important to understanding how modern-day racism is expressed, particularly by people who believe themselves to be progressive or nonracist. Works such as David Wellman's *Portraits of White Racism* and Eduardo Bonilla-Silva's *White Supremacy and Racism in the Post–Civil Rights Era* and *Racism without Racists* expose the rhetorical strategies highly educated European Americans use to deny racism without making overtly racist comments. Bonilla-Silva has characterized this manifestation of racism as "racism-lite."[8] Wellman challenges notions that racism is simply irrational and argues that contemporary racism serves the rational self-interests of European Americans. That is, contemporary racist ideologies allow European Americans to deny they are racist while at the same time supporting policies that benefit them and marginalize people of color. More recently, Nancy DiTomaso has made a similar argument, adding to Oliver C. Cox's critique of Gunnar Myrdal's *American Dilemma* as well as Lawrence Bobo and Ryan Smith's. Bobo and Smith argue that overt Jim Crow racism was merely replaced with a subtler "laissez-faire" racism that viewed African Americans as culturally rather than biologically inferior. DiTomaso argues that European Americans have not faced the moral dilemma Myrdal believed they would, because they do not see their actions as racist. This body of work, which shows how expressions of racism shift in different historical and political eras, is important to my own conceptualization of racism-evasiveness and liberal white supremacy as strategic practices and ideologies that uphold systemic racism.

Black Feminist Thought

In 1892 Anna Julia Cooper wrote *A Voice from the South*, which argued that African American women were overlooked because they did not fit neatly into one category.[9] Their marginalization was reflected in the national dialogue on voting rights, which was framed as a pressing issue for either African American men or European American women, leaving women of color completely out of the equation.[10] Cooper put forth a basic tenet of Black feminist thought: identities and status positions intersect and cannot be neatly separated. In 1972, Joyce Ladner published an important sociological study on the lives of multiply positioned African

American adolescent girls living in St. Louis, Missouri, and, among other issues, how they navigated ideas of social class.[11] In 1977, the Combahee River Collective put forth a statement calling for an "integrated analysis," one that understood systems of oppression as interlocking.[12] Black feminist theorist Kimberlé Crenshaw conceptualized this process as intersectionality, showing how privilege and disadvantage overlap and why it is important to center women of color, particularly Black women, who continue to be marginalized politically, representationally, and structurally.[13]

The field of intersectional studies has grown with several important works addressing the experiences of people of color who are multiply positioned.[14] Patricia Hill Collins has examined intersecting oppressions within a "matrix of domination." Collins demonstrates that where there is domination, there is also resistance. Important to Black feminist thought is a commitment to social justice. Indeed, a central purpose of this book is to understand and fight against practices, ideologies, and behaviors that reproduce inequality. I address how European American liberals misapply intersectionality through racism-evasiveness. In chapter 5, I draw on Black feminist thought and intersectionality to advance *action-oriented* and *racism-centered intersectional approaches* to social justice.

Theories of Class Oppression

In 1848, Karl Marx and Friedrich Engels argued that society was "splitting up into two great hostile camps . . . bourgeoisie and proletariat."[15] The bourgeoisie, or capitalist upper class, owned the means of production (which is what Marx meant by private property), while the proletariat, or working class, was exploited.[16] The working class is propertyless; they do not own or control the means or relations of production and have only their labor to sell. Marx and Engels tied human freedom to labor. Freedom was the ability to work for more than mere survival but also for the means to express one's creative potential.[17] This human need for creativity was denied to the working class, who were required to produce ever more for the capitalist class and in the process became ever more alienated from their work, themselves, and each other.[18] Marxist analysis typically relegates racism to class oppression. Enslaved African Americans, in Marx's view, would be viewed as part of the working class, the solution to their oppression being a unification of all the proletariat.

In *The Distribution of Power within the Political Community: Class, Status, Party*, Max Weber defined social class as propertied workers versus non-propertied workers but emphasized additional dimensions of status or prestige and power.[19] According to Weber's theories one can have social class in the form of money, but not status and power. These dimensions intersect such that one does not have to be among the power elite, which in the U.S. context C. Wright Mills defined as including the president and the cabinet, top-ranking CEOs, and top-ranking military officials, to have prestige and exert authority over others. Status competition and status anxiety can occur among people of very similar incomes. For example, people with higher levels of education may make similar incomes as those with less education but view themselves as superior based on the status they gain from their occupations or degrees. Influenced by W. E. B. Du Bois, Weber's analysis addressed people of color as an excluded status group.

Oliver C. Cox, probably one of the most well-known contemporary Marxist theorists, contributed to theories on class oppression that included people of color in his books *Caste, Class, and Race* (1948) and *Race Relations* (1976). Cox was among the first scholars to distinguish between caste and racial systems of endogamy. He was concerned that fashionable comparisons of caste systems in India oversimplified race relations in the United States and were merely "distractions" to understanding inequality.[20] Although Cox used historical examples to illustrate the socially constructed nature of "race," his analysis remained largely class centered rather than racism centered. Like Marx, he believed that the key to overcoming racial injustice was a unification of the working class.

Erik Olin Wright, also a contemporary Marxist theorist, produced several highly regarded works on social class, including *Class, Crisis and the State*; *Class Structure and Income Determination*; *Classes*; *The Debate on Classes*; *Class Counts*; and *Approaches to Class Analysis*. One of Wright's main contributions was his analysis of contradictory class locations, such that one could have common class interests with both capitalist employers and with exploited workers. For example, managers, who are themselves controlled by capitalist owners, supervise workers beneath them and impose the class interests of the capitalist class upon them. This work is important to understanding the position of the middle class today.

These theoretical frameworks inform my conceptualizations of liberal color-blind ideology, racism-evasiveness, racial oppression, class oppression, and elitism and how these produce liberal white supremacy within a system of racism. Having discussed the relevant literatures, I now define my central argument and key concepts.

Key Argument and Concepts

My main argument is that white supremacy is maintained, not only by right-wing conservatives or stereotypically uneducated and/or working-class racial bigots, but by highly educated progressives who operate from a liberal ideology of color-blindness, racism-evasiveness, and class elitism. By explicating the differences between liberal and radical approaches to racism, class oppression, capitalism, and social movement tactics, I show how progressives continue to be limited by liberal ideology and perpetuate rather than dismantle white supremacy, all while claiming to be antiracist. To clarify this argument, I present my key concepts.

LIBERAL COLOR-BLIND IDEOLOGY AND RACISM-EVASIVENESS

John Locke is often referred to as the father of classical liberalism based on the ideas he developed in *The Two Treatises of Government* (1689). Locke believed that people in any society had natural rights to "life, liberty, and estate" and that government intervention should be limited, as it interfered with such rights.[21] Locke's writings influenced the work of other philosophers, such as Voltaire and Rousseau, and informed Thomas Jefferson's writing of the Declaration of Independence. He and other philosophers, including Thomas Hobbes, wrote about a social contract, which involved an agreement among the people to relinquish some of their freedoms to a powerful state in the interest of everyone's comfort and safety. In 1997, Charles W. Mills argued that the social contract was inherently racist and that the writers purporting such ideas were essentially justifying European control and dominance over people of color and other subordinated groups. Mills stated, "European humanism usually meant that only Europeans were human."[22] This is a key point at which liberal and color-blind ideology converge. *Liberal-informed color-blind ideology* is a belief system that rests on a seemingly positive and humanist notion that people do not and should not see or make judgments about differences in skin color. Achieving color-blindness is then seen as the key to equality. However, claiming that one does not see skin color produces the negative action of *racism-evasiveness*—refusing to see racism and strategically downplaying it or avoiding it. In this way, liberal color-blind ideology can only uphold humanism and equality for people of European descent, as Mills argues. No actions are put forward to challenge racism so long as people can claim they are color-blind. This only works to further harm people of color, whose experiences with racism are easily dismissed by color-blind falsehoods and racism-evasive maneuvers.

CLASS OPPRESSION AND ELITISM

Class oppression involves the dominance of the power elite and social upper classes over the working class that is simultaneously exploited for their labor and alienated from it. *Class elitism* can occur among people of roughly the same social class but who enjoy different levels of status, prestige, social capital, and cultural capital. The middle class is defined as people who make between $39,800 to $119,400 in a three-person family.[23] This income range is broad and includes people who have very different occupations, educational backgrounds, and lifestyles. People who identify as "middle class" can make class elitist and status distinctions among themselves. For example, administrative assistants may make less than plumbers or construction workers but view themselves as more sophisticated and enlightened due to the professional setting of their workplaces. They may define themselves as "middle class" and not "working class." Although anyone can engage in class elitism, and I reference examples of class elitism by people of color, the central focus of my book is on class elitism among middle class, professional European American liberals, which they exert over working-class people, particularly those with less formal education. This class elitism and disregard for working-class people helps sustain class oppression.

CLASS OPPRESSION, ELITISM, AND LIBERAL WHITE SUPREMACY

Liberal European American middle-class elitism toward other European Americans is class supremacist behavior, but it also reinforces white supremacy. Whiteness is not about skin color but is a social and political construction that reaffirms dominance and maintenance of the status quo. As Charles Mills argues, "Whiteness is not really a color at all, but a set of power relations."[24] Historically, there was a hierarchy of whiteness with some European Americans denigrated beneath others.[25] To gain the social and political advantages of whiteness, European Americans had to show their support for the racial and economic status quo by distancing themselves from blackness and expressing their political support for the system in place (e.g., Irish Americans supporting the U.S. system of slavery).[26] When European American liberals assert their superiority over other European Americans as the better "white"[27] people, they are constructing a hierarchy of whiteness, not one based on biology but on morality, where they are the most superior. They do this to shift blame for perpetuating racism onto another group. Thus, because they identify as liberal and "white," support a hierarchy of whiteness (intentional or not), and assert supremacy over others, they embody liberal white supremacy.

RACIAL OPPRESSION

Racial oppression is the continued dehumanization, devaluation, harassment, and marginalization of people of color at every class level. Racial oppression is sustained through the interaction of an oppressive economic structure, the actions of political elites, and a racist culture that includes ideologies, controlling images, and discriminatory practices, policies, and laws.[28] It is based on the inherently dehumanizing idea of "race," a concept developed with the intended purpose of ranking and dividing human beings, whose common interests posed a threat to political elites.[29] Right-wing conservative European Americans who openly discriminate against people of color perpetuate racial oppression, but so do liberal, antiracist European Americans who act paternalistically toward people of color. When liberal European Americans talk down to or speak for people of color, use them as sounding boards for their white fragility, or befriend them to gain legitimacy as antiracists, they uphold liberal white supremacy.

LIBERAL WHITE SUPREMACY

I define *liberal white supremacy* as a set of beliefs and practices progressive European Americans engage in to assert their moral superiority over other European Americans and people of color they see as less intelligent or sophisticated in their understanding of racism and injustice. These beliefs and practices help European Americans maintain control of the discourse and retain their dominant positions, as people of color make progress toward social justice. These liberals privilege their perspectives and methods as the best suited for challenging inequality, but, ultimately, they reproduce it. Liberal white supremacy is sustained by liberal ideology, which informs color-blind approaches and racism-evasiveness, and supports racial and class oppression.

The Plan of the Book

In chapter 1, I distinguish between different manifestations of racism and further develop my concept of liberal white supremacy. Past research has shown that liberal discussions on racism often reproduce racist behaviors, even as they attempt to combat them.[30] These problematic talk-centered discussions are tied to a key weakness in liberal organizing: *nonconfrontational behavior* and *aversion to discomfort*. Historically, liberals have preferred a conflict-averse and color-blind focus on unity and harmony.[31] I show how this liberal approach to racism interacts with class bias to uphold liberal white supremacy.

In chapter 2, I review the history and conditions that led to the division between liberals and radicals and present my model, which illustrates key differences in discourse and tactics. In general, liberals tend to emphasize civil discourse over direct action and disruptive tactics. Radicals, on the other hand, favor action-centered and more confrontational approaches. Liberals emphasize talking about racism; radicals emphasize working-class solidarity.

Chapter 3 examines a radical group's confrontation of questionable educational policies and the role of nonconfrontational tactics and liberal ideology in stifling dissent. Their unwillingness to be confrontational, their tendency toward comfort, and their alliance with established power ultimately prevented liberal activists from achieving social justice. Not only did liberals fail to express anger when needed, but they chastised radicals for directly calling out corruption and attempted to silence them. When the confrontational methods of the radical group worked in ridding the school district of a corrupt superintendent, liberals attempted to claim credit for their success.

Chapter 4 addresses racism-evasiveness in an interracial nonprofit group. As with the preceding case study, this group faced a political machine that portrayed radical activists as troublemakers. However, in the second case, fighting racial injustice was more explicitly part of the organization's mission. Despite this fact, activists were hesitant to explicitly discuss racism, opting instead to emphasize interracial class solidarity. I address this tactic as a kind of *strategic* racism-evasiveness that was influenced by an action-centered organizational culture and that was a response to dominant liberal discourse and racial ideologies that emphasize civility and color-blindness. Therefore, this second case study helps illustrate the class-over-racism perspective and action-centered approach of radicals compared to liberals, as well as the limitations external liberal ideology impose on more radical organizations.

Finally, in chapter 5, I conclude with an analysis of how liberal white supremacy continues to limit community organizing, national politics, and interracial alliances. Here I discuss my experiences with self-identified progressive academics. I have interacted with faculty who engage in all the behaviors of white fragility while simultaneously vilifying liberal European Americans who engage in those very same behaviors. It is a very troubling paradox that often leads me to question the role of liberal European Americans in the movement against racism and prompted one prominent African American philosopher to ask, "Should I give up on white people?"[32] For people of color engaged in antiracist work to not give up on progressive "white" people, the latter must be willing to forgo their need to be validated as antiracist heroes. Instead they must be motivated by a deep sense of social justice and feel obligated to do the work whether or not they receive any credit for it. They have to constantly examine the way their own internalized white superiority and privilege affect their work with people of color. They have to realize what Becky Thompson called "a promise and a way of life."[33] European Americans who cannot move away from their need to be validated by people of color as "good white people" are ultimately barriers to social justice.[34] They continue to emotionally drain and infuriate people of color, whom they constantly seek out for validation. Addressing these issues in this final chapter, I call for a move toward *action-oriented* and *racism-centered intersectional approaches*, which I find exemplified in the Movement for Black Lives.

A Note on Terminology

Following the murder of George Floyd on May 25, 2020, scholars and journalists began questioning whether the term "Black" should be written with a capital letter.[35] A debate on whether to capitalize "white" soon followed.[36] For several years, I have addressed the complexities of these terms in my teaching and writing. In my academic writing, I have consistently used the pan-ethnic terms "European American," "African American," and "people of African descent," while placing the terms "white" and "Black" in quotation marks when referring to people. When I refer to institutions, I use the term "white" without quotation marks, as in "predominantly white institutions." Here, the term "white" is not referring to a socially constructed category of people, but a pervasive ideology of whiteness that permeates institutional culture and practices. The category of "white" was created intentionally by economic elites to divide English indentured servants and African slaves, who were constantly rebelling under a common class identity.[37] The ruling elite used a system of rewards and punishments to coerce working-class European Americans to identify with a "white race." Interracial fraternizing and marriages were punished severely, and whiteness was deemed superior by law, attached to property and citizenship rights, as well as public deference and respect denied to people identified as "Black."[38] This system of racial classification did not immediately make sense to those we now view as "Black" and "white," because it was peculiar to a population, who did not naturally identify by such racial categories. Nor was this system built without objection. The Virginia General Assembly had to justify new laws based on skin color to officials in England tasked with evaluating them, and such laws were not immediately accepted.[39] Irish and Italian Americans, who were a type of "in-between peoples," engaged in performances of blackface minstrelsy to assert a "white" identity. They had to work toward whiteness.[40] Given this history, I encourage my European American students to question their "white" identities. They are not just "white," and uncritically identifying in this way can normalize whiteness. I ask them to consider why we generally prefer the terms "indigenous" and "Asian Americans" to the terms "reds" or "yellows."

There are also problematic ways to use the term "European American." Some European Americans use the term to sound politically correct or to express what Mary C. Waters calls an "optional ethnicity" that often denies the existence of white privilege.[41] I do not use the term for these purposes but rather to show that whiteness is not biologically real and that European Americans also have a stake in dismantling racism. As Noel A. Cazenave states, "race should be problematized and ultimately relinquished not only because it is confusing...but because it is erroneous, and most importantly because it is injurious."[42] Johnny Eric Williams also problematizes the concepts of "white" and "Black" and often uses the term "self-identified 'white' people" or "people who think they are white."[43] I argue that whiteness is, among other things, imbued in places, spaces, and ideology. Whiteness is not a human being, although people can embody whiteness in all sorts of harmful ways. As such, people of color can also uphold whiteness as superior. If European Americans and people of color understand this history, they may begin to comprehend how racial categories rob them of their own humanity. By uncritically accepting a "white" identity, we contribute to the maintenance of white supremacy.

I recognize that the term "African American" is also problematic because it is not inclusive of people who do not identify with this group. This term does not include all people of African descent who are affected by white supremacy around the world. For example, I see the Movement for Black Lives as combatting police violence and social control across the globe, not just in the United States. Furthermore, we could argue that there is a difference between the term "Black," capitalized, and "white" or "White." When activists use the term "Black," they are referring to a positive political identity. To say that one is "unapologetically Black" is an empowering response to a system of white supremacy that has subordinated people of African descent for centuries. This system created and perpetuated an internalized oppression among people of African descent that kept them silent and compliant. Those embracing a "Black" identity are reclaiming this term to counter that history and the self-hatred it built. As I suggest to my students, the term "Black" has been used by people of many different ethnic backgrounds to assert a shared political identity against oppression, as can be seen in African-Caribbean movements and youth movements in Britain, where people of Asian descent identified politically as "Black."[44] The term "White" (capitalized) is also a political identity, but rather than uniting people to fight against systemic racial oppression, it is used by white supremacists to reinforce the superiority of "white" identity and continued division. Whiteness is "politically ... the willingness to seek a comfortable place within the system of race privilege."[45] Thus, white nationalists make an inaccurate comparison when they try to compare "white pride" to "black pride." To say that one is proud of being "white" is to say that one is proud of racist segregation that allows only those with a so-called pure "white" identity to accumulate privilege. Whiteness is about exclusion. As Melanie E. L. Bush states, "If race was constructed as a tool to dominate and subordinate, how can we render it (white identity) positive?"[46] This is not the same as being proud of one's ethnic heritage—Irish, Italian, Scottish, and so forth. White nationalists often conflate these two ideas.

In sum, there is no perfect term, because racial categories were socially constructed within a system of white supremacy. Up to this point, I have placed the terms "white" and "Black" in quotation marks when talking about people to signify that these terms are problematic and we have much more thinking to do on the matter. Having explained these issues, I will now refrain from using the quotation marks, to assist with readability, and use European American, African American, and Black where appropriate. When I am speaking about Black Lives Matter or the Movement for Black Lives, I capitalize the "B" without quotations, as it represents a movement against white supremacy.

In my case studies and examples, where possible, I use the terms individuals use to self-identify. For example, if I know a person to self-identify as Latino instead of Latinx or Hispanic, I use the term "Latino." The term "Latinx" was developed to offer a gender-neutral alternative to the terms "Latino" or "Latina." However, the Pew Research Center reports that "most Latino adults have not heard of the term Latinx," few use it, and college-educated people are most likely to have heard of it.[47] Some have argued that Latinx is also problematic because it does not conform to the Spanish language and is an example of "linguistic imperialism," and that the term "Latine" is more consistent with the language.[48] Following this argument, I use the term "Latine" when referring to these groups, in general. The need for continued thinking on terminology can be better understood by addressing the origins and development of "race" and racism. I turn now to a discussion of this history to promote this understanding and to further explain the concept of liberal white supremacy.

CHAPTER 1

Racism, Class, and Liberal White Supremacy

> If you think of race as assigning meaning to whole groups of people, ideologically convincing others that some people are inferior to others, that some people are designed as beasts of burden and other people are designed to accept, to embrace the wealth of that, then what you end up getting is a system of extraction that allows for a kind of super exploitation of Black and brown people.
>
> —Robin D. G. Kelley, 2020

> In the United States, "white racism" is a centuries-old system intentionally designed to exclude Americans of color from full participation in the economy, polity, and society.
>
> —Joe Feagin, Hernán Vera, and Pinar Batur, *White Racism*, 2001

One of the central points of this book is that liberals and radicals have different approaches to racism and class. Their approaches to both of these systems are interrelated. Of the two intersecting systems, racism remains a more controversial and easily misunderstood concept, because there is such a long history of denying its existence in the United States and other nations.[1] Central to this denial is academia's preference for the "race relations" paradigm, which problematizes people of color rather than the system of racism.[2] Sociology, often seen as the most liberal of the social science disciplines, contributes to this denial.[3] What is more, people have different definitions and understandings of racism. When I first began studying racism as a student in the 1990s, I constantly had to explain the differences between so-called individual and institutional racism and rarely found references to systemic racism in mainstream media. Today, the terms "institutional racism" and "systemic racism" have become more prevalent. I find that my students are much more familiar with these terms than they were even in the early 2000s. However, I am not convinced that everyone knows what these terms mean, how they are connected, or how they should be defined. Therefore, it is important to distinguish between different manifestations of racism, how I define racism in this book, and what this has to do with the most modern forms of color-blind ideology as well as what I call liberal white supremacy.

Color-blindness and racism-evasiveness are connected to a liberal ideology that focuses on nonconfrontation. Historically, liberals have preferred a color-blind focus on unity and harmony.[4] Using the words "racial," "race," "minorities," or talking about the "race issue" is much less confrontational than defining the issue explicitly as racism. Ironically, when liberals do name racism and engage in discussion about it, they help reinforce racism-evasiveness, because these discussions are meant to assert their moral superiority over other less educated, stereotypically working-class European Americans. This liberal approach to racism and class reinforces liberal white supremacy. To understand this process, we must first address how we should define racism: its origins, sustenance, and consequences.[5]

Defining Racism

THE ORIGINS OF RACE

Any definition of racism must begin with the origins of "race" as an idea. There are various theories on how racism emerged in the Americas. Audrey Smedley's and Theodore Allen's are probably the most accepted and supported in the social sciences. They and other scholars find that skin color was not a precursor to slavery.[6] People of African descent were not automatically seen as inferior or uncivilized because they were darker in complexion. In fact, prior to the development of slavery in colonial Virginia, the English saw Africans as more civilized than the Irish.[7] Most Africans came to Virginia as indentured servants and some were able to become landowners. Court cases show that Africans of landowning status had certain rights.[8] Smedley notes that social interaction, collaboration, and marriage between English and African people were not uncommon.[9] These factors indicate that skin color was not viewed the same way as it is today and was not an automatic indication of social status as much as class was. The idea of "race" as a scientific hierarchy of white over black did not exist until slavery developed in colonial Virginia.[10]

Even as Africans were enslaved, they still interacted and rebelled with English servants, who did not see their treatment as vastly different from slaves. Moreover, as indentured servants of all ethnic backgrounds were freed, they began demanding land and more rights as part of their freedom. Smedley talks about a growing number of unhappy, unruly former servants who were lacking opportunities and "on the make."[11] African and English servants would take part in small and large rebellions: stealing hogs, running away together, and destroying property. The most troubling rebellion to the English ruling class was Bacon's Rebellion in 1676, which resulted in the burning of Jamestown, Virginia. These rebellions prompted the Virginia General Assembly and ruling elite to develop laws that would create specific racial categories of people for the purpose of branding African Americans.[12]

In 1691, anti-miscegenation laws called for the banishment of any free white person who intermarried a "Negro, Mulatoe, or Indian man or woman."[13] People were whipped and fined for engaging in such marriages or other interracial interactions. In 1705, slave codes were passed by Virginia's ruling class proclaiming that all "white" people were superior to "black" people.[14] Servants now identifying as "white" were offered a greater number of benefits that were previously denied to them. Indentured servants were also allowed more days off, could testify in court, and were admitted into social clubs. Poor European Americans did not own slaves but were given the status of overseer on the plantations. They were given public deference that was denied to Africans, regardless of class background. This gave them a public and psychological wage over Africans.[15] In short, the Anglo-Saxon ruling class in colonial Virginia created a society where the interests of poor people diverged and freedom depended on tying oneself to whiteness.

At this time, the Virginia General Assembly remained subjects of the King of England and had to justify the laws and practices they were developing in the New World. A British attorney, Richard West, was tasked with overseeing these new laws. In 1723, the Assembly passed a measure titled "An Act directing the trial of Slaves, committing capital crimes; and for the more effectual punishing conspiracies and insurrections of them; and for the better government of Negros, Mulattos, and Indians, bond or free."[16] West's reaction to this measure indicates that skin color was not viewed as a natural way to divide people. In response to the measure, he stated, "I cannot see why one freeman should be used worse than another, merely upon account of his complexion . . . it cannot be just, by a general law, without any allegation of crime, or other demerit whatsoever, to strip all free persons, of a black complexion (some of whom may, perhaps be of considerable substance) from those rights, which are so justly valuable to every freeman."[17] In this response, West registers his confusion about why the Assembly would want to take rights away from people who were of substance and had property, regardless of skin color. The Assembly had to convince West, and others in England, that skin color now mattered more than class status.

William Gooch, who later became governor of Virginia in 1727, sent England a justification for stripping Africans of certain rights that emphasized his concern that free African Americans and "Mulattos" were engaged in a conspiracy against the English. He argued that there was no proof to convict the conspirators, which was all the more reason to "fix a perpetual Brand upon Free-Negros & Mulattos" and "to make the free-Negros sensible that a distinction ought to be made between their offspring and the Descendants of an Englishman."[18] Gooch had heard of plans for revolutions and uprisings and wanted to quash them. He wrote about "the Nature of Negros, and the Pride of a manumitted Slave," who thought themselves "as good a Man as the best of his Neighbours" upon acquiring their freedom.[19] He wanted to put African Americans who had freedom, and property in some cases, in their place; to brand them forever so that they would know their place. He had to convince West, and others in England, that Africans were not their equals regardless of their landowning status and class position, and that unification between the English and African servants and slaves was a threat to profit. As Smedley points out, the scientific study of "race" did not occur until after it was already a social, legal, and political construct.[20] In *Notes on the State of Virginia*, Thomas Jefferson called on science to provide answers to biology and "race."[21] The pseudo-scientific hierarchies of "race" that then followed supported the economic system of slavery and formed the basis of racism.

SUSTAINING RACISM

Carter Wilson develops a theory on the reproduction of racism from slavery to advanced capitalism.[22] He argues that racism is sustained through the interaction of three entities: economic structure, political elites, and racist culture. In Figure 1, I offer my conceptualization of Wilson's work. Wilson analyzes the evolution of racism, which, he argues, changes forms depending on the mode of production in place. Out of the economy of slavery, for example, came a sadistic racist culture that in turn maintained this oppressive economic system. Wilson states, "Increasing profits in this system required increasing the level of sadistic control over the slave."[23] This racist culture included imagery, ideologies, and sadistic acts such as castration, all of which helped maintain the oppressive economic structure. The image of Sambo, for instance, "functioned in southern society to reinforce whites' views of themselves as Christian and civilized and their perspective on the slave as happy and childlike. Whites had to see the slave as Sambo, or they would have been driven to the brink of insanity by their fear of the slave and by their inhuman-

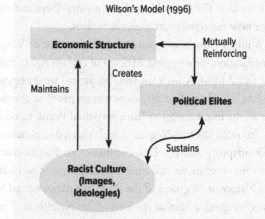

FIGURE 1
Carter Wilson's Theory
on Racial Oppression
Note: Wilson (*Racism*) does
not diagram his theory. This
visual is my conceptualization
of the model I see in his work.

ity."[24] Political elites are also deeply connected to the economic structure and racist culture. Wilson contends, "This concentration of wealth produced a powerful planter class with the resources and resolve to protect slavery. This class dominated southern regional politics and strongly influenced national politics ... Members of this class used wealth and prestige to either run for office or support pro-slavery candidates."[25] Political elites have the power to control discourse and promote racist imagery and ideologies that support their positions.

Political elites helped create the racist culture we face in the twenty-first century. That racist culture includes ideologies of color-blindness and liberal white supremacy. We can point to President Richard Nixon's role, for example, in using color-blind ideology as a political strategy. In his diaries, H. R. Haldeman quotes Nixon as stating, "You have to face the fact that the whole problem is really the blacks. The key is to devise a system that recognizes this while not appearing to."[26] Then, in 1980, Ronald Reagan's campaign consultant, Lee Atwater (who would later serve in the administrations of Reagan and George H. W. Bush), stated:

> You start out in 1954 by saying, "N——, n——, n——." By 1968 you can't say "n——" ... So you say stuff like, states' rights ... You're getting so abstract now [that] you're talking about cutting taxes, and all these things you're talking about are totally economic things and a byproduct of them is [that] blacks get hurt worse than whites ... if it is getting that abstract, and that coded, that we are doing away with the racial problem one way or the other ... because obviously sitting around saying, 'We want to cut this,' is much more abstract than even the busing thing, and a hell of a lot more abstract than "N——, n——."[27]

The dilemma conservative political elites faced after the civil rights movement was that it was no longer acceptable to make openly racist comments. Therefore, they had to develop new discourses and ideological support for the racist economic structure from which they benefited. Conservative political elites, therefore, helped create a racism-evasive and color-blind discourse that worked to their advantage. As Wilson's work implies, racism evolves in every historical period, taking whatever form is necessary to support the racial and economic status quo.[28]

Origins, Prevalence, and Consequences of Liberal Color-Blind Ideology

Contemporary racism is sustained by color-blind ideology. One of the earliest uses of color-blindness is found in constitutional law. In his argument against "separate but equal," Justice John Marshall Harlan stated, "Our constitution is color blind and neither knows nor tolerates class among citizens."[29] Yet, in his book *"Color-Blind" Racism*, Leslie G. Carr argues that most people conveniently ignore the implications of Harlan's first paragraph, which states: "The White race deems itself to be the dominant race in this country. And so it is, in prestige, in advancements, in education, in wealth, and in power. So, I doubt not, it will continue to be for all time, if it remains true to its great heritage and holds fast to the principles of constitutional liberty."[30] Here, Harlan subscribes to liberal doctrines of color-blindness, but the result is a text that can be used to further racial inequality. As Carr states, "Justice Harlan tried hard to make the majority of the court understand that the law and the constitution must remain blind to the existence of 'race' because color blindness was the best way to maintain white supremacy."[31] Carr argues that conservatives have easily used Harlan's sentiment and color-blindness, in general, to argue that any policies that take "race" into account are unconstitutional and even racist.[32] Carr also contends that because liberals promote a free marketplace, they have trouble defending arguments for policies such as affirmative action that require government intervention. Here we see the problems of liberal's pro-capitalist attitude interacting with their color-blind approach to racism (see chapter 2). Therefore, both liberals and conservatives have helped perpetuate modern-day color-blind ideology.

Eduardo Bonilla-Silva's work played a pivotal role in drawing attention to the significance of color-blind racism. Bonilla-Silva analyzed attitudinal data to conceptualize the tropes and frames of color-blindness.[33] First, there is "abstract liberalism."[34] Here, there is a focus on individual rights and abstract ideas of equality—the notion that we are all equal regardless of skin color. Using the frame of abstract liberalism, racism can come across as very reasonable. In fact, this theme and its focus on equal rights is what helps fuel white nationalist movements today.[35] A central point in Bonilla-Silva's conceptualization of color-blind racism is that while many European Americans deny the significance of whiteness, they navigate a "white habitus": a "racialized, uninterrupted socialization process that conditions and creates whites' racial tastes, perceptions, feelings, and emotions and their views on racial matters."[36]

The second theme, biologization of culture, places the blame for racial inequality on the cultural deficiencies of African Americans, who are viewed as lacking proper values of hard work. Bonilla-Silva's respondents recognized that African Americans have had to deal with racism but argued that they have "thrown in the towel" and are not willing to work hard anymore. Bobo and Smith referred to this as "laissez-faire racism" and argued that it has taken the place of Jim Crow racism.[37] It never occurs to respondents making these claims that middle-class people of color, those who have good jobs, who have internalized all of the "right" values, still face racism.[38]

The theme of naturalization was most prevalent in perspectives on racial segregation in Bonilla-Silva's study. Bill, a manufacturing manager in his forties, explains segregation this way, "I don't think it's anybody's fault. Because people tend to group with their own people . . . Doesn't mean if a black person moves into your neighborhood, they shouldn't go to your school. They should and you should mix and welcome them and everything else, but you can't force people together."[39] Bill misses a point I have been teaching my students for the past twenty years, which is that, historically, laws forced people apart. Laws were necessary to prevent integration. If anything, this implies that segregation is *unnatural*.

In Bonilla-Silva's final theme, minimization of racism, European American respondents argued that racist discrimination had all but disappeared.[40] They denied the existence of racism by emphasizing other factors responsible for poor outcomes, such as individual behavior. They also argued that social class or gender was more important than racism in determining life chances. Bonilla-Silva's work offers a concrete understanding of what color-blindness sounds like. However, conceptually, the term "color-blind racism" conflates two separate yet related issues, the ideology of color-blindness and systemic racism, of which it is itself a part. Some clarification is in order, then, if we are to understand how contemporary racism works.

There are at least three separate issues scholars attempt to address through the concept of color-blind racism. First, there is systemic racism, which is a centuries-old and highly organized system of "race"-based oppression that operates at every level of society.[41] Systemic racism refers to the entirety of racist ideologies, institutional practices, and individual behaviors. Within this system, there are different levels of racism that interact to reinforce each other and uphold the larger system.

In their book *Black Power*, Stokely Carmichael and Charles Hamilton distinguished between two levels of racism by using the city of Birmingham, Alabama, as an example.[42] They argued that bombings of African American churches and the forced movement of African Americans out of white neighborhoods in Birmingham were both examples of individual racist acts that were quickly condemned by most people. In the same city, however, they pointed to a less recognized institutionalized racism, which was evident in a lack of proper food, shelter, and medical facilities. They argued that while this manifestation of racism was not as quickly condemned as individual racial bigotry, it resulted in equally devastating effects on human life, including the death of five hundred African American babies each year. As author Tim Wise states, institutional racism is "the gasoline, allowing the otherwise stationary combustion engine of individual racism to actually function."[43] For example, the institutional practice of redlining helped create racial segregation, divesting resources from predominantly African American neighborhoods and enriching predominantly white neighborhoods.[44] That institutional practice would not have been successful without individual racial bigotry and vice versa. Individuals make decisions that help reinforce patterns of racism at the institutional level, and those individual decisions are enabled by institutional practices. As a Levittown resident stated in the film *Race: The Power of an Illusion*: "I can understand an individual . . . being racist, but for your country . . . to condone it, give him the tools to do that, there's something definitely wrong there." All these interactions compose the system of racism.

The second issue jumbled into the term "color-blind racism" is the ideology of color-blindness. Color-blindness is the belief that one can actually be blind to color in a highly racialized society. People who make this color-blind claim express that no one should be treated differently because of the color of their skin. This is largely a liberal belief that relies on Dr. Martin Luther King Jr.'s assertion that people should be judged by the content of their character. Third, there is the negative outcome of this seemingly positive color-blind ideology. Claiming not to see color often results in refusing to see or talk about racism. This is racism-evasiveness, and it is very often strategically employed.

Thus, systemic racism is held together by ideologies of denial and avoidance. Color-blind ideology can operate in any institution and result in racism-evasiveness in a way that interferes with progress. For example, many primary and secondary schools emphasize color-blindness as an ideal and as a result do not talk explicitly about racism. This can lead to a failure of schools to adequately address any racist incidents that do occur. In Mica Pollock's study of race talk in California high schools, students and teachers deliberately avoided using "race words" or any description of people by their ethnicity, such as African American, Samoan, Chinese, and so forth.[45] She describes this phenomenon as color muting. Ironically, Pollock notes how even she was affected by her respondents' silences on racism and at times would use color-muted language to describe racial issues. Pierce finds a similar phenomenon in her study of a law firm that was sued in the 1970s for "egregious discrimination."[46] Because of the lawsuit, the firm worked hard to present itself as "excellent in diversity." That public presentation silenced any discussion on racism, because the firm was supposed to be color-blind in its practices. Talking about racism, then, was seen as doing something wrong. That is precisely what Barbara J. Risman and Pallavi Banerjee find in their study of schoolchildren, who feel guilty for noticing racial inequality and talking about it.[47] What all these studies show is that liberal color-blind ideology creates an environment that confines racial discourse to uncritical conversations on "multiculturalism" or "diversity." The larger ideology of color-blindness leads to racism-evasiveness.

Finally, the concepts many scholars have developed to explain color-blind ideology are themselves racism-evasive. Just as Pollock was affected by color-mute practices in the schools she studied, I believe racism scholars, in general, are impacted by the very racist ideologies they are trying to address. Cazenave attributes the lack of conceptual clarity on color-blindness and racism in the social sciences to what he calls Linguistic Racial Accommodation (LRA).[48] He argues that most academics are conflict averse. Scholars examine the "race issue," "minorities," "culture," and the like, never conceptualizing what "race" is or how it operates in a larger system of racism.[49] Moreover, academia as an institution rewards those who remain in the LRA tradition while punishing scholars who engage in Linguistic Racial Confrontation (LRC). This perpetuates a cycle that sustains LRA over LRC to the detriment of honest and intellectually sophisticated scholarship on racism.

Cazenave's model explains the conceptual confusion I find within the scholarship on color-blind racism and reveals the power color-blind ideology and racism-evasiveness have in the larger society.[50] Scholars of color-blind or so-called post–civil rights racism critique respondents for denying racism, yet the terms these scholars develop also underplay the central importance of racism. Ruth Frankenberg recognizes that the term "color-blind" obscures complex political and social dynamics.[51] Yet Frankenberg's concept of color evasion fails to capture the central issue of racism, again refocusing the discussion on color. Her concept of power evasion is better at identifying the central issues in racial discourse today. Frankenberg explains that power evasiveness in racial discourse downplays "differences of racial identity and their connections to positions of domination and subordination."[52] Still, the issue of racism is not centrally named. Power operates on many levels, and one can talk about power in a way that avoids racism. Power with regard to class inequality is often more comfortably addressed than racial inequality. In fact, a student in my racial and ethnic relations course used an analysis of power to deny racism. She argued, "It all comes down to power; if you have money, you have power regardless of ethnicity." Scholars must develop concepts that will adequately capture this kind of avoidance and denial of racism that maintains white supremacy. My conceptualizations of racism-evasiveness and liberal white supremacy pinpoint these issues more centrally. What people are ultimately avoiding when they say they do not see color (color-blind), when they overlook differences in power (power-evasion), or avoid "race words" (color-mute) is *racism*.

Cazenave defines racism-blindness as "the dominant ideology and practice of not seeing systemic racism in highly racialized societies in which strong sanctions are applied in the denial of its existence, pervasiveness, and consequences."[53] He defines racism-evasiveness as "the deployment of various processes and practices that avoid treating systemic racism as a social problem by keeping society blind to the pervasive racism that would otherwise be obvious."[54] Further, he defines racism denial as "the refutation of the existence, pervasiveness, or seriousness of systemic racism despite overwhelming evidence to the contrary."[55] I address *strategic* racism-evasiveness as the product or consequence of societal color-blind ideology. I argue that the shared ideology in U.S. society, and among progressives in particular, is not that we should be blind to racism, but that we should be blind to color. The result of this seemingly well-intended ideology is racism-evasiveness and denial.

Building on my previous work, I see racism-evasiveness as a *strategic action*; the response to and negative consequence of *color-blind* ideology.[56] In my past work, I found that activists did, in fact, see racism. They had sophisticated understandings of racism and never denied its central significance but were afraid to address it explicitly. I expand on this case study in chapter 4. I address racism-evasiveness as an action individuals strategically deploy within their organizations, particularly because organizational cultures are influenced by larger societal ideologies and liberal discourse on civility and color-blindness. Just as scholars are punished for addressing racism centrally,[57] progressive activists may be portrayed as too controversial, radical, and divisive if they make racism an explicit part of their agenda.

Furthermore, in her study of predominantly white law firms, Tsedale Melaku states, "White male discriminators disappear into vague or abstract terms (e.g., society discriminates)."[58] In such professional settings, European Americans do name systemic racism, but they may do so to hide their individual agency in contributing to racism in their workplaces. I have found the same behavior in academic workshops meant to educate European Americans about racism. They point to the institution or the system as the problem rather than examining their own potentially racist behavior. They consciously and strategically evade racism, when it serves their rational self-interests to do so, even while they explicitly name racism as a problem.

Conceptualizing Liberal White Supremacy

Liberal white supremacy includes the behaviors, practices, beliefs, and rhetorical moves by progressive European Americans who deny their role in perpetuating racism to maintain their position as morally superior, not only to people of color, but to other European Americans. Like color-blind ideology and racism-evasiveness, liberal white supremacy is part of the racist culture Carter Wilson identifies. To understand how, I magnify the racist culture component of Wilson's model to more closely examine how all the parts within it interact. Figure 2 shows that color-blind ideology leads to racism-evasiveness, and both work together as key components of liberal white supremacy and contemporary racism.

Racism-evasiveness can be further broken down to show the tropes it involves. Racism-evasiveness includes arguments that position class, gender, and culture over racism as the more important variables in social life, "race-talk," linguistic racial accommodation, and race-craft.[59] There are also liberal behaviors that are tied to racism-evasiveness but are more immediately about promoting a virtuous pro-white core.[60] White fragile behaviors of crying, defensiveness, pointing to friends of color, diverse workplaces, neighborhoods, and schools as justifications of one's antiracist politics uphold liberal white supremacy. When European Americans

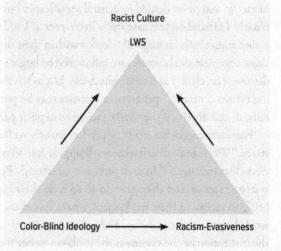

FIGURE 2
Liberal White Supremacy
as Part of Racist Culture
Color-Blind Ideology leads
to Racism-Evasive actions,
practices, and behaviors.
Both of these help maintain
liberal white supremacy. The
interactions between these
ideologies, behaviors, and
practices are part of the racist
culture conceptualized by
Carter Wilson, which I model
in figure 1.

engage in these behaviors, the focus and concern remains on their feelings and need for validation rather than the actual injustices people of color face and how to combat these injustices. Such conversations easily come to center around convincing European Americans, responding to *their* feelings and addressing *their* criticisms so that they may feel comfortable about racial inequality. In this context European Americans may dominate the discussions and may even be seen as the experts on racism or what is more often addressed as "diversity, equity, and inclusion" rather than people of color who have actually experienced and researched these issues. Asserting moral superiority above working-class white racists and poorly behaving radicals represents the class-elitist behaviors of liberal white supremacists, defined in the introduction (see figure 3).

Liberal white supremacy reinforces a white racial frame that positions European Americans as superior and people of color as inferior.[61] When liberal European Americans use various rhetorical and other tools to assert their level of enlightenment on racism, they are viewing themselves as superior and placing people of color in a subordinate position to be used as needed. For example, when they point to their friends or relatives of color, the diverse schools their children attend, the people of color they admire or vote for, and so forth, they *use* and objectify people of color. European Americans position themselves in the dominant role even on a subject, such as racism, where people of color are the more likely experts. In contradiction to Anna Julia Cooper's famous statement, European Americans who operate in this white racial frame are deciding when and where people of color may enter the conversation.[62]

Liberal white supremacy is also furthered by political elites, who benefit from oppressive economic and racial arrangements and work to sustain them. I have al-

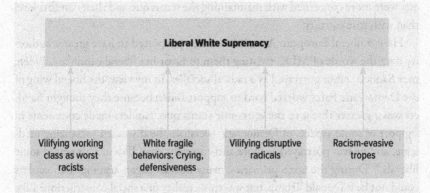

FIGURE 3
Practices That Uphold Liberal White Supremacy

ready outlined how conservatives, such as President Nixon, have contributed to liberal color-blind ideology to support their positions in the economic and racial order. Liberal elites secure their positions in electoral and local politics and gain access to important occupational roles that exist because of the liberal ideals of equality they allegedly support. For example, positions in "diversity management" operate within liberal principles of equality but address racism in a nonconfrontational way that ultimately protects predominantly white institutions. These kinds of positions help contain radicalism, as diversity becomes something to manage. Workshops and conversations on "race" are not really about combatting racist practices that impact people of color but controlling radical discourse and challenges to the institution.[63]

Politicians draw on liberal ideologies that support "diversity" to further their own success. President Bill Clinton was able to secure support from African Americans on a liberal, diversity platform. He claimed to support a liberal cause that was inclusive of people of color and was credited for having a diverse cabinet. At the same time, he developed policies that hurt working-class African Americans, other people of color, and working-class European Americans.[64] We continue to see liberal white supremacy in today's political debates and campaigns. In March 2020, Joe Biden supporter Hillary Rosen attempted to lecture Nina Turner, Bernie Sanders's campaign cochair, on Martin Luther King Jr.'s "Letter from Birmingham Jail." Rosen, a European American woman, claimed that King was only criticizing silent moderates, not people like Joe Biden. She further stated to Turner that she had no standing to criticize Biden by using the words of MLK. Turner, an African American woman, responded, "Don't tell me about Martin Luther King. Are you kidding me? Don't tell me what kind of standing I have as a black woman in America! How dare you!"[65] Furthermore, Turner explained that to MLK, white moderates were more concerned with maintaining the status quo and their comfort level than with true equality.

Here, a liberal European American women purported to have greater authority over the words of MLK, twisting them to favor her liberal candidate, Biden, over Sanders, often portrayed as a radical socialist. In my view, the liberal wing of the Democratic Party worked hard to support Biden because they thought Sanders was a greater threat to the economic status quo. Sanders made comments in support of some aspects of Democratic socialism, he discussed socializing medicine, and he was portrayed as more anti-capitalist than Biden. This scared some liberals.[66] During the 2020 primaries, many liberals began arguing that Sanders could not beat Donald Trump, but was this a reality or a social construction? Like Trump, Sanders had the ability to mobilize marginalized working-class European Americans and those who felt like outsiders. At the same time that liberal Democrats were claiming that Sanders could not win, people were stating they would vote for anyone but Trump. So was liberal Democratic support of Biden really about his ability to beat Trump, or was it about their commitment to maintaining capitalism at all costs? This is also a question we should pose when examining the debates and disagreements between representatives such as Alexandria Ocasio-Cortez and Ilhan Omar, who represent a more radical wing of the Democratic Party, and House Speaker Nancy Pelosi, who represents the liberal, mainstream Democrat. What we have been witnessing is a radical/liberal split within the Democratic Party, and that split is tied to racism-evasiveness and liberal white supremacy. In the next chapter, I further develop this connection by presenting my model that distinguishes liberal and radical perspectives and approaches.

CHAPTER 2

Liberals and Radicals, a Conceptual Model

The white conservatives aren't friends of the Negro either, but they at least don't try to hide it. They are like wolves; they show their teeth in a snarl that keeps the Negro always aware of where he stands with them. But the white liberals are foxes, who also show their teeth to the Negro but pretend that they are smiling. The white liberals are more dangerous than the conservatives; they lure the Negro, and as the Negro runs from the growling wolf, he flees into the open jaws of the "smiling" fox... the wolf and the fox both belong to the (same) family. Both are canines; and no matter which one of them the Negro places his trust in, he never ends up in the White House, but always in the dog house.

—Malcolm X, 1963

The original commitment in Vietnam was made by President Truman, a mainstream liberal. It was seconded by President Eisenhower, a moderate liberal. It was intensified by the late President Kennedy, a flaming liberal. Think of the men who now engineer that war—those who study the maps, give the commands, push the buttons, and tally the dead... They are all honorable men. They are all liberals.

—Carl Oglesby, *Let Us Shape the Future*, 1965

Brief History of the Liberal/Radical Split

This chapter clarifies the distinctions between political liberals and radicals. While there is a perception of a fragmented left, few have outlined what this fragmentation involves. I review the scholarship on divisions within the left and draw distinctions between liberals and radicals based on this literature, my twenty years of experience in professional, so-called liberal academia, ten years living in a racially diverse liberal community, and my past research on progressive organizations. There are four key elements I examine that distinguish liberals from radicals: perspective on capitalism, approach to racism and interracial organizing, approach to class and working-class people, and mode of activism (confrontational versus nonconfrontational tactics). By confrontational, I do not mean violent. Confrontational tactics are disruptive, but they do not have to be violent. In fact, the Student Nonviolent Coordinating Committee was one of the more confrontational organizations of the 1960s. Confrontational tactics go against standard procedures. Such tactics may include open disobedience to unjust or unreasonable rules, taking the unpopular position such as refusing to salute the flag, or occupying buildings until one's position is heard. Activists using confrontational tactics are not concerned with staying on the good side of their opponents or making their institutions look good.

While I offer some clear distinctions between liberals and radicals, it is best to think about them as existing on a continuum. People are often contradictory and rarely subscribe to one set of beliefs or actions. Thus, a person may be liberal in their beliefs but radical in their actions. I have met many people who identify as liberals but are radical in their beliefs and behavior. This was the case for Micaela, one of the three key activists in my case study of Essex Town (see chapter 3). She self-identified as a liberal, but her tactics were radical, and she was constantly berated for using these tactics. Liberals and conservatives may also be more alike than either would care to admit. One key similarity between liberals and conservatives is their embrace, or at least noncritique, of the capitalistic power structure. Liberals have a history of aligning with this power structure against radicals. Historically, this difference played a key role in their division from each other.

Liberal Apologists, Radical Communists

Historian Doug Rossinow traces the history of conflict and cooperation between liberals and leftists.[1] He argues that liberals and radicals had an amicable relationship between the 1880s to 1940s. This alliance was particularly significant during

the era of the "Popular Front," 1935 to 1948. At this time, liberals actually supported revolution in some parts of the world. However, a severe wedge between
liberals and radicals began to grow during the late 1930s with their different approaches to capitalism and communism. As the United States turned more conservative between the years 1940 to 1960, liberals attacked the left to appear more
reliable to the power establishment. Radicals at this time were staunchly critical of American capitalism and saw liberals as "handmaidens to America's ruling
cliques."[2] Rossinow argues that radicals showed more passion and less care to public opinion than liberals. Radicals did not view capitalism as a system that could be
tweaked to benefit society. To radicals, capitalism was inherently "immoral and exploitative."[3] Radicals were often dubbed communists, whether they self-identified
this way or not, and targeted for their political views.[4]

During the McCarthy Era of the 1940s and 1950s, suspected communist sympathizers, often simply people who openly opposed war, were fired by their employers. Political leaders arrested, imprisoned, and censored those who spoke out
against war and actively promoted propaganda to portray radicals as enemies.[5]
College courses, newspapers, and other publications were monitored to ensure a
pro-war message dominated. Left-leaning theaters and papers were monitored and
defunded. When the United Electrical, Radio, and Machine Workers of America refused to produce records for the Joint Anti-Fascist Refugee Committee, they
were physically attacked with no help from police.[6]

Woodrow Wilson was unrelenting in his efforts to discredit anyone who spoke
or wrote against the US involvement in World War I. Wilson created the Committee for Public Information, headed by George Creel, who admitted that the
commission's intent was to discredit anyone who opposed the war.[7] To protect
themselves, liberals participated in this war propaganda machine and blatantly col-
luded with the political elite. Liberal organizations, such as Americans for Democratic Action (ADA) took part in silencing radicals.[8] In the 1940s and 1950s, the
ADA backed the search for communists. According to journalist Chris Hedges,
they did so because they were careerists who desired prestige.[9] The newspapers liberals have come to rely on and view as legitimate sources participated in this de-
monization of the left. The *Washington Post* called Eugene Debs "a public menace"
who should be behind bars, after he was arrested for denouncing the war and ad-
vocating direct action.[10] The *New York Times* called Jane Addams unpatriotic after
she was booed for speaking against the war at Carnegie Hall.[11]

The rift between liberals and radicals was also played out in the film industry
and involved liberal filmmaker Stanley Kramer. While Carl Foreman was working
with Kramer on the film *High Noon*, he was called to testify in front of the House

Un-American Activities Committee. During his testimony, Foreman renounced his Communist Party membership but refused to give the names of his friends.[12] Kramer allegedly bent to political pressure, pushing Foreman off the movie set of *High Noon* and denying Foreman a production credit. After McCarthy's hunts had all but ended, Kramer went on to create films with clearly leftist themes in 1958, 1959, and 1960.[13] Rossinow states, "Those on the left no doubt felt that the moral elitism of well-placed liberals such as Kramer rested on a rotten foundation, with the liberals championing causes pioneered by leftists whom they had knifed in the back."[14]

In the 1940s, the American Civil Liberties Union (ACLU) issued a statement intended to chill any members within the Popular Front who might have communist sympathies. Historian Judy Kutulas asserts that the ACLU was at first radical but took on the image of "liberal respectability" as it became a mainstream, institutionalized organization, and opposed communists out of fear.[15] They monitored candidate statements to make sure that none of their leaders were pro-communist. Rossinow notes, "The ACLU embraced the official orthodoxy of cold war America before there was a cold war."[16] Once the cold war was underway, however, the ACLU and other anti-communist organizations were only emboldened by wartime propaganda. In 1949, the Congress of Industrial Organizations (CIO) expelled left-leaning unions that may have included anarchists, communists, or socialists.[17] During the Vietnam War, the American Federation of Labor and Congress of Industrial Organizations (AFL-CIO) attacked radicals opposed to war and issued a statement in support of the war. At the end of the day, Hedges concludes, "Unions, formerly steeped in the doctrine of class struggle and filled with those who sought broad social and political rights for the working class, collaborated with the capitalist class and merged with the liberal establishment."[18]

After the war, in 1947, the organization Americans for Democratic Action was determined to make liberalism anti-communist and divide the left/liberal coalition within the Popular Front by any means necessary.[19] To achieve this, "diversity," a liberal concept, was exploited. Communism was such a sticking point for the power elite that they were willing to concede on the issue of racism.[20] The economic and political elite were not bothered by liberal attempts to promote civil rights, which had become a clear marker of liberal identity. They were more concerned with purging the Popular Front of communists and anyone who may have supported communism even in the slightest.[21] Thus, liberals (including Martin Luther King Jr.) were allowed to pursue civil rights as long as they denounced communism at the same time. They embraced racial inclusion but not insurgency.[22] The conclusion we can draw from this historical moment is that the power elite, and middle-class liberals, would ultimately accept people of color, women, and the LGBTQIA (lesbian, gay, bisexual, transgender, queer/questioning, intersex, asexual) community, as long as they would conform to the capitalist status quo. Middle-class liberals turned their backs on radical scholars, such as W. E. B. Du Bois, who continually criticized capitalism.[23] Du Bois remained popular among the African American working class.[24]

By the mid-1950s, liberals and conservatives were united in their stand against communism. In fact, Roderick Bush argued that it was the liberal collusion with the political right and repression of radical leftists that fractured any burgeoning liberal-left consensus.[25] The National Association for the Advancement of Colored People (NAACP) removed any members suspected of communism, "refusing to associate with them for fear that they too would be red-baited."[26] European American liberals in the Student Nonviolent Coordinating Committee (SNCC) pressured members to disassociate from organizations that were suspected of housing communist sympathizers, but working-class people of color in SNCC refused to do so.[27] Radicals within the new left of the 1960s "routinely denounced a 'liberal establishment,' led by men such as President John Kennedy and Lyndon Johnson, as in fact far too conservative, too close to the 'power-elite,' and insensitive to the plight of the social excluded."[28] In 1963, Students for a Democratic Society (SDS) wrote a statement called "America and the New Era," which detailed their concerns with "corporate liberalism." Doug Rossinow analyzes the significance of this manifesto:

> They [SDS] thought street politics and open conflict formed the true path to progress, and they lamented that sincere liberals in unions and elsewhere had abandoned "protest marches, local reform movements, and independent bases of power." . . . Contemporary liberals had forsaken activism for lobbying, an outside role for an inside one. They had been captured, perhaps bought . . . "corporate liberalism" was . . . an attempt by conservatives to *fool liberals into thinking they had friends in power* (emphasis mine).[29]

Indeed, Carl Oglesby of Students for a Democratic Society argued that there were two types of liberalism, a humanist one and one that masqueraded as humanist. He named anti-communist corporate liberalism as the type that worked for the corporate state. It promoted the propaganda that U.S. capitalism and imperialism were rescuing poorer countries from their savage ways. I see this pro-capitalist agenda continue to play out in K–12 curriculum, PTA-led fundraisers, and other events in progressive communities. This is the first key factor that separates liberals from radicals: their perspectives on capitalism.

Perspectives on Capitalism

In Table 1, I distinguish between liberal and radical perspectives on capitalism, their approaches to racism, approaches to class, and tactics.[30] Liberals are apologists for capitalistic exploitation. They see problems in this system but have not embraced a "shift change,"[31] and in this way, they are similar to political moderates and conservatives. Like moderates and conservatives, liberals do not want to be associated with Marxism and are likely not familiar with his writings beyond *The Communist Manifesto*, which they may not have even read. With regard to communism, liberals have what Noel A. Cazenave calls the IPA syndrome, which is "the *ignorance* of not knowing, the *privilege* of not needing to know, and the *arrogance* of not wanting to know."[32] *The Communist Manifesto* is less than one hundred pages long. Karl Marx wrote thousands of pages on capitalism in his multivolume work *Das Kapital*. Liberals tend to regurgitate standard critiques of communism and socialism as failed experiments in the Union of Soviet Socialist Republics (USSR) and rarely do any reading beyond that common critique. They fail to distinguish between communism or socialism in name versus communism or socialism in practice. Hence, they do not get the oft-cited joke among radicals that Karl Marx said of people misapplying his ideas, "If that is Marxism, then I am not a Marxist." Using a Marxist analysis, economists Satya Gabriel, Stephan A. Resnick, and Richard D. Wolff explained that the USSR and People's Republic of China (PRC) were not examples of realized communism but feudalism en route to state capitalism in the PRC and a form of state capitalism in the USSR.[33] True communism, by Karl Marx's standards, would allow the working class to control and distribute the surplus they created.[34] In both the USSR and the PRC, the state controlled the surplus and made decisions about its distribution. In the PRC, the state was quite abusive of their workers, which would certainly not gain Marx's approval. The city of Magnitogorsk in the Soviet Union was actually designed by *American* engineers, and it was made to mimic the American *capitalist* city of Gary, Indiana.[35] The USSR also censored its intellectuals, more in line with fascism than communism.

Liberals fail to grasp these nuances. Instead, they think capitalism is the best system possible and believe it can be reformed, whereas radicals debate significant alternatives to capitalism. Worker cooperatives are one such alternative of which liberals seem to have very little knowledge. Mondragon, a federation of worker cooperatives in Spain, which includes universities, engineers, food service, construction, and many more industries, has received much attention by economists, such as Wolff and Resnick, as well as independent news media, such as *Democracy*

TABLE 1
Liberal versus Radical Approaches

	Capitalism	Class prejudice and working-class issues	Racism and interracial organizing	Tactics
Liberals	Uncritical embrace of capitalism as best system. Focus on limited reforms. Feel-good charity initiatives in schools preferred to critiques of capitalism as a system perpetuating poverty.	Dismissive of working-class issues and negative stereotyping of working-class people as "backward," "rednecks," "deplorables." Limited examination of liberal class prejudice, class exploitation, internalized class superiority.	Talk-centered on racism rather than action-centered. Book clubs and neighborhood groups value "diversity" and "inclusion." Tend to fall for figureheads (people of color in power). Need for validation as "good white people" and alleviation of "white guilt." Expressions of "white fragility," paternalism, attempts at "color capital." Use of people of color as tokens. Outrage at racism, but failure to discuss class prejudice.	Nonconfrontational tactics including discussion groups or workshops, book clubs, candlelight vigils, unity dinners. Fear of and aversion to disrupting established rules. Conformist. Offer testimony at board of education, aldermanic, or other meetings, participate in popular marches, but rarely march or occupy spaces, especially in one's own community. Heavy reliance on and faith in electoral politics.
Radicals	Focus on revolutionary reform of capitalism. View capitalism as inherently exploitative. Discussion on alternatives to capitalism, such as worker self-directed enterprises. Critique of charity as a limited reform.	Focus on working-class issues as a central concern. Interracial unity through common class oppression. Greater sympathy for living and working conditions of poor and working-class people. Some groups examine racist attitudes among working-class "white" people.	Action-centered on racism rather than talk-centered. Prefer taking direct action against oppression. Less focus on white guilt. Practical class-centered focus. Not afraid to challenge people of color in power. Tend not to fall for figureheads.	Mix of confrontational and nonconfrontational tactics. Willing to be uncomfortable and make those in power feel uncomfortable. Disrupt meetings, challenge unjust rules, express open dissent. March and occupy spaces, even when unpopular to do so. Participate in, but not rely on, electoral politics. Little faith in elections.

Now and *Thom Hartmann*. Mondragon cooperatives give the workers a voice in decisions that affect them. These cooperatives are profitable, but wages are regulated so that executives do not make more than five times what the average worker makes. This is different from the typical scenario in the United States, where the top CEOs make more than three hundred times what the average worker earns, a gap that has increased over the years, controlling for inflation.[36]

Mondragon is just one example of a successful cooperative. Catherine Mulder published one of the first in-depth studies of what she calls Worker Self-Directed Enterprises (WSDEs) around the world.[37] She examines six case studies of WSDEs, where workers have more control over the production and distribution of the surplus. These include the London Symphony Orchestra, the Green Bay Packers, New Era Windows, Organopónico Vivero Alamar, Lusty Ladies, and the Syracuse Cooperative Federal Credit Union. Currently, Mulder is writing about a cooperative system in Italy, where children are taught cooperation rather than competition as part of their formal education. In the United States, there is more of a focus on capitalistic competition in many public schools and a curriculum that focuses on rational choice business and individualism. U.S. students do not seriously debate alternatives to the prevailing ideology on capitalism.

When WSDEs fail, many liberals take this as evidence of capitalism's superiority to other systems. What liberal thinking fails to examine are the reasons behind the failure of some WSDEs that cannot compete so long as extreme profit and exploitation continue to be accepted as the norm. Liberals know less about WSDEs than radicals, because they tend to read and watch only mainstream liberal news, such as the *New York Times*, the *Economist*, and the *Huffington Post*. They do not, as often, view or read more radical, independent news, such as *Democracy Now*, *Pacifica Radio*, *Economic Update with Richard Wolff*, *Counterpunch*, and *Democracy Works*. During 2018–2019, the *New York Times* published five stories that included the term "worker-owned." Two of these stories were theater reviews of a play that referenced a worker-owned cooperative. Another was a wedding announcement about a couple, one of whom works with a cooperative. The fourth article was an opinion piece that criticized democratic socialism and claimed that worker-cooperatives *always* led to crisis. The fifth article, on home health care, quoted a person who worked for a cooperative. None of the articles provided a careful or even cursory look into the actual workings of existing cooperatives. *Counterpunch* published twenty-one stories in the same year that included the term "worker-owned." These stories did not merely quote someone who happened to work for a cooperative; they offered a deeper examination of problems in current economic conditions and cited in-depth studies of cooperatives. They compared cooperatives and discussed their strengths and weaknesses. Eleven of these articles offered an in-depth look into existing cooperatives or dedicated significant space to discussing how cooperatives run. The rest briefly named worker-cooperatives as an alternative but did not describe them in detail. However, even these articles, unlike those in the *New York Times*, did not shy away from offering in-depth analyses of capitalism's limitations, citing research rather than relying solely on opinion and evaluating possible alternatives. Not all of these articles embraced cooperatives unequivocally. In previous years, *Counterpunch* also shared interviews with Noam Chomsky, who has characterized Mondragon as worker owned but not worker managed and pointed out that when profit is the driving force, exploitation (even in cooperatives) will continue.[38] The *New York Times* and other liberal-minded news sources are not completely blind to radical ideas, such as worker cooperatives, but they offer less space to these ideas. This is because they have to appease a mixture of corporate sponsors and liberal audiences.

In my own liberal community, schools focus on creating change by partnering with corporations. My daughter's seventh-grade class discussed how a company could help end poverty. One sharp student stated, "Make the rich pay," and was swiftly attacked by other students, who stated that this would never work. The student followed up with another idea of lowering food prices and was criticized again by classmates who said, "How is a small business supposed to make money if they lower their prices?" This debate would have been wonderful if the students were being moved to truly think critically about the system of capitalism and imagine alternatives to capitalism. Instead, this was a class based on entrepreneurship, where you were supposed to create a product to better the world. It was a nice idea, but the class was never taught the true reasons for why a small business in a capitalistic world could not put a dent in poverty. Students must first understand how power and politics work. They must be given the tools to analyze strengths and weaknesses in antipoverty policies. They should be advised that, in fact, the rich did pay higher taxes in recent history, things were not as they are today, and food prices can be manipulated. They could be taught about food deserts and question why healthy food is more expensive as well as why food provided to poor people is so high in fat. Students could be taught about WSDEs and asked to come up with creative ways to start one and imagine ways to counter challenges they would face.

I often wonder if the liberal parents promoting this entrepreneurial education and fundraisers for the "underprivileged" really want to change poverty. If school children (and all of us) engaged in critical discussions about redistribution of wealth, universal health care, making the rich pay as they did in the past, reorganizing the federal budget, and serious alternatives to capitalism, then perhaps we would achieve greater equality. However, that would mean these parents would have to find something else to do with the time they put into clothing drives and "kindness matters" campaigns that make them feel good about themselves. Noam Chomsky sums up the issue by stating that liberals "perceive themselves as challenging power, as courageous, as standing up for truth and justice . . . They say 'Look how courageous I am.' But do not go one millimeter beyond that. At least for the educated sectors, they are the most dangerous in supporting power."[39] For many liberals, the point is to show that they are on the right side. They are the good ones. They want credit. But that is their only motivation. Beyond that, they do not challenge capitalism, read people who seriously challenge capitalism, or think hard about alternatives to capitalism. What we are left with now, according to Hedges, is a "liberal class, cornered and weak, engaged in the politically safe game of attacking the barbarism of communism—and, later, Islamic militancy—rather than attempting to fight the mounting injustices and structural abuses of the corporate state. The anemic liberal class continues to assert, despite ample evidence to the contrary, that human freedom and equality can be achieved through the charade of electoral politics and constitutional reform."[40] In fact, Marx saw electoral politics as a type of illusory human freedom. We have all sorts of abstract freedoms: the freedom of speech, religious freedom, freedom of assembly. These are all important, but when we actually assert some of these freedoms in a way that truly challenges power, we are often squashed by pepper spray, rubber bullets, and policies of "expressive conduct" that limit where and when we get to assemble on college campuses. This will not change so long as liberals uncritically accept capitalism as a necessary evil. The weak, reform-based liberal perspective on capitalism and morally superior attitude also translate into their preferred brand of activism and approach to racism.

The Liberal Approach to Racism:
Liberal White Supremacy in Interracial
Friendships and Progressive Organizations

I have conceptualized liberals as more racism centered (although superficially) and radicals as more class centered. Ironically, the opposite used to be true. In the 1930s and 1940s, European American liberals thought the class-based policies of the New Deal would take care of all forms of inequality. They had an aloofness to racism that did little to attract people of color. Radicals challenged liberals to become more staunchly antiracist and criticized white chauvinism.[41] It was not until "the Second Progressive era as white liberals with *painful slowness* [emphasis mine], began to see the political wisdom of competing with the left for the mantle of Friend to the Negro" that liberals began to strategically welcome African Americans into their ranks.[42]

African Americans continued to voice suspicions of European American liberals throughout the 1960s. At a SNCC meeting in 1965, John Lewis stated that
white liberals and wealthy African Americans would "sell us down the river for
the hundredth time in order to protect themselves."[43] James Baldwin often questioned the actions of white liberals, and Kenneth Clark noted the tendency of
white liberals to be all talk. Stokely Carmichael stated flat out that SNCC did not
need white liberals, and a Harlem activist asserted, "White liberals are the slimiest
snakes on earth."[44] This distrust had to do with liberals' long history of behaving
badly in interracial organizations. In 1966, SNCC wrote a position paper, entitled
"Black Power," that addressed the role of European Americans in the Black liberation movement. Among other issues, this paper highlighted key problems with
European Americans' superior attitudes, a flawed focus on unity, paternalism, and
liberal insensitivity to both Black and white workers. The paper also noted the re-
actionary stance of the middle-class NAACP, which they thought was controlled
by the white liberal power structure.[45]

SNCC argued that the presence of European Americans in their movement
silenced African Americans and perpetuated their own inferiority. They maintained that guilt and fear was what motivated European American liberals to organize with African Americans, who were not seen as able to effectively organize
by themselves. Therefore, SNCC put forth a new role for European American liberals. They should get their own house in order by examining the racism within
their own white communities. SNCC addressed the same issue Baldwin questioned, "Do I really want to be integrated in a burning house?"[46] Baldwin also
wrote a scathing critique of the white liberal psyche. He argued that beneath the
white liberal's desire for integration was a need to reassure themselves of their own
self-worth. Therefore, Baldwin suggested, "A vast amount of energy that goes into
what we call the Negro problem is produced by the white man's profound desire
not to be judged by those who are not white ... at the same time a vast amount of
the white anguish is rooted in the white man's equally profound need to be seen as
he is, to be released from the tyranny of his mirror."[47] He criticized the white liberal tendency to paternalistically congratulate African Americans on their progress, as in Bobby Kennedy's assurance that one day an African American would be
president.

Today, some of what SNCC requested has been answered. European Americans are organizing among themselves, teaching each other about racism, and having discussions on racism. However, they have not overcome or even begun to address the fundamental flaw James Baldwin raised: the tendency to see people of
color either as symbols or victims.[48] It is here that I believe liberal tears over racism
and the overly enthusiastic praise of President Obama fits. Both reactions are dis-

honest. I argue that this behavior, white anguish and guilt, continues to plague liberal organizing today. Being guided by this need to be released from their own history of tyranny prevents liberals from being effective organizers.

I have witnessed a range of liberal practices, when it comes to talking about and acting directly against racism and have dealt with these practices in many academic conversations on white privilege and racism.[49] These practices include denial, where liberals desperately try to deflect attention from racism as a central issue by pointing to gender or class. Some of these same individuals exhibit white fragility that includes crying or dominating discussions in a way that keeps the focus on them.[50] This denial practice also includes pointing to family or friends of color as evidence that they know more about racism than the average white person. These practices are all part of the liberal white supremacy I outlined in chapter 1. Rather than listening to people of color or trying to understand their experiences with racism, European Americans attempt to control the discussion and compete with each other for the title of most enlightened white person. Decades of research has documented these racism-evasive, color-blind approaches among liberals.[51]

Liberals in neighborhood groups and talk-centered book clubs reproduce the same behaviors. What is the purpose of these talks? Are they intended to challenge systemic racism or merely to clear one's conscience and get on the right side of the "good nonracist/bad racist" binary? Bethan Benwell offers one answer. She finds that liberals in book clubs manage their antiracist impressions by disparaging "racist others," who are older or less educated.[52] Benwell studied discussions in the UK, Africa, the Caribbean, India, and Canada. These same strategies are common in the United States as well. Liberal European Americans distinguish themselves from racist others by region, age, social class, and education. The southern, uneducated, "redneck," especially the Trump supporter, is the racist other against which many liberal antiracists juxtapose themselves today.[53]

Some members of liberal, antiracist groups have begun to express dissatisfaction with aimless lengthy meetings, where the psychological aspects of racism and white identity are discussed with little focus on methods to combat institutional racism.[54] These talks also manifest the liberal white supremacy I have conceptualized here. Members of antiracist organizations share that there is a superior attitude among antiracist European Americans. Respondents in sociologist Eileen O'Brien's study of such groups described antiracists as "condescending," "arrogant," and "judgmental."[55] Elaborating on this behavior, they stated: "Humility is something that white people need big time, because even in this antiracist organization I have found that many of them develop this notion that I am better than anybody. Some of them develop the belief that they are better than the average white because they're 'beyond' and then some of them believe they're better than us because they understand."[56] Reflecting on the behavior of white antiracists, a person of color stated: "Often times I find white antiracist workers a bit judging. I think that they set themselves above their white peers. I think that often this marker of antiracism gets worn as a banner that yeah, I'm down with the black people, the colored people, the 'whatever' people."[57] O'Brien writes extensively on the tendency of antiracist European Americans to separate themselves from other racist European Americans. These antiracists lack empathy for those who do not share their progressive beliefs and tend to get angry at every racist incident they see, making a scene and berating other European Americans for their behavior. Since people of color may face racism every day, we often do not and cannot cause a scene every time we see an injustice. Indignant, self-righteous white antiracism in these cases can actually cause more harm for people of color or put them in danger. I have had this experience multiple times with white antiracist friends and partners who feel the need to talk loudly with me about how horrible white people are or point to every noticeable racist incident, even when we are supposed to be enjoying a relaxing outing together. They may view their behavior as protective, but it is often the opposite.

European American antiracists may feel so compelled to protect their friends of color that they monitor their friendships with other European Americans.[58] In one case, this kind of paternalistic behavior went so far as a European American antiracist woman refusing to cosign her Latina friend's loan because she did not agree with her living in a predominantly white neighborhood. This liberal European American antiracist woman, who organized a multicultural book club, would only cosign if her Latina friend agreed to live in a neighborhood that was more diverse and suitable for people of color![59] In another case, a European American antiracist advised his friends of color against pursuing doctoral degrees because it would be too hard for them to navigate the white spaces and racism of higher education. These antiracists see people of color as incapable of knowing what is best for ourselves without the help of a superior European American liberal.

European American liberals also use people of color to show that they are sophisticated, progressive, and cool. This has been referred to as "color-capital."[60] Equally problematic is the tendency of liberals to overemphasize their diverse workplaces, neighborhoods, and organizations. One of Matthew Hughey's respondents (a self-identified antiracist white man) illustrated various aspects of this behavior in his enthusiasm for living in a diverse neighborhood. This respondent equated bringing one of his African American neighbors to his antiracist organization meeting as being like "show and tell" in elementary school.[61] Having African American neighbors gave this respondent more credibility among antiracists and showing his friend his membership in the organization made him look like one of the good nonracist white people.

Sociologist Megan Underhill finds that middle-class, liberal, European American parents seek out racially diverse neighborhoods for similar reasons.[62] These parents hope to raise sophisticated children by exposing them to diversity. They see living next to people of color as their contribution to social change. Robin DiAngelo characterizes this as "color-celebrate" behavior among liberal European Americans.[63] As long as people live or work in diverse areas, have people of color in the family (perhaps a child or grandchild), marched in the 1960s, or adopted a child from China, they feel they cannot be racist. Another element I would add to DiAngelo's color-celebrate list is the overly enthusiastic love of ethnic food or *performance* of eating ethnic food with the proper utensils (e.g., chopsticks). This performance becomes a signifier of their alleged cultural sophistication. What these liberal parents do not admit, and likely do not realize, is that they are using people of color as props, just as they might display an obscure piece of artwork, to maintain their image as cultured and progressive individuals.

I have previously written on European American liberal friendships with people of color as a component of emotional segregation. Emotional segregation is an inability of European Americans, due to historical and structural realities, to see people of color as emotional equals.[64] This is easily viewed as a problem with outspoken racists who openly dehumanized people of color in the Antebellum and Jim Crow South and "The New Jim Crow" through policing of African Americans today.[65] However, liberal European American antiracists also treat people of color in emotionally unequal ways. In interracial friendships, European Americans often expect their friends of color to be their teachers or someone to unload on as they learn how to be antiracist. In these friendships, the person of color acts as the European American's confidant. The person of color is expected to hold the European American's hand as they cry about the racism they see in the world, ultimately striving to convince their friend of color, and themselves, that they are good people. This is emotionally draining for people of color, and because these relationships are often based on the European American's comfort and well-being, they are not emotionally egalitarian relationships. Thus, liberal ideology is problematic not only in its inability, since the civil rights movement, to dismantle physical segregation, but also because it supports a kind of *emotional* segregation as well. Contrary to liberal beliefs, having friends of color, marrying people of color, or having multiracial children does not exempt them from racism or realize the dream of Dr. Martin Luther King Jr.

The problem James Baldwin identified in 1962 remains. Liberals are not dealing with their own feelings of superiority but addressing racism for the purpose of feeling better about themselves. Their guilt makes them ineffective at truly challenging white supremacy. They have not applied SNCC's vision for European American liberals accurately. What they must accept is that if they are to challenge racism, they have to be confrontational when it is uncomfortable to do so, join protests in the poor neighborhoods they are afraid to enter, and often *not* get credit, awards, or compliments for their activism. If they are truly committed to equality, the work cannot be about stroking their egos. Any European American liberal interested in creating significant change must have an honest conversation with themselves and truly examine why they are in the movement.

Liberals remain defensive about these critiques. On May 19, 2016, the ninety-first anniversary of Malcolm X's birthday, I shared Malcolm X's criticism of liberals on my Facebook page:

> The white liberal differs from the white conservative only in one way: the liberal is more deceitful than the conservative. The liberal is more hypocritical than the conservative. Both want power, but the white liberal is the one who has perfected the art of posing as the Negro's friend and benefactor; and by winning the friendship, allegiance, and support of the Negro, the white liberal is able to use the Negro as a pawn or tool in this political "football game" that is constantly raging between the white liberals and white conservatives.[66]

I also shared Malcolm X's comparison of conservatives to wolves and liberals to foxes. This post elicited some backlash from white liberals who were offended by Malcolm's comparison of them to animals. When Johnny Eric Williams, a respected scholar on racism who has been targeted for his views on white supremacy, shared my post of Malcolm's quote, a European American liberal begged, "Gentle friends; I hope that you view me as a person, not as a fox, wolf, donkey, or elephant." On the surface, this post calls for humanism, but it does so in a color-blind, nonhumanistic way that dismisses the importance of what Malcolm X had to say about racism among liberals. This reaction is a defensive one and indicative of a larger inability among liberals to be self-critical. What Malcolm X was expressing is still a fact of life for many people of color dealing with well-meaning liberals. In fact, one of the respondents in my case study of racism-evasiveness (see chapter 4) made this distinction when addressing southern and northern racism. She stated: "Don't grin in my face and act like you like me, but you're prejudiced. You really don't care for Black people." She characterized people in the Northeast as being "behind the closet" in their racism. Dealing with this subtle racism at work was what ultimately wore her down and informed her decision to retire. I have made the same remarks as this respondent about my time with political conservatives in western Pennsylvania versus my time with liberals in Connecticut, New York, and New Jersey. When racism is overt, I at least know where people stand. When it is subtle, expressed in paternalism, seemingly innocent questions of "Where are you from," assuming that I am nanny to my white-looking daughter, shock and jealousy, when European Americans, particularly women, learn of my success, or when they freely interrupt me but express irritation when I interrupt them, it adds another layer of frustration. When people of color deal with this form of racism, we have to exert greater emotional energy in reading and managing our emotions as well as the emotions of the people directing these so-called microaggressions at us.[67]

Liberals have a hard time accepting that they are part of the racism that Malcolm X lays out. This was especially apparent during the 2016 presidential election. Identifying as a liberal against Trump's tyranny seemed to constitute social justice action all by itself. Likewise, "embracing Barack Obama allowed 'white' liberals to prove they didn't have a racist bone in their bodies."[68] Liberals tend to fall for figureheads or token people of color and fail to criticize them when criticism is warranted. Many self-identified antiracist liberals are so immobilized by the fear of being called a racist, by guilt, and by their need to appear morally righteous that they can end up contributing to racism. Radical leftists were much more critical of Obama than liberals, who saw any criticism of Obama as promoting racism. Obama's rise to the presidency worked in line with liberal ideology; it was about gaining power and not seriously challenging the racial and economic status quo. By now, the story of Obama's assurance to Wall Street that he "had their back" is well known.[69]

Historian Jakobi Williams documented how liberal African Americans, such as Jessie Jackson and Barack Obama, appropriated the radical Black Panther Party's rainbow coalition politics for their own gain.[70] Barack Obama's rainbow politics, however, focused on courting middle-class, elite, and college-educated European Americans, whereas the Black Panthers focused on uniting the working class.[71] Thomas Frank notes that Obama sought out the most highly educated people he could find, a population that was far removed from the everyday lives and needs of the working class.[72] Frank states, "When the left party in a system severs its bonds to working people—when it dedicates itself to the concerns of a particular slice of high-achieving affluent people—issues of work and income inequality will inevitably fade from its list of concerns."[73] More than this inability to understand working-class *issues* is a deep-seated prejudice against working-class *people*. I turn now to this aspect of liberal white supremacy as another key distinction between liberals and radicals.

Approach to Class:
Liberal White Supremacy in Attitudes toward
Working-Class European Americans

In 2016, when Hillary Clinton was running for president, liberal class bias against the working class seemed to be at its peak. On September 9, HRC gave her now infamous speech at an LGBT fundraiser in New York City. She stated, "You know, to just be grossly generalistic, you could put half of Trump's supporters into what I call the basket of deplorables ... The racist, sexist, homophobic, xenophobic, Islamophobic—you name it."[74] Many have noted that Trump's behavior emboldened white supremacists, giving them national permission to be more forthright in their racism. We could make a similar claim about HRC and the liberal class. Her condemnation of Trump supporters gave liberals permission to openly denigrate the group of people they had long despised, working-class European Americans and so-called rednecks.[75] I shared my concerns about the liberals who supported HRC, and my analysis of why working-class voters did not trust her, right after the start of the Democratic National Convention. In an article for the progressive newspaper *Counterpunch*, I described the class divisions in working-class Appalachia.[76] Appalachian towns, like the one where I grew up, are not completely poor and white. They include solidly middle-class and upper-middle-class people. Poor and working-class children go to school with and live near small business owners, farmers with money and land, and the professional upper middle class—doctors, lawyers, and even public school teachers. As I stated in my article:

> Many public school teachers viewed themselves as elite and compared to us they were rich ... For many of us, HRC represents that upper crust of our towns whose family got to hang out at the country club while we worked in the supermarkets and fast food restaurants. Completely out of touch with the bread and butter issues we faced every day like putting food on the table, she was the rich kid in high school, who would use you for a vote, but look down on you when your back was turned. When we look at her, we see the kid who got to travel, wear nice clothes, and make fun of our torn up hand-me-down clothes. She was the kid who was on every page of the yearbook. She was in all the clubs and the teachers loved her.[77]

I went onto discuss how apparent political opposites like Trump, Sanders, and Warren could speak in a way that connected to these working-class people, but HRC could not. I argued, "Many people in these towns don't identify as middle class but are proud to be working class and they aren't going to trust a politician who doesn't speak passionately about the struggles they face every day." The reaction I got from middle- and upper-middle-class European American liberals showed a complete disconnection to the lives of the people I was describing. Their reaction was markedly different from that of my radical friends of color. The latter responded with praise, noting that I had gotten to the heart of the issue. One radical Black scholar shared my article, stating, "I hope the big shots in the Democrat party are reading... many people do not like Hillary Clinton, and [I] am not talking about the conservatives... At the end of the day, that article may seem like an attack on Hillary, but it is doing her a favor." Some of the radical-minded readers of *Counterpunch* also contacted me by phone and email informing me that the essay spoke to their experiences and concerns with HRC. A reader from Arkansas thanked me for "penning a powerful essay about the struggles of common people" and stated that, as a resident of Arkansas, he was "all too familiar with the Clintons' vanity and their narcissistic character."

The response from radicals was quite levelheaded. Liberals, on the other hand, responded in panic and accusation. One European American male liberal was horrified, accusing me of abandoning my commitment to social justice. My friends could not understand why I, as a woman of color who has studied racism for over a decade and experienced open racism from "Middle American," working-class European Americans, did not immediately participate in their distrust and hatred for Trump's so-called deplorables. Some worried that my article was pro-Trump simply because it pointed to Hillary's weaknesses. Others, likely because they were panicked, missed a central point of my article. What I clearly stated was that Trump was never working class, but he could connect emotionally with them through his evocative rhetoric. What I suggested Hillary Clinton should do was make a sustained emotional connection to this abandoned working class: "If Hillary wants to win us over, she has to do something bold. She has to start talking about us like she understands what our lives are really like. She has to show us that she's not like all the other spoiled, rich kids who make fun of us. Her latest decision, playing it safe with a Kaine VP, is not going to cut it for the people she just flies over and forgets."[78] Ironically, the day after I wrote this, HRC went to Johnstown, an Appalachian town very near mine in western Pennsylvania. She also put a little more emotion into her profile during the Democratic National Convention. She spoke about the difficulties her mother faced growing up in poverty and working as a housekeeper. However, as I predicted, she could not sustain a genuine, emotional connection to the lives of the working class. She continued to run a campaign that courted middle-class, well-educated liberals; voters she already had in her corner and was not likely to lose.

In the end, the image liberals had of Trump's deplorable rednecks likely did not even vote. Very poor European and African Americans living in isolated areas have low voter turnout. Pre-election data showed that Trump's supporters were financially secure and had more education than the general public.[79] These are the very people in Appalachian towns like mine who prided themselves on being better than the poorer "rednecks" in their own communities.[80] There is a status competition among the working and middle classes. Middle America includes conservative people with blue-collar jobs who identify as middle class rather than working class. These conservatives strive for status above the working class, go off to get college educations, and dismiss the working class they leave behind as trash in the same way middle-class liberals do. Conservatives and liberals are often portrayed as drastically different but are more ideologically similar than many realize.[81] The *National Review*, a magazine that prides itself as defining the "modern conservative movement," communicated a very similar stance on Trump voters as the pro-Hillary liberals. Writing for the magazine, Kevin D. Williamson scolded the working class for their alleged support of Trump:

> The truth about these dysfunctional, downscale communities is that they deserve to die. Economically, they are negative assets. Morally, they are indefensible. Forget all your cheap theatrical Bruce Springsteen crap. Forget your sanctimony about struggling Rust Belt factory towns and your conspiracy theories about the wily Orientals stealing our jobs ... The white American underclass is in thrall to a vicious, selfish culture whose main products are misery and used heroin needles.[82]

In response to this article, Nicholas Carnes and Noam Lupu stated: "This kind of stereotyping and scapegoating is a dismaying consequence of the narrative that working-class Americans swept Trump into the White House. It's time to let go of that narrative. What deserves to die isn't America's working-class communities. It's the myth that they're the reason Trump was elected."[83] Citing data from a 2016 NBC survey, Carnes and Lupu note that only a third of Trump's voters had household incomes at or below the national median of $50,000. Another third had household incomes that ranged between $50,000 and $100,000 and a third had incomes at or above $100,000. Carnes and Lupu state, "If being working class means being in the bottom half of the income distribution, the vast majority of Trump supporters during the primaries were not working class."[84]

Arlie Hochschild found that working-class European Americans in Middle America were more complex and not as stupid as liberals made them out to be.[85] They had ambivalent feelings about a man they saw scolding the "line-cutters" that they disliked, but they were also disgusted by his callous attitude. For Hochschild, liberals were missing something important about Trump voters:

> A lot of the people I talked to were doing really well now—but they had grown up in poverty, or their parents had—they'd struggled hard, and they'd worked hard. They

were also white men, and they felt that there was no cultural sympathy for them; in fact, there was a tendency to blame the categories of whiteness and maleness. I came to realize that there is a whole sector of society in which the privilege of whiteness and maleness didn't really trickle down. And I think we have grown highly insensitive to that fact."[86]

Hoschild's analysis works in line with the Bernie-Trump voter phenomenon. That is, people who supported Bernie Sanders but voted for Trump when Sanders lost to HRC.[87] I also speculate that these same voters preferred Elizabeth Warren, a political opposite to Trump. Like Trump and Sanders, Warren could reach working-class voters on an emotional level that HRC could not. Thus, it was not only sexism that caused HRC's defeat, as many liberals wanted to believe.

In fact, while middle-class liberal women were pointing to working-class European American men as the problem, it was working-class women who felt most abandoned by the "I'm with her elite feminism" that did not include them.[88] As public policy researcher Kathleen Geier stated, "If you're a woman living paycheck to paycheck and worried sick over the ever-diminishing economic prospects for you and your children, you're unlikely to be heavily invested in whether some lady centimillionaire will shatter the ultimate glass ceiling."[89] Columnist Liza Featherstone took a similar position, arguing, "A feminism that revels in its identification with people like Clinton—forming groups with names like Pantsuit Nation—is not a feminism that values the lives of most women."[90] Featherstone asserts that it was this bourgeois white feminism that gave us Trump, not working-class voters.

Liberals may be right that Trump's voters were motivated by racism. However, they save their nastiest vitriol for the stereotypical image of Trump voters: toothless, dirty, and poorly dressed rednecks who do not know what is best for themselves. The reality is that Trump voters probably look and speak a lot like the liberals who hate them. How often do liberals go head to head with the Trump voters who are just as educated and well spoken as they are, perhaps their children's conservative teachers, principals, school officials and staff, journalists, doctors, or respected members of their own communities? These are their neighbors and coworkers. They serve on the local board of education and town council. They are softer in their racism than the stereotypical pickup truck–driving, poorly spoken, narrow-minded, Middle American working-class voter that liberals quickly dismiss. The latter are easy targets for liberals. The former may have some power to share, especially if they occupy an important role in one's community. Therefore, liberals are not as likely to chastise them too harshly or dismiss them.

Class bias against working-class people may have become more visible during the 2016 presidential campaigns, but it did not start there. Classism is deeply rooted in liberal ideology and approaches to poverty. In 1979, Pierre Bourdieu put forth a theory on social class.[91] Among other points, he argued that the elite fetishize poverty. The display of Van Gogh's paintings of peasants in elite homes is a case in point. The economic elite's long-winded discussions of beauty, art, and architecture are a way of distancing themselves emotionally from people living in deep poverty. Like people of color are to liberals, the poor become objects to display for the elite. The liberal middle class, which aspires to be elite-like, tries to mimic the rich in their tastes. Bourdieu was studying social class in France, but his work has become a staple in college courses that address approaches to class in the United States, where there is a long history of highly educated liberals acting as if they know what is best for the working class, and this superior attitude was coupled with well-intentioned attempts to promote the welfare of working-class people. Doug Rossinow shows that social reform–focused liberals in the 1880s were somewhat influenced by British Fabianism, an ideology that favored a top-down approach.[92] Jane Addams was among these social reform liberals. Addams was an advocate for the working class, living and working among them, but she was not keen on putting working-class people into leadership positions.[93] Thus, similar to the paternalism SNCC experienced, European American liberals of the 1880s showed a concern for working-class issues but no confidence in their ability to organize themselves.

The Intersection of Racism and
Class Bias in Liberal White Supremacy

In 1944, Gunnar Myrdal argued that working-class European Americans would never accept African Americans, because the former were jealous of the latter's progress.[94] He felt progress depended on educated, upper- and middle-class European Americans, who were more willing to befriend African Americans. This line of thinking could only fuel liberal white supremacy, which relies on feeling morally superior to people of color and other, less enlightened European Americans. Inspired by Myrdal, liberals focused their antiracism on educating the prejudice out of individual bad apples. This approach to racism as an individual, attitudinal problem has been thoroughly critiqued by racism scholars.[95] Sociologist Nancy DiTomaso recently took Gunnar Myrdal's *American Dilemma* to task, arguing that Americans have not faced the dilemma Myrdal assumed they would.[96] Myrdal thought that European Americans would eventually have to fight racial injustice, because the disconnect between American values of equality and the fact of racial discrimination would cause a psychological dilemma for European Americans. Instead, DiTomaso finds that we have an American *non*-dilemma; Americans are not racked with guilt over racism, because they do not see their role in sustaining it. They benefit from white privilege by living in neighborhoods with good schools, clean streets, and plenty of resources. DiTomaso sees this as "opportunity hoarding," but European Americans simply see it as doing what is best for their children. Despite their professional appearance, research shows that highly educated European American liberals are just as racist as their working-class counterparts. They are just better educated in how to hide their racism.[97]

John Hartigan notes that "white, middle class liberals learn very young not to use epithets with racial connotations, while they receive different messages from their parents concerning labels for poor white people, the most naturalized of which is 'white trash.'"[98] This prejudice is also not limited to middle-class liberal European Americans. Class-privileged people of color can also feel superior to their working-class counterparts, just as they can participate in racial bigotry against European Americans and deny that racism is a significant problem for people of color.[99] I have witnessed some of this behavior within my liberal racially diverse community. For example, on Halloween my daughter's thirteen-year-old classmate dressed up as a "redneck." Her classmate was biracial. His father identified as African American and his mother as white. He was from a liberal family. His mother supported diversity initiatives at the schools but at the same time denied the centrality of racism as an issue. At one time, she claimed that she was an authority on what counts as racism because she had two biracial children. She made this claim while arguing against some children who pointed out that horror films were racist. With regard to costumes that year, the school had issued a statement that outfits should not target specific groups or promote hate. Still, no one batted an eye at this "redneck" costume. I asked my daughter what kind of "redneck" her friend was going to be: the ones who wore a red bandana around their necks when they marched on Blair Mountain in West Virginia to protest class exploitation, the ones who worked closely with the Black Panthers against oppression, or the ones from Redneck Revolt, an organization that confronts class exploitation and racism? Of course, he was none of these. He meant to be a stereotypical, brainless, white working-class buffoon. I cannot entirely fault this young man for his costume choice. He is being socialized into the same racist and classist system most of us experience in the United States. Some of us are better equipped than others to challenge this system, but with a superficial, tolerance-based school curriculum and liberal parents, who minimize racism to overt acts of bigotry against people of color and do not examine stereotypes of the poor, where would this child gain the information he needs to question the problems in his costume choice? After all, there have been incidents of college students and college staff, who should know better, wearing racist costumes on Halloween and for other events.

Most liberals are clueless about the social and political significance of the term "redneck." A member of Redneck Revolt explains:

> The word redneck has always been used pejoratively, but we don't see it that way ... look back at the Harlan County wars, and those folks would wear bandanas to keep the sun off their necks, and that's where the term redneck comes from. We embrace that term, and say, "Yeah, that's who we are. We're working-class people who are out in the streets." ... Your comfort is still built on a system of White supremacy ... the things that you're enjoying are a byproduct of 150 years of working-class struggle. If you like the weekends, thank a union man. You like your 40-hour work week ... thank a union worker. It's working-class people who brought those changes. It wasn't [the] middle-class bourgeois who brought that change. It was working-class people out fighting in the streets.[100]

Redneck Revolt likely descended from the deep connection between working-class European Americans and the Black Panther Party. The first people the Illinois Black Panther Party (ILBPP) attempted to organize outside of Chicago were poor European American Appalachian coal miners in a group called the Young Patriots Organization (YPO). Jakobi Williams describes the accidental meeting of these organizations.[101] Bob Lee, a leader of the ILBPP, was struck by the classism among middle-class European Americans when he first attended an event with the YPO on police brutality. Lee stated: "I had never seen whites attack poor whites before. I had never seen poor whites having to explain themselves to other whites before ... I made my speech and it was an emotional tie-in with the [Young Patriots] because I felt the hostility toward them. And that was the beginning of [our alliance]."[102] Williams contends that the class-solidarity focus of the Black Panthers and unification with working-class European Americans caused the latter to reassess their use of the Confederate flag. Young Patriots talked about unlearning racism. Bob Fesperman of the YPO traveled to Chicago sharing what the Black Panthers taught him about racism. He stated that white people like him were never seen "until we met [the] Illinois Chapter of the Black Panther Party and they met us."[103] Learning from the Black Panthers, the YPO developed free health clinics and breakfast programs in their own communities. In line with radical politics, the ILBPP emphasized the need to build a revolution against poverty, which they saw as a key source of exploitation. In 1968, Lee spoke about unifying the Black Panthers with the Young Patriots:

> We are going to erase the color thang, see ... There's welfare up here ... There's police brutality up here, there's rats and roaches. There's poverty up here. That's the first thing we can unite on ... Once you realize that your brothers have been brutalized by

the cops the same way the Westside and the Southside [are]. Once you realize that you are getting an inadequate education in these high schools and junior high schools over here, the same way the Southside and the Westside [are]. Once you realize that you are paying taxes, taxes for the same cops to whoop your ass … The same thing is happening on the Southside and the Westside, and if you can realize that concept of poverty … a revolution can begin.[104]

Lee understood what John Hartigan has noted: "Poor whites are not the bank officers who deny mortgages and other loans to African Americans of all classes at rates two to three times that of their white counterparts; poor whites are not among the landlords who refuse housing to African Americans, nor are they the human resources managers who are racially influenced in their hiring and firing decisions."[105] The ILBPP's empathetic, nonpaternalistic class-centered analysis is missing from most liberal perspectives on injustice.

The Black Panthers were not only class focused. They were one of the few groups that could maintain a racism focus at the same time that they emphasized class unity. Likewise, the Southeast Michigan chapter of Redneck Revolt argues that racism must be dealt with immediately and examines how racism and class exploitation are integrally tied:

Our stance is that our entire capitalist system is built on a bedrock of White supremacy, and as White folks we have access to spaces that people of color don't. So we try to exploit the spaces and put ourselves in those positions to reach the White working class because it's like the old IWW [Industrial Workers of the World] saying, "If we don't get to them first, the Klan will." … [I]n order to address capitalism, in order to address economics, the issue of systemic racism first has to be addressed.[106]

All of this contradicts elite white liberal perspectives on working-class people. Moreover, left out of their whole discussion of Trump's deplorables is the fact that Middle American, Appalachian towns are not all white. When middle-class European American liberals disparage the working class, they abandon poor people of color as well and tend not to interact with poor people in general. The people of color with whom they do interact share their class privilege. In other words, they prefer their "diversity" to be middle class and professional. Indeed, sociologist David Embrick finds that "diversity" has become a professional norm in the business world, but this does not translate to actual practices to combat racism.[107]

Liberal approaches to working-class concerns and people intersect with their approaches to racism. Liberal white supremacists are concerned with finding evil racists who allow them to look good and befriending middle-class, liberal (rather than radical) people of color who play by their rules.[108] Hartigan notes that the real issue middle-class European Americans have with rednecks is that they don't conform to white norms of respectability.[109] Professional, middle-class people of color may be more likely to conform to these standards of behavior and, in fact, may feel compelled to follow such rules to survive white-normed institutions and surroundings.[110] This would explain why liberal European Americans prefer to befriend and use middle-class people of color as color-capital. Thus, liberal approaches to people of color and the issue of racism, and to working-class people and the issue of social class, combine to reinforce their moral superiority and liberal white supremacy.

Ultimately, if liberals were concerned about Trump's reign of terror, they should be more engaged in activism to thwart fascism and authoritarianism in society. Authoritarian attitudes were a better predictor of Trump's win than social class alone.[111] However, conformity to experts and authority is a liberal tradition, and to challenge such things is too radical a move for them.[112] This is all tied to the last component of liberal versus radical behavior, and that is their social movement tactics.

Tactics: Liberals of the Worst Sort

In *Radicals of the Worst Sort*, Ardis Cameron details the life histories of working-class women who engaged in confrontational tactics to fight exploitative working conditions.[113] One of these stories involved a group of women working in the Everett Mill in Massachusetts. On January 11, 1912, they discovered their pay was short. They immediately threw down their aprons, took to the streets, began destroying machinery at Everett Mill and neighboring mills, and swept through the city's major mills to inspire others. These women occupied the bottom rung of society not only because they were women, but because they were poor, working-class women. Cameron states, "Armed with 'lots of cunning and lots of bad temper,' they brought their demands to the center of national debates calling into question not only low wages but the whole of 'corporate power.'"[114] If these women, and people like them, are radicals of the worst sort, because they challenged oppression in confrontational ways that defied middle-class norms of femininity, then liberals of the worst sort are the opposite. Liberals of the worst sort claim to care about social injustice and express this care in nonconfrontational, subtle ways that do not upset the class and capitalistic status quo. They go along with middle-class norms of respectability and fruitlessly work within the power structure's rules while they attempt to challenge injustice. This allows them to appear morally righteous, while keeping intact their chances for gaining access to power and influence.

There is a long history of tension between radicals and liberals on which sorts of tactics to use in struggles against oppression. This tension does not just involve European American liberals and radicals but people of color as well. In the late nineteenth and early twentieth centuries, two schools of thought were popular among African Americans: Booker T. Washington's liberal/conservative accommodation ideology and W. E. B. Du Bois's more radical approach that would later be applied by the Black Panthers to merge racial and class struggles.[115] Booker T. Washington's approach was the more conformist stance at the time. Those who agreed with his perspective deemed it necessary to secure funding and keep liberal allies.

This conformity has often been a political strategy for people of color. It has also been a matter of survival. During World War II, many Japanese Americans complied with authorities, leaving most of their belongings behind, and were marched into internment camps. Yuri Kochiyama, an Asian American activist and Black Panther, shared in an oral history the sentiment that many Japanese Americans had about conformity and safety at the time: "At the beginning no one realized how long this would go on. I didn't feel the anger that much because I thought maybe this was the way we could show our love for our country, and we should not make too much fuss or noise, we should abide by what they asked of us."[116] Kochiyama's experience with internment radicalized her. She realized that abiding by the rules would not bring acceptance and change. She joined the Black Panthers and spent the rest of her life fighting for social justice.[117] The "no-no boys" are another case in point. They were so named because they refused to fight for the United States in segregated ranks while being denied citizenship at home. Many served time in federal prison for their defiance.[118] No-no boys were also stigmatized as troublemakers among Japanese Americans who *did* choose to conform.

These kinds of divisions between liberal and radical people of color carried over into 1960s civil rights organizing. Activists in SNCC were known to be more radical than other civil rights organizations, such as the Southern Christian Leadership Conference (SCLC) or NAACP. SNCC engaged in "drop out" movements, arguing that their time was better spent fighting for real change that would affect their lives than in school learning middle-class, white norms.[119] Fighting injustice in education was a central part of what SNCC did in their own Freedom Schools.[120] SNCC activists learned about alternatives to capitalism and revolutions around the world.[121]

Compared to the more liberal NAACP, SNCC took a much more militant, confrontational approach. Stokely Carmichael stated, "SNCC will work with anybody who supports our programs, shares our goals, honors our principles, and earns our trust . . . you don't worry about the Communists, worry about SNCC. We way more dangerous, Jack."[122] Carl Oglesby, president of Students for a Democratic Society, challenged liberals on their brand of humanism:

> If your commitment to human values is unconditional, then disabuse yourselves of the notion that statements will bring change, if only the right statements can be written, or that interviews with the mighty will bring change if only the mighty can be reached, or that marches will bring change if only we can make them massive enough, or that policy proposals will bring change if only we can make them responsible enough. We are dealing now with a colossus that does not want to be changed. It will not change itself. It will not cooperate with those who want to change it . . . They don't need study groups, they need a movement.[123]

Likewise, SNCC characterized the liberal style of activism as "cocktail parties and seminars."[124]

In 1957, Martin Luther King Jr., often portrayed as the political opposite to the more radical Malcolm X,[125] identified northern liberals as a weakness in the movement toward equality:

> A second area in which there is need for strong leadership is from the white northern liberals . . . What we are witnessing today in so many northern communities is a sort of quasi-liberalism which is based on the principle of looking sympathetically at all sides. It is a liberalism so bent on seeing all sides, that it fails to become committed to either side. It is a liberalism that is so objectively analytical that it is not subjectively committed. It is a liberalism which is neither hot nor cold, but lukewarm. We call for a liberalism from the North which will be thoroughly committed to the ideal of racial justice and will not be deterred by propaganda and subtle words of those who say: "Slow up for a while; you're pushing too fast."[126]

King became increasingly frustrated with European American liberals, and like Malcolm X, he questioned the trustworthiness of European American moderates. In his 1963 "Letter from Birmingham Jail," he responded to a group of European American southern religious leaders who had concerns about his actions, which they saw as "unwise and untimely":

> I MUST make two honest confessions to you, my Christian and Jewish brothers. First, I must confess that over the last few years I have been gravely disappointed with the white moderate. I have almost reached the regrettable conclusion that the Negro's great stumbling block in the stride toward freedom is not the White Citizens Councillor or the Ku Klux Klanner but the white moderate who is more devoted to order than to justice; who prefers a negative peace which is the absence of tension to a pos-

itive peace which is the presence of justice; who constantly says, 'I agree with you in the goal you seek, but I can't agree with your methods of direct action'; who paternalistically feels that he can set the timetable for another man's freedom; who lives by the myth of time; and who constantly advises the Negro to wait until a 'more convenient season.' Shallow understanding from people of good will is more frustrating than absolute misunderstanding from people of ill will. Lukewarm acceptance is much more bewildering than outright rejection.[127]

In this letter he repeatedly addressed the need for direct action, confrontational tactics, and the creation of discomfort or "tension," something moderates and liberals like to avoid. King's identification of the liberals' unwillingness to challenge authority, and their concern for peace and order at the expense of justice, is remarkably similar to the reaction I documented in my case study of Essex Town (see chapter 3). In this case, activists using radical tactics were constantly scolded for being disruptive and out of order.

Thomas Frank identifies an "obsessive pining for consensus" as a central feature of liberalism.[128] He defines liberalism as a politics of professionalism. This professionalism and focus on consensus and respectability, he argues, is a political ideology that "carries enormous potential for mischief."[129] Professionalism is "inherently undemocratic, prioritizing the views of experts over those of the public."[130] Ultimately, consensus, even when well intended, can work to reproduce the status quo. In my piece on Occupy Wall Street, I questioned the ability of consensus-based organizing to truly challenge racism, since the default position is to avoid controversial issues.[131]

It is not expert knowledge by itself that is the problem. It is the application of that expertise to shut down dissent that is the issue. The "experts" in my case study of the Essex Town Board of Education (BOE) claimed to have expert knowledge that the town residents did not have. In reality, radical residents, also experts with college degrees, had more knowledge on what was happening with education and politics than the so-called experts on the BOE. What distinguished them was not their education, but their liberal versus radical approaches. Experts on the BOE did not want to dig further into the background of those they hired or confront the political machine, because they ultimately wanted to become part of that machine. Their goal was to maintain it. To create change, liberals in this town, and elsewhere, tended toward safe, nonconfrontational tactics, such as petitions, brief school-sanctioned walkouts, and testifying at meetings (e.g., BOE meetings). When they did join rallies outside of their communities, it was likely a popular, highly anticipated rally, such as the Women's March in Washington, D.C. A more radical activist in my case study of Union City, (see chapter 4) had this to say about European American liberals in such marches: "Anglos have a way of doing things, being so conniving... And they are not in the fight, in the trenches. But if the publicity is there and the newspapers are there... they'll show up and the colored people hate that... It's important... to see them but then when are you going to step down into the trenches and do something?"

Unlike liberals, radicals use more confrontational methods. We need a mix of both confrontational and nonconfrontational methods to be successful. What aggravates the left, I believe, is liberal posturing. They limit their tactics to the safest, most comfortable ones and act as if they are creating large-scale change. At the same time, they chastise radicals for being disruptive rather than welcoming radical methods as a much needed, effective alternative and complement to their own methods. Radicals were activists at some of the very first Black Lives Matter protests and showed sustained commitment to the Occupy Wall Street movement. Even at its most popular time, I never saw an Occupy poster or lawn sign in my racially diverse, liberal community. I also never saw visible support for the activists opposing the Dakota Access Pipeline. When I mentioned these issues, I would get blank stares. However, after the election of Donald Trump, I saw plenty of signs declaring "Hate Has No Home Here" in multiple languages with the American flag shaped into a heart. Also very popular is the sign that proclaims:

IN THIS HOUSE, WE BELIEVE:
BLACK LIVES MATTER, WOMEN'S RIGHTS ARE HUMAN RIGHTS,
NO HUMAN IS ILLEGAL, SCIENCE IS REAL, LOVE IS LOVE,
KINDNESS IS EVERYTHING.

By 2018, I also saw a few "Black Lives Matter" signs and some European American liberal neighbors donning Black Lives Matter T-shirts. These same neighbors did not participate in or talk much about the high school Black Lives Matter protest that took place in our town in 2014. I was the only parent at the bus stop holding an "I can't breathe" sign to support the high schoolers as they marched by. One resident drove by and attempted to scold me for doing so. Other parents at the bus stop tried to avoid me. Eric Garner was murdered in 2014. The Black Lives Matter movement was being vilified, and liberals were not sure which way the wind would blow. Especially after the murder of George Floyd, the Movement for Black Lives gained momentum, and presidential hopefuls had to at least give it lip service. It became safer for European American liberals to express their support, even as African American radicals involved in the movement remained *unsafe*.

The Movement for Black Lives is important and should continue. My critique is not with the movement, but with the way liberals, particularly European American liberals, have co-opted it for their own emotional reassurance, and what this says about the limitations of their style of activism as well as their motivations. Middle-class European American liberals would rarely pursue the confrontational tactics, such as those used by the working-class European Americans in Young Patriots, who were increasingly harassed and threatened by police officers after associating with Black Panthers. Instead of backing away from their radical politics, the YPO only stepped up their coalition with the BPP. When Bob Lee of the YPO was harassed by police officers after a meeting in Chicago and placed in the backseat of a police cruiser, residents surrounded the vehicle until he was released.[132] Lee stated, "I'll never forget it because Preacherman [a leader in YPO] was standing in front of the police car with his wife and two children along with other white families . . . and the cops couldn't move."[133] These kinds of anti-authority, potentially dangerous methods that place people in uncomfortable positions do not sit well with liberals, especially those of the professional middle class.

Sociologist Robert Merton informs us of a type of fair-weather liberalism similar to what I am describing.[134] Fair-weather liberals do not hold prejudiced beliefs but reluctantly carry out discrimination when it suits their interests to do so. Merton used the example of liberals who do not hire people of color because doing so would hurt their businesses. They also do not speak out against discrimination because they might lose respect among their colleagues. The problem with Merton's work is that he mostly considers overt acts or bad feelings as discriminatory. What we have learned from decades of research on color-blind-ideology-driven racism is that someone may appear to be nonracist and still uphold the racial status quo through racism-evasiveness—various attempts to deny that they are individually racist—and softer manifestations of racism, such as fetishizing people of color or using them to prove their own antiracist moral superiority. What we have today are liberals who may speak out on discrimination in nonconfrontational ways within the proper forums and especially when it gets them praise from friends and neighbors. This allows them to divorce themselves from those bad, uneducated racial bigots in the South, or the North, who voted for Trump. If we placed these liberals in the segregation-era South, or the North for that matter, would they still put "Hate Has No Home Here" signs in their yards or choose not to because of the discomfort it might bring their families? Perhaps many would find themselves sharing the perspective of the pastors who agreed with Martin Luther King Jr.'s goals but not his methods.

In summary, liberals tend toward reform, not revolutionary change. This is tied to their perspectives on capitalism. Liberals are system sustaining because they benefit from the status quo. Their vocal recognition of systemic racism does not significantly alter their economic positions or get them in trouble. Recognizing the need for diversity has been a part of the Democratic Party at least since the

1940s. It is not particularly brave for a white person to call out racism today. It is so socially unacceptable to be called a racist today that even some white nationalist organizations are careful to say they are not racist. These organizations want to exhibit professional, middle-class behavior.[135] In this way, the white nationalist's presentation of self is not so different from liberals. It is now politically viable for Democrats to appear "woke" and speak intelligently against racism.

SNCC predicted that middle-class people of color would limit their focus to racism while working-class people of color would focus on class. They also argued that middle-class European Americans would be less likely to push for what they saw as the key issue, "political and economic changes of substantial benefit to both the Negro and poor white."[136] Just because Democrats and liberals are now naming racism as a problem does not mean they will take significant action to deal with it, especially if doing so puts them in an unpopular or uncomfortable position, and it certainly does not mean they will simultaneously address working-class issues. Ultimately, this behavior and ideology of liberals does nothing to disrupt the system of racism and, in fact, upholds it. Liberal self-indulgent discussions on racism, embrace of capitalism, and disregard of working-class issues reinforce liberal white supremacy. Their discussions result in a false sense of efficacy and moral superiority. Middle-class people of color who subscribe to standard rules of liberal conduct also help sustain liberal white supremacy. They provide liberal European Americans with examples of respectability and friendships that supply the color-capital they crave. They and their European American counterparts speak against systemic racism in acceptable ways, accepting capitalism and maintaining ties to those in power. There remains today a recognition and aggravation among those on the radical left with this liberal posturing. In the next chapter, I analyze a case study that illustrates these ongoing divisions between liberals and radicals, especially with regard to liberals' emphasis on civil discourse and their choice of tactics.

CHAPTER 3

The Friendliest Town

Confrontational Tactics and
Liberal Acquiescence

Consequently, it is becoming evident that the hope for
real reform lies not in alliances with established power,
but with the recreation of a popular left opposition—an
opposition that expresses anger when it is called for, not mild
disagreement.

—Students for a Democratic Society,
"America and the New Era," 1963

We will have to repent in this generation not merely for the
vitriolic words and actions of the bad people but for the
appalling silence of the good people.

—Martin Luther King Jr.,
"Letter from Birmingham Jail," 1963

The purposes of this chapter are to show how liberal and radical tactics differ in general, provide examples of radical methods that are both nonviolent *and* confrontational, illustrate persisting liberal elitism toward other progressives, and illuminate a fundamental weakness of liberal organizing—an aversion to discomfort and confrontation. The case study presented in this chapter is not directly focused on racism, but it offers key lessons on understanding how racism-evasiveness and white supremacy are maintained by basic tenets of liberal ideology and methods. Liberals are averse to confrontation, in general, and advocate for civility as a central goal. This informs other liberal tendencies, such as evading racism, which is an uncomfortable topic and often seen as divisive. Thus, liberal nonconfrontation and racism-evasiveness are mutually reinforcing (see figure 4). If liberals are averse to confrontation, they will not explicitly address racism but will focus on more com-

FIGURE 4
Liberal Nonconfrontation and Racism-Evasiveness as Mutually Reinforcing
Addressing racism explicitly requires confrontation and discomfort. The liberal tendency toward
nonconfrontation prevents liberals from centering racism and instead leads to racism-evasiveness.
Racism-evasiveness is, by definition, nonconfrontational. Thus, liberal nonconfrontation and
racism-evasiveness are mutually reinforcing.

fortable topics, such as "diversity," and they will not effectively challenge the power
structure. Without confronting the power structure, white supremacy cannot be
dismantled.

In this chapter, I investigate a community movement to remove an allegedly
fraudulent superintendent as a case study in confrontational versus nonconfrontational tactics and the role of liberal ideology in stifling radical dissent. I examine the conversation between liberals and radicals in a politically progressive town
I call "Essex Town." The town of Essex is a fairly large suburb located in northern
New Jersey with a population of 46,207.[1] The town has five elementary schools,
two middle schools, and one high school. Essex Town residents often praise the
town's racial diversity. According to the 2010 census, the town is 57.15% white,
26.58% Black or African American, 16.20% Hispanic or Latino of any race, 0.38%
Native American, 7.96% Asian, 0.02% Pacific Islander, 4.82% from other races, and
3.09% from two or more races.[2] The average median household income is $88,917.
Essex is characterized as a "stigma-free town" welcoming to LGBTQIA people and
often celebrated by townsfolk as "the friendliest town." The town is largely Democratic. According to the Voter Registration Summary from the New Jersey Division of Elections, 46.4% of registered voters are Democrats and 10.7% Republican.
A large percent, 42.9%, are unaffiliated. Essex Town showed overwhelming support for Barack Obama in 2012 (71.3% of the vote versus 27.9% for Mitt Romney)
and for Hillary Clinton in 2016 (74.7% versus 23.2% for Donald Trump).

The response of liberals in Essex Town after Donald Trump was elected mirrored the patterns I noted across the nation in the introduction. On a national level,
progressive organizations were springing up to oppose Trump, most focusing on
electoral politics. The election of Trump shocked liberals in Essex Town, who responded by holding candlelight vigils and discussions on racism as a means of resist-
ing Trump's anti-immigrant and other policies. Neighbors voiced their depression,
frustration, and fear of a Trump presidency. Many of my daughter's friends parroted

their parents' concerns that "If Trump is elected, I am moving to Canada!" Several of my European American neighbors jokingly shared their need for therapy to get through this awful Trump era. By all these standards, Essex Town is certainly a liberal town, and as such, I argue that the town is limited by liberal ideology, namely the desire to remain nonconfrontational while pursuing progressive change.

Background on the Activists

The success of this community movement was largely attributable to the effective confrontational tactics and remarkable synergy of skills between three radical leaders: Tom, the professor, Micaela, the attorney, and Barry, the street captain or public character. Tom, a European American man in his late thirties, was my partner, a college professor, and Essex Town resident with two children attending schools in the district. He openly identified as a political radical and regularly published studies on the political economy, white-collar crime, and racism from a critical Marxian approach. Tom became involved in the movement as we observed increasingly authoritarian methods and control of both children and parents at our daughter's elementary school. This school was 36.3% white, 30.9% Black, and 21.7% Hispanic.[3] The principal during the time of this study was a European American woman. She was later replaced by the assistant principal, who was an African American woman. Tom and I had reached out repeatedly to the school's principal, assistant principal, mayor, and superintendent over the course of five years about our concerns over lack of recess, denying recess as a form of punishment, children being yelled at to "eat faster" at lunch, constantly surveilling children's every movement through school cameras—and scolding them through the loudspeakers.

Tom was particularly concerned about the treatment of children with special needs. Parents reported that school administrators encouraged them to hire a lawyer instead of meeting with the child study team to deal with conflicts. This was especially troubling, because the superintendent brought in an expensive law firm as his first order of business and fired the in-house board of education attorney, who had been working with the board for twenty-eight years. Tom characterized the new law firm as "an unnecessarily overly expensive crony law firm that exacerbated problems to create billable hours."[4] Tom discovered that the new law firm cost the district more than the in-house lawyer, who was allegedly fired because the superintendent said he was too expensive.

Tom suspected the overly authoritarian treatment toward children was partly the result of racist attitudes toward a district with a large population of African American and Latine children. Several studies have found that African American,

Latine, and American Indian children are disciplined more often and more harshly than European American children.[5] A report from the U.S. Department of Education's Civil Rights Data Collection indicates that rates of discipline are higher in racially diverse and suburban schools.[6] Studies on welfare racism are informative here. Such research finds that when European Americans believe that mostly African Americans use public assistance, they are less sympathetic to these policies.[7] These racist attitudes toward welfare, in general, can then negatively impact all people on public assistance, including European Americans.[8] Likewise, school staff may react with less sensitivity toward all children in schools that have a high percentage of students of color. Tom offered public comment on these conditions at BOE meetings. He stressed the physical and emotional costs that resulted when children had no time to eat, were offered little unstructured free time, and were overly controlled. These conditions, he argued, led to the very misbehavior school staff were trying to control.

Micaela's concerns were similar to Tom's. Micaela was a European American woman in her early fifties, an attorney, and a social justice activist with one child in the school district. Micaela identified as a liberal Democrat but was critical of liberal ideology. In fact, when she first met her husband, an African American man, he insisted that she read about the Black Power movement and critiques of white feminism. Micaela's son also encountered authoritarian attitudes at his elementary school, which was 37 percent white, 27 percent Black, and 18 percent Hispanic. His principal was a European American man. Micaela reported an incident of harassment, intimidation, and bullying by school staff toward children to the school principal, superintendent, and BOE. According to Micaela, lunch aides punished the entire fourth-grade class due to the misbehavior of four or five children. As punishment, lunch aides demanded that all sixty-five children in the fourth grade sit on a stone wall in ninety-degree weather in complete silence for five minutes. Because all sixty-five students were not completely silent, the entire class lost their recess and had to remain sitting on the wall. Micaela stated, "This is illegal since [Essex Town] schools count recess minutes as total PE minutes and therefore cannot withhold recess AND recess can never be withheld as punishment unless parents consent."[9] Multiple children brought the incident to their parents. The principal assured parents the punishment would not happen again, but it continued for three days. After her child asked to stay home from school, Micaela observed the recess. The principal and lunch aides scolded the children by yelling, "Tomorrow's supposed to be high 90s—you'll cook like eggs on this wall tomorrow" and "Shut up or roast."[10] According to Micaela, the office assistant alerted the principal that Micaela was filming. At that point, the principal allowed the children to sit in the shade. Micaela stated of the superintendent, "I asked him to investigate, report if necessary and make sure the students received the message that this was wrong. He did NONE of the above and the BOE never followed up."[11]

The third leader, Barry, also expressed discontent with the superintendent's disregard of parental concerns. Barry was a Jewish European American man and lifelong Essex Town resident in his late fifties. He moved to Essex Town in 1963. He and his wife have two daughters, who graduated from high school in 2012 and 2015. I characterize Barry as the "street captain," because he was a beloved member of the community. This proved to be a valuable asset to the movement. Barry developed his own town social media page after being censored multiple times on the town community page. The community page existed for several years and had 9,356 members. Barry's page was only up for seven months when it gained 5,783 members. Other people in town attempted similar pages with little success compared to Barry's. Barry identified his politics as "somewhere in between" and characterized himself as a social liberal but fiscal conservative. Barry stated that he was, at first, a "cheerleader" for the superintendent, but his views changed after he witnessed the superintendent's dismissal of parent concerns. Barry contacted the superintendent numerous times and was ignored until he posted his concerns to social media. Immediately after that he received a patronizing phone call from the superintendent. Barry stated, "He called me and was like 'Hey buddy, I saw your post' and he asked me to take the post down ... I began to suspect that the superintendent had a checkered past."[12]

I refer to Tom, Micaela, and Barry as "the radical group." I identify these three leaders as "radical," not because of their political identities, but because of the tactics they used and because liberals viewed them as a radical contingent that stepped outside of the normal methods of "civil discourse" for creating change in education. Liberals from other groups often referred to them as an "angry mob" who were too "rough" in their tactics. These three radical residents joined forces after the BOE voted to renew the superintendent's contract. They shared a dissatisfaction with the liberal group's response, which was to focus on future elections.

While this case did not involve explicit racist behavior, radical activists suspected there was a racial fear among European American politicians who wanted to remain in control of the town. By supporting candidates of color and working to expose corruption, radical activists posed a threat to that control. The political corruption of central concern to the radical group was the connection of the superintendent and BOE to the town mayor and former governor. The town had a board of education whose budget was twice the amount of the town's budget, $160 million and $80 million, respectively. According to Tom, "The mayor, the former senator, and other players are recognized as a 'political machine' by people who know New Jersey politics."[13] Tom investigated the superintendent, the mayor, and the BOE through Open Public Records Act requests (OPRA). One such OPRA yielded several text messages between the superintendent and the mayor in which they discussed the opposition against the superintendent and personnel matters. In these text messages, the mayor inquired about applicants for various school positions. As Tom stated, "This is totally improper because personnel matters cannot be discussed outside of a closed executive session of the BOE."[14]

Tom believed that this largely white political machine controlled the BOE and that the mayor and the senator lobbied behind closed doors to keep the superintendent employed. He, and several other town residents, also believed that the mayor and former governor heavily influenced who was elected to the BOE by running loyal candidates and making generous contributions to their campaigns. According to a few town employees, the mayor went so far as to encourage them to attack the radical group on social media and in public. In one particularly troubling incident, a man drove past Micaela's son and yelled, "Tell your n—— loving mom if she doesn't like the town, then get out!"[15]

Methods

To study the differences between liberal and radical tactics, I analyzed three town social media pages, the "community page," "Barry's alternative community page," and "the progressives for education page." I focus mainly on the first two pages, because that is where most of the evidence against the superintendent was communicated. Barry's page developed as a result of more outspoken community members being censored on the community page. Barry was one of the three radical leaders who were repeatedly censored. The progressives for education page was organized by a liberal group of residents. I found that many liberals on this page grew silent as the opposition to the superintendent became more intense. After the superintendent resigned, liberal factions that went quiet on social media or chastised the radical group for their "tone" came back into the mix to refocus the discourse and claim credit for the movement's success. My analysis of the progressives for education page focused on this framing of the liberals' role in the movement. I downloaded and analyzed 2,591 pages of these social media sites using a keyword search for the term "superintendent." This eliminated any commentary on other town issues not pertaining to the superintendent, including conversations on town events, trash pickup, or other business. I expanded all posts, comments, and replies on the superintendent and then moved the content into a Microsoft Word file. I limited my search dates between February 2018, the month when the BOE renewed the superintendent's contract with a raise, and October 31, 2018. The BOE announced the superintendent's resignation on October 19, 2018, but I followed the commentary through the end of the month. I then examined the liberal organization's page for their responses to the resignation in October. I looked for key turning points in the movement and the point at which the radical group began sharing the evidence that eventually led to the demise of the superintendent. In addition to my analysis of these social media pages, I read the minutes of BOE meetings and transcribed comments at public meetings concerning the superintendent. I compiled data on the political context for this movement through conversations with the three community members who led the investigation of the superintendent and corrupt practices in Essex Town. These leaders shared with me the evidence they gathered through the Open Public Records Act and personal communications, including personal messages they received via social media and emails. There were four key turning points in the controversy over the superintendent. Table 2 illustrates the differences in how liberals and radicals responded to these key moments. Table 3 summarizes the tactics liberals used to marginalize and discredit radical activists throughout the movement. Below I summarize the significance of these moments and what they tell us about liberal versus radical tactics.

TABLE 2
Liberal versus Radical Responses to Significant Turning Points

	Liberal response	Radical response
Contract renewal	Focus on elections in November, letters and comments from community to change SI's behavior.	Confront BOE and SI about accusations of unethical behavior. Investigate accusations of unethical behavior.
Alleged embezzlement	Protect alleged embezzler. Focus on kindness and civility while attacking radical group. Disagree with radical group's confrontational methods. Label radical group "angry mob."	Post evidence of embezzlement, naming the embezzler and social media tagging BOE members. Confront BOE on lack of action. Contact county prosecutor.
Alleged résumé fraud and criminal conduct	Mixed response—growing support for radicals as evidence mounts, but continued calls for civility and labeling of radicals as "angry mob." Accuse radicals of bullying. Liberal page remains silent, posting mostly on school events.	Post evidence to social media confronting BOE members by tagging them. Post embarrassing email communication with SI. Confront BOE at public meetings. Continued involvement of county prosecutor.
SI's resignation	Claim credit for success by posting announcement of SI resignation on liberal page. Focus on upcoming elections. Call for continued civility.	Disrupt BOE meeting. Demand resignation agreement. Post resignation agreement to social media. Demand report from independent law firm. Begin investigation of candidates running for election.

TABLE 3
Tactics Liberals Use to Marginalize and Discredit Radicals

Tactic	Examples
Emphasizing proper procedure	Liberals publicly blame radicals for disrupting meetings. Superintendent publicly stated that the radical group was preventing the BOE from "determining next steps," "understanding both sides," allowing "things to work out." BOE vice president stated the radical group should use "appropriate channels." BOE members equated "dissent" with following proper process and speaking for two minutes.
Emphasizing civility	Liberals claimed radicals were "uncivil" on social media. Liberal town leaders called for civil discourse when radicals interrupted meetings with questions or tagged leaders in posts on social media, which BOE characterized as bullying. BOE made a public announcement emphasizing "kindness, respect, and propriety" to quiet radical dissent. Liberal parents sent personal messages to the radical group asking them to "tone it down."
Using threats and intimidation	Radical activists received threatening messages; family members were harassed in public.
Shaming and name-calling	Liberals posted to social media calling radicals "shameful," "childish," "mean-spirited," "obsessive," "unstable," "out for blood." Liberals referred to radicals as "angry mob." Liberals falsely accused radicals of holding "personal vendettas." BOE made a public announcement falsely accusing radicals of defamation. Superintendent publicly stated the radical group was hurting peoples' feelings. BOE vice president publicly stated the radical group was "hurting careers," "hurting lives."
Appropriation of radical success	Liberals attempted to appropriate the success of radicals as their own, attempted to erase the significant role radical methods played in achieving desired goals by attributing the success to "many voices."

Significant Turning Points

RENEWAL OF THE SUPERINTENDENT'S CONTRACT
AND COMMUNITY RESPONSE

The BOE hired the superintendent in 2014 with a four-year contract. He quickly developed a reputation for being authoritarian and disrespectful to teachers because of his and the BOE's refusal to settle the teachers' contract. During this struggle, the teachers' union criticized the superintendent for using the memory of the Sandy Hook tragedy to shame teachers, who were upset about their contract. In a letter addressed to faculty, the superintendent referenced the tragedy and encouraged the teachers to "think about what's really important."[16] Residents critical of the superintendent believed that he should not have tied together the teacher's contract struggle, which dragged on for over a year, and the Sandy Hook tragedy. In 2018, the teacher's union conducted a survey, where four hundred out of seven hundred members voted "no confidence" in the superintendent. Parents complained that the superintendent would not return their emails or phone calls when they had concerns about special education, bus safety, inappropriate punishment of children, and limiting or taking away recess time.

After four years of these complaints and outrage from the community, more people became confident that the BOE would not renew the superintendent's contract. The liberal organizations in town were certain that their focus on electoral politics would prove effective. These organizations helped elect a BOE member who they thought would stand up to the superintendent and vote him out. It was a shock to them when this person voted *in favor* of the superintendent, and the BOE renewed his contract with a raise, despite numerous public comments against him at the February 26, 2018, meeting. In true liberal fashion, this liberal-supported BOE member had aligned himself with the white power structure, as evidenced by his vote and emails in which he instructed other BOE members on strategies to protect the superintendent.

As shown in table 2, liberals immediately responded to the contract renewal by focusing on elections and civil discourse. When people complained on social media about the state of education in Essex Town, liberal groups encouraged everyone to vote in November (nine months later), when two members of the board would be up for reelection. The organizers of the progressives for education page sent an email to its members the day after the contract renewal. Even though the board renewed the superintendent's contract and gave him a raise, the leaders of this liberal organization wrote that they thought the public comment was enough to humble the superintendent and get him and the board to become better listeners. Leaders of this organization also stressed a concern about remaining civil to one another and focused their tactics on conversations with neighbors, asking questions, and writing letters. In the spirit of that civility, they invited community members to view a film related to corporatization and privatization of public schools.

Leaders of another liberal organization posted their complaints about a poorly constructed robocall parents received regarding a student bringing a knife to school. They found this poor communication unbelievable after they just spoke to the board about a need for better communication. These parents were very careful in their posts to say that they respected the board and did not want to say anything negative about them. Furthermore, they asked for people to be nice when they posed any disagreements to the original post. At one point, when there was a potential disagreement over the robocall, the original poster detracted from the disagreement by talking about her puppies and posting cute photos. This focus on "respectful," "nice" discourse and aversion to confrontation yielded little results from the BOE. The lack of communication parents received the day after nicely presenting their concerns at the BOE meeting was evidence of that.

The radical group was more confrontational in their response to the contract renewal. Unlike the liberal group, they did not think that civilized public comment was enough to change the superintendent's behavior. They thought the contract renewal and raise only emboldened the superintendent, making him feel invincible. They also had little faith that elections, on their own, would solve the larger issues of corruption in Essex Town. After all, there were five votes on the BOE, and even if they got their two dream candidates elected, it would not provide a numerical majority.

The radical group immediately began investigating the superintendent. Barry posted to social media sites in neighboring towns and asked if anyone had any information on the superintendent. A woman contacted Barry and shared with him a detailed story of how the superintendent faked cancer, going so far as to shave his eyebrows to keep up the lie in one of the schools where he previously worked. This story became important later, because this was one of the schools the superintendent omitted from his résumé, possibly to cover up his problematic employment history. The superintendent was also accused of leaving his special needs child in his car while he attended a lengthy board meeting. Barry investigated this incident, finding that a police report was filed but was missing. Tom stated, "These claims are backed by an attorney, who took a deposition from a police officer. The superintendent was friendly with the police chief and the chief had a pattern of covering up crimes and tickets for his friends."[17] Throughout the course of Tom's investigation, interviewing former employers and colleagues and filing OPRA requests, he discovered a case of embezzlement at an elementary school in Essex Town. Publicizing this finding on social media, after the BOE failed to respond, elicited some of the strongest objections to the tactics the radical group was using.

ALLEGED EMBEZZLEMENT AT THE ELEMENTARY SCHOOL

Tom came across evidence of an embezzlement at the elementary school when he received audits of the school district. In one of the reports, an auditor flagged the elementary school, noting than an employee paid her property taxes with school funds. Tom researched this further, obtaining a town resolution to return the money, a bank statement, and a letter from the superintendent to the town where the employee paid her property taxes. These documents indicated that the funds were not returned until three months after the embezzlement occurred.[18] When the radical group told the president of the BOE about this incident, he was unaware that it had occurred and was surprised to learn that it happened two years earlier. The superintendent never informed the BOE about the incident and did not consult with them before writing the letter to return the funds. Furthermore, the staff member was not held accountable and continued to have check-signing authority.

When the BOE did not respond to the radical group, they confronted board members at the next meeting during public comment. At this point, the superintendent falsely stated that the embezzlement had been investigated and no evidence was found. The radical group escalated pressure on the board by involving the Essex County prosecutor. The prosecutor's office stated that the investigation was still open and that the superintendent should not have been commenting on it. Thus, the superintendent could not conclude that there was no embezzlement, if the investigation had not even been closed. Micaela posted documentation of the embezzlement, which included the alleged embezzler's name, and cover-up on the community social media page. Her post yielded over four hundred responses revealing many of the key tactics liberals use to marginalize and discredit radicals: emphasizing proper procedure, emphasizing civility, using threats and intimidation, and shaming and name-calling (see table 3).

In response to Micaela's post, liberal members of the community accused the radical group of making inflammatory accusations and referred to them as "mean-spirited" and an "angry mob." They implored the radical group to leave the "poor woman" (alleged embezzler) alone. They stated that the radical group did not know anything about the school employee and that she was a nice person. In response, Micaela refocused the conversation on the superintendent's role in these crimes and his indiscretions. In addition to covering up the embezzlement, she stated that the superintendent hid the abuse of children, including the police report on the neglect of his own child, committed résumé fraud, disguised his criminal conviction for driving while intoxicated, and failed to disclose his conflict of interest in recommending the board attorney, district insurance, and personal relationships with principals and other subordinates.[19]

While liberals focused on a need to be nice, the radical group continued to confront the superintendent and the board about the embezzlement. Micaela tagged a board member in a social media post and stated, "Question for you, [tags board member], is love for children a defense to embezzling their student accounts monies for personal property taxes?"[20] The board member she tagged was the one who betrayed his liberal supporters by voting in favor of the superintendent's contract renewal. However, rather than join the radical group in their confrontation of this board member, liberals dismissed their complaints by continuing to label them as "angry," "uncivil," "childish," and "shameful." In doing so, liberals employed both the emphasis on civility and the shaming and name-calling tactics to marginalize and discredit radicals (see table 3).

Very soon after the evidence of embezzlement was revealed, the principal of the elementary school suddenly retired. The radical group connected the retirement to her role in covering up the embezzlement. Elementary school parents began defending this principal on social media, both on the community page and Barry's page. They tried to argue that there was no connection between her retirement and the embezzlement, but Micaela pointed out that the principal gave no notice of her retirement, and it had not been discussed or recommended by the board. Her letter of retirement came suddenly after public announcement of the embezzlement. Parents opposing the radical group provided no evidence or documents that supported their position on the embezzlement or the principal's retirement. Liberal opponents to the superintendent continued to shame radicals on social media, stating that they agreed with the goal—removing a corrupt superintendent—but they did not like the radical group's tactics. An outspoken supporter of the superintendent asked the radical group to apologize to the school employee. A liberal elementary school parent *who opposed the superintendent* stated that she agreed 100 percent! Another elementary school parent accused Micaela of being a "horrible person," "spewing hatred," and having "inner demons." In response to a post with three exclamation marks that accused Micaela of hurting the community and scolding her to get over herself, Micaela stated, "Thanks for sharing your opinion. I'll remove it [the original post] when the BOE removes the SI. Fair?"[21] She later added, "The only reason this post was necessary is because rather than do their job, the Board of Ed renewed the contract of a man who had no business being the steward of our children's education."[22] An administrator of the community social media page closed the comments on this post and listed a number of problems with Micaela's posts. He stated that the administrators had received many complaints about her posting the documents, which named the school employee. At this point, Micaela had also been receiving threatening messages, and her family was being harassed in public, both liberal tactics to marginalize radicals (see table 3). As liberals called for kindness and civility toward the alleged embezzler, they attacked the radical group's character.

Two European American teachers attended the board meetings and contributed to the attacks. They reiterated the narrative that the radical group had "personal vendettas." They offered no evidence of these vendettas. They accused Micaela of wanting people to be fired. They also stated that teachers were being bashed on social media. Yet, there were no negative comments about teachers on social media. In fact, the opposite was true. Any comments about teachers on social media were positive. Clearly, the issue for these elementary school teachers was the image of the school.

The superintendent also used the tactics of emphasizing civility, procedure, and shaming. He expressed concern that people who worked in the elementary school heard about the accusations, and it was hurting their feelings. He further claimed that only the board had all the information, and they were the only people who could possibly know what really happened at the elementary school. He encouraged the community to have faith in the process, while he simultaneously shamed the radical group. He stated:

> It would be nice if we, uh, allow things to work out so we can show that . . . you may only know one side of the situation and that's really important, understanding both sides and we have both sides of that information, so when we're doing investigations, and we're talking to individuals and we're determining what next steps are, we have all the information, and individuals that go out and try to hurt people intentionally, whether it be social media, whether it be going around talking to people on the playground, that gets back to those individuals that have worked in that building for a very, very long time.[23]

At this meeting, the superintendent inaccurately responded to the evidence presented on the embezzlement, and Micaela interrupted him to correct the misinformation. The board vice president used the tactics of emphasizing procedure and civility to discredit Micaela for being disruptive. He stated: "While people are coming up to the microphone or while the Board is responding, I just want us to think about, and once again, we want to hear everything that you have to say, but let's treat each other with the same respect that we're teaching our children, that we're trying to teach our children, and uh, snickering, you know, to mock somebody or, let's just be respectful and listen, and uh, and everyone can have a chance to speak, and speak their mind."[24] The VP also echoed the superintendent's concern about hurt feelings, stating: "I've seen some very upset teachers and administrators . . . when they see some of the comments on social media, It's appropriate to bring things to the Board if you've seen something that is, that you feel was wrong, bring it to us . . . Please be careful about attacks on social media. It's hurting feelings. It's hurting lives. You can hurt careers and reputations permanently . . . go through the appropriate channels . . . and we will look into it."[25] The most recently elected board member reinforced the narrative that the radical group was damaging the community with their accusations. Using the shaming and emphasis on civility, tactics, he stated:

The tone, the casual collateral damage that is being done to people who are peripher-
ally related at best to the core issues that are being discussed is in my personal opinion
just disgusting, it's beyond the pale, it's outside the bounds of common decency, and
I think we can do better ... An awful lot of us have these blue signs on our yard that
say "hate has no home here" and it's not feeling that way and I think we need to keep
that in mind ... we're all dealing with the education of children who get their examples from the adults they see.[26]

Micaela could be heard in the audience stating "Shameful." She saw the statement
as shameful, because this European American board member compared the radical
group's calls for an investigation to the hate experienced by immigrants in deten-
tion camps. The lawn signs he referred to proliferated in Essex Town after the election of Donald Trump in protest of his anti-immigrant policies.

After this meeting, a resident who supported the superintendent asked everyone on the community social media page to watch the video and note how "uncivil" the radicals were being at the meeting. This yielded a mix of feelings on
the topic. Some people argued that the evidence was clear and that people had
tried to deal with the board "civilly" to no avail; that the time for being polite was
over. Others stated that "snickering and murmuring" in the audience was disruptive and reasserted the need for "civil discourse." Several people wanted to know
more about the wrongdoings and wanted action to be taken by the board, but they
wanted this to be done in a calm and respectful manner.

The liberal discourse that occurred in this case was not unlike liberal, racism-
evasive discourse. The people being confrontational and tackling injustice head on
were cast as angry troublemakers just as anyone who raises the uncomfortable issue
of racism is often viewed as angry and divisive.[27] This gets us nowhere on fighting
racism or other injustices, because there is too much concern about politeness and
comfort. Often the people trying to raise the issue of injustice are the ones who are
viewed as irrational, when in reality the people denying it are being irrational in
their fervor to discount racism and corruption, even when all the evidence points
to it. As with "white fragility," the feelings of white persons crying, often because
they have been accused of wrongdoing, takes center stage, stripping focus away
from the real issues.

In this case, liberals joined forces with town conservatives to marginalize and
discredit the radical elements in the community. There were a few vocal opponents
of the superintendent, who were always vocal and confrontational in their tactics.
These individuals continued to support the radical group's work. However, liberal groups that shared the goal of removing the superintendent fell silent when
the radical group were publicly accused of being unstable and uncivil. They did

not approach the radical group to help them with their investigation or support them publicly at board meetings or on social media. Some members of these liberal groups contacted Micaela and asked her to change her aggressive tone. The strongest attacks on the radical group came from parents with children at the elementary school. I believe they were upset, not because they truly cared about the school employee, but because they did not want their school to have a bad reputation. This could hurt the chances of some of the parent leaders being elected to the board in the future. There are five elementary schools in the district. Parents with political aspirations likely feared that any parent on a ballot from this school would immediately be excluded by voters, if the radical group continued to make them look bad. After all, the newly elected board member who recently failed the community by voting in favor of renewal was formerly from this elementary school. I believe the other issue parents were concerned about was property values. Maintaining the image of a friendly town with good schools was important to the resale value of homes. Indeed, there were frequent posts about property values. Either way, in this case, liberals privileged their reputations over what was socially just and worked to disassociate themselves from radicals until it became clear that the radical group was going to be successful.

EVIDENCE OF FRAUD AND CRIMINAL CONDUCT

Amid discussion of the embezzlement, the radical group shared evidence of the superintendent's criminal conduct and résumé fraud. It took the group three months to obtain the résumé. The BOE refused to provide it on the grounds that it was a "personnel matter." The radical group finally obtained the résumé through an OPRA request of files from a board of trustees serving school districts on which the superintendent served. Micaela posted her summary of the issues with the superintendent's résumé. First, the superintendent claimed that he was "Dean of Students" at one school, School A, whose records did not confirm this position. Second, he claimed to be working at School A during a time when he was, in fact, employed at another school, School B. He resigned abruptly from School B, where he allegedly faked having cancer. Furthermore, he claimed to have started employment at yet another school, School C, in 2000, when he actually did not begin until October 2001. When I read the superintendent's résumé, I also noticed that he named two schools in Connecticut where he claimed to have done his student teaching. I spent several years working in the very city he listed, and I did not recognize the names of these schools. Upon further investigation, I learned that these schools, in fact, did not exist. This issue was never resolved, but it raised questions about the validity of the superintendent's teaching certification.

Micaela posted a screen shot of her email communication with the superintendent, where she confronted him on this work history. In these emails, he accused her of "making things up" and denied ever having a position in Ohio. She then posted the superintendent's resignation letter from Ohio, showing the community that he was, in fact, employed in Ohio as an assistant principal and that he lied to her about it in the email. She further pointed to his confirmed arrest for driving under the influence as the reason he was fired from the Ohio position and why he did not report it on his résumé. The radical group also posted the police reports on social media, which indicated that the superintendent asked a gas station attendant where he could find a "good time," and when the police approached him, he fled in his car. After he was apprehended, the superintendent failed three sobriety tests.

With this mounting evidence, the board finally yielded to pressure from the radical group and hired an independent law firm to investigate the accusations. However, in making this announcement, the board maligned the radical group, using the shaming and emphasis on civility tactics to discredit them:

> Recently, a few individuals have made inflammatory, and possibly defamatory comments concerning various District employees and professionals, at public meetings and on various social media sites, attempting to vilify certain individuals. The [Essex Town] Board of Education does not condone this conduct and is gravely concerned by its negative impact on our staff and the District's excellent reputation ... While private citizens enjoy a First Amendment right to speak at public meetings and/or post information on social media, the [Essex Town] Board of Education wants to remind everyone that we should all be working together to ensure that our District embodies the same values of kindness, respect, and propriety that we all endeavor to impart to our children.[28]

Here, a largely liberal board used the principles of "kindness, respect, and propriety" to silence people fighting against injustice and typed them as angry, divisive, and impolite. As expressed in the statement, their key concern was with the "reputation" of the district. Policing their image was of "grave concern."

After multiple posts stating that the radical group was "mentally unstable," "obsessive," and "out for blood," Micaela responded to those who supported the superintendent:

> I realize ... you're Team [superintendent], Kool-Aid and all ... blindly following and ignoring all truth afforded you. But that speaks much more about how you operate than what we do ... stay your course, keep thinking you're chosen for committees because of you're [sic] brain and not your penchant for bobbleheads ... that's what nar-

cissistic sociopaths do ... they get you and the PTA/PAL moms, the BOE and the community leaders to do their bidding, they stroke your egos and tell you how great you are so that they can use you like pawns.[29]

In this response, Micaela laid out a formula for how liberal parents helped maintain the status quo through their blind support of town politicians, who were likely using these parents to further their own ambitions. The behavior of liberals who supported the superintendent during this movement was akin to the corporate liberalism that Students for a Democratic Society conceptualized.[30] That is, liberals who aspire to have friends in power fail to effectively challenge injustice as a result. Members of the board posted much more freely and comfortably on the progressives for education page organized by liberals, where they were less likely to be directly confronted than on the pages where the radical group was more active. When board members did post to the progressives for education page, it was often to cheerlead the town's programs, awards, sports victories, prominent students, and the like. They were not offering valuable information on this page, often gave standard responses, and were likely using this organization's base to promote their successes. I argue that this liberal page allowed such posts to go unchallenged, because maintaining a friendly relationship with board members and town politicians with power was most important to them. On Barry's more confrontational page, the board rarely went unchallenged. Barry continually tagged board members and asked them to respond to the radical group's direct questions. In response, both supporters and opponents of the superintendent used the emphasis on civility tactic to accuse the radical group of bullying. The bullying accusation was so commonly employed by the board that Barry would often preface his social media posts where he tagged board members with "#taggingisnotbullying."

The board was troubled by these social media posts and the radical group's continued disruption of meetings. At an October board meeting, the most recently elected member reprimanded the radical group for calling out. Noticeably irritated, he blurted out, "Is this the behavior you want to model for your children?" Micaela and Tom responded, "Yes, dissent!" To this, the board member emphasized procedure, stating, "That's not how it's done," and indicated that dissent was modeled by following the process and coming to the microphone when it was their turn. He shouted "My turn" when the radical group interrupted. Disrupting business as usual is a common social movement tactic, and one often used by activists who challenge the status quo. This is true of athletes, who take a knee during the national anthem, Code Pink activists, who are often arrested for interrupting meetings, civil rights activists, who shut down streets during marches, and people who occupy buildings in protest, as was done during the student protests at

City College, City University of New York, which led to the admittance of students of color and the creation of Black and Latino Studies Departments. The radical group employed these disruptive methods regularly, and liberals attempted to discredit them by arguing that they did not follow proper procedures, the rules of civil discourse, attempting to scare them through threats and harassment, and shaming them through name-calling (see table 3).

By October, the superintendent had not been showing up to the meetings, and it was clear that he was going to resign. More residents, especially on Barry's alternative town page, began supporting the radical group. By this time, Tom had compiled the evidence in a handout, with his notes on what the evidence meant. The radical group shared this handout at a board meeting. Interestingly, a liberal parent posted on social media that the documents were a smoking gun! This same person messaged Tom earlier in the movement to ask that he and Micaela change their "tone" on social media. She characterized their posts as "classless" personal attacks. Now, with the growing amount of evidence in the radical group's favor, the independent investigation, and rumors that the superintendent was going to resign, she expressed support for what they were doing. The independent law firm contacted the radical group for a meeting, where the radical group shared all their findings. This law firm confirmed everything the radical group found.

SUPERINTENDENT RESIGNATION
AND REAPPEARANCE OF SILENT LIBERALS

The resignation of the superintendent was finally resolved on October 19, 2018, a Friday morning, which the radical group viewed as purposely inconvenient, since most people were at work, and meetings usually took place at night. As with the last few board meetings, the superintendent was not present. In what follows, I recount the events of this important meeting to further illustrate the kind of nonviolent confrontational methods radicals used that liberals deemed too disruptive and how these methods worked to obtain information.

After the vote in favor of the resolution regarding the superintendent's resignation, the most recently elected board member (the one liberal groups supported) read from a prepared statement in which he claimed that the board was not legally able to share more information with the community. He thanked the superintendent for his service and stated, "I greatly appreciate the many positive impacts he's had on our district and I wish him all the best." As other board members continued to praise the superintendent, the radical group continually called out "Fraud! Vote accordingly!" The vice president attempted to silence them and implored them to keep order—a key tactic used to discredit radicals.

As the board VP attempted to close the discussion and move on, the radical group called out, "How much are we paying him?" The board business administrator then stated that the superintendent would be getting three months of pay for every year left on his contract, which amounted to approximately $130,000. Again, the VP attempted to move on, but Micaela repeatedly insisted that the public had a right to hear the entire agreement. The board attorney finally shared that in addition to the $130,000, the superintendent would receive payment for his merit goals, payment for unused vacation, totaling $4,536, and a complete release, meaning that the superintendent could not sue the board.

During public comment, Tom made a statement to expose the history of corruption by the superintendent and the board. He stated, "You just sent a message to anyone out there who wants to commit fraud, come to Essex Town! [applause] Lie on your résumé! Falsify documents! [applause] And guess what, when you go home, they might give you a hundred thousand dollars." He then mimicked the newly elected board member, who reprimanded the radical group for setting a bad example for their children. He stated, "You talk about 'Is this how you want your children to behave?' [mimicking the board member's voice]. I don't want my children to grow up and think 'Oh you can just violate contracts [applause]. You can sign agreements and then violate them and get money for them!'" He spoke directly to the board attorney, accusing him of corruption: "You came in. Your law firm. You worked with [the superintendent] for three years and nine months as board attorney [in another town]. He comes in. He subverts all the checks and balances with the board attorney and then slowly edges your law firm in. Your law firm pushes everybody to litigation . . . special needs parents, who are draining their retirement accounts to pad your law firm's pockets!"[31] He then shamed the board for not properly vetting the superintendent:

> He submitted a different employment history for [another town] than he did for here! And you think it's OK! This man can be in three places at one time according to all his employment records. How is that possible? He can exist in two different time zones . . . I'm so disappointed in you [names the two board members who continued to compliment the superintendent]. I thought you had learned your lesson and I can see very clearly that you haven't learned a goddamned thing![32]

There was applause and calls of "Yes" throughout Tom's statement as well as applause emojis on Barry's social media page. It seemed that Tom articulated the disgust and frustration many watching the meeting were feeling. After Tom spoke, the VP stated that they only had time for one more comment. Tom shouted, "C'mon! You hog all the talking time, Xxxx!" He was referring to the VP, who was known for being long-winded and pedantic. Micaela chastised the board for wasting the taxpayers' money: "The superintendent cost another town lots of money and what did they do? They passed the trash. And you accepting a resignation from a super-intendent who fraudulently violated the contract that you wrote for his employ-ment, you are passing the trash [applause]."[33] Micaela was referencing a news ar-ticle that New Jersey journalists wrote on this problematic process.[34] By "passing the trash," the journalists meant that educators accused of child abuse settle with school districts, resign, and move onto other positions. To get these educators to go away, the school district agrees to say nothing about the accusations to potential employers. The superintendent's employment history indicated that he had been moved from school to school after being accused of or being fired for inappropri-ate conduct.

Had the radical group not interrupted repeatedly during the October meet-ing, the board attorney would have gotten away with not reading the entire agree-ment. The liberal tactics of focusing on "proper channels" and civil discourse were designed to discredit radicals and quiet dissent. In 1966, Carl Davidson expressed this point in a position paper: "Working through existing channels. This phrase really means, 'Let us stall you off until the end of the year.' If we listen to it at all, we ought to do so just once and in such a way as to show everyone that it's a waste of time."[35] Martin Luther King Jr. also made this point to fellow liberal-minded clergy in his "Letter from Birmingham Jail (see chapter 2). David Wellman doc-uments this silencing tactic as a cultural norm in the United States used to repro-duce racism. In his work *Portraits of White Racism*, he interviewed several liberal and conservative people, who revealed their racism in contradictory doublespeak. For example, during an in-depth interview with a man Wellman calls Dick Wil-son, the respondent stated that he disliked the confrontational tactics of the Black Power movement. He believed that people had a right to march and protest, but they had to honor the restrictions placed on this right. During the interview, he found himself in a dilemma that he could not resolve. That is, where would peo-ple of color be today if they were not willing to be disruptive and purposely break racist laws, such as those that enforced segregation? The respondent admitted that he did not know and concluded that these questions just did not have easy an-swers. This conservative respondent sounded very similar to many of the liberals within Essex Town, who argued that activists should exercise their First Amend-ment right quietly. They only differed from Wellman's conservative respondent in that they supported disruptive tactics *outside* of their community, but only to the extent of putting up lawn signs or going to marches when it was popular to do so.

The proper procedure liberals preferred in Essex Town of bringing complaints to the board of education through public comment makes them think they have a voice. It is similar to Noam Chomsky's critique of college newspapers. In the film *Manufacturing Consent*, Chomsky argues student newspapers give students the illusion of having a voice. If they truly were able to upset the power establishment at universities, the administration would not allow them to exist.[36] Similarly, public comment can make people feel powerful. They give a speech, receive compliments on their speeches, and are told that the board will look into their concerns. They may sometimes get the board to pass resolutions, and this can make members of the community feel good about doing something positive. However, these resolutions may result in little more than an awareness raising event, not something that significantly challenges the status quo. This is a key difference between liberal and radical tactics. Liberals follow standard procedures. Radicals disrupt them, even when using them.

Nonconfrontational Fair-Weather Liberals
Appropriate the Movement

In chapter 2, I described Robert Merton's discussion of fair-weather liberals and put forth my own conceptualization of nonconfrontational fair-weather liberals.[37] These liberals follow the path of least resistance, showing up to fight for progressive goals when it is convenient to do so and when they are least likely to be attacked. I discovered a reemergence of these liberals after the board's announcement of the superintendent's resignation. There was an outpouring of gratitude toward the radical group on Barry's social media page. Members recognized that these three individuals persevered despite many personal attacks on them. The social media comments during the October 19 meeting also focused heavily on the brave efforts of the radical group. It was here that I noticed liberal groups attempting to take credit for the work of these three activists. They also contributed to the discourse on civility and refocused the discussion on electoral politics.

The first person to speak during public comment after the board announced the superintendent's resignation was a European American organizer for the progressives for education page. She was one of the people who believed that Micaela's methods were too aggressive. Her statement echoed those of other liberal members who attempted to take credit for the superintendent's resignation by pointing to the "many voices" that opposed him in February. In addition to pointing to these many voices, she demanded that the board search for a new law firm. The radical group's "mean-spirited" investigation of the superintendent was what yielded the information on this crony law firm and their problematic practices with parents of children with special needs. At no point throughout the movement to remove the superintendent did this speaker publicly support the radical group in finding this information and alerting the public. On social media, other members from the liberal organization supported this narrative that "many voices" opposed the superintendent months ago. These public statements exemplify the fifth tactic liberals use to marginalize and discredit radicals: Appropriation. Through appropriation, liberals take the success of the movement away from radicals and reconstruct it as a liberal success (see table 3). None of the people who vocally supported the radical group, including a person who had a long history of activism in the community and conducted her own OPRAs, engaged in this kind of appropriation.

More brazen than the comments that "many voices" were responsible for the superintendent's resignation was an announcement on the progressives for education page informing the community that the superintendent was officially out. This post excitedly proclaimed that the board terminated its relationship with the superintendent and that the separation agreement was going to be discussed at the October 19 meeting. This post did not tag the radical group and gave no credit to them. The post gave the impression that this liberal organization was responsible for the resignation. In fact, when I spoke with a community member after the October 19 meeting, he stated that he thought the radical group worked with this liberal organization. They did not. The radical group knew from their inside sources that the superintendent was resigning at least three weeks before the announcement on the liberal organization's page. In response to the post on this page, a member reiterated that she and many others had been voicing their concerns about the superintendent respectfully and that the community must return to civility. She also posted multiple times that anyone would be lucky to be superintendent of "our great town" and that we should all move forward. Like other liberals, her posts revealed that her key concern was with the town's image as the "friendliest town." This person never reached out to the radical group during their investigation and, in fact, was one of the people who wanted Micaela to "tone it down." When community members asked specific questions on this page about the separation agreement, only the radical group could answer them. Also, the newspaper stories that came out in the town quoted the radical group extensively, because they were the people who secured the documents and were the only people who could tell the story of how these documents were discovered. This was the reason for the independent law firm's meeting with them. They did not meet with the liberal organizations.

To his credit, a resident who was a key organizer of a liberal organization that developed after the election of Donald Trump posted a thank-you to the three activists. He stressed that many people criticized these three individuals for their "tone," but in the end, their methods worked. This person came back to the social media discussions when it was clear that the radical group had solid evidence of the superintendent's résumé fraud. Early in my research, I characterized this person as a *potential* liberal defector; someone who was not completely averse to confrontation and had the potential to push liberals to be more confrontational. There seemed to be a few individuals who wanted to use more confrontational tactics but were limited by their group's or the town's liberal ideology. One of these residents continually voiced support for the radical group and often pointed out that the town was full of "DINOs"—Democrat in Name Only. Another member of a more radical, direct action group called twice for a march against the superintendent's renewal and against the terms of his resignation. These marches never happened. Past research on liberal organizations has noted similar frustrations among activists who want to take more direct action but who are confined by the cultures of their organizations.[38]

Amid the celebration of the radical group, there was also an immediate focus by liberals to "vote, vote, vote!" Once again, liberals prepared to put all of their eggs in the electoral basket. During the livestream of the meeting on Barry's social media page, liberals continued to remind the community that there were two seats up in November. There were three candidates running, two of whom the liberal organizations supported. Both of these candidates were people of color. The European American liberals in Essex Town were all too excited to be organizing the campaigns for candidates of color. Their strategies mirrored those of European American liberals in national politics. They focused on voting as the morally right and intelligent thing to do, especially when voting in people of color. The third candidate in the election, a European American woman, was rumored to be the mayor's pick for the board. There was evidence that she supported the superintendent. Micaela warned the European American liberals, who opposed this candidate, that if they did not work harder to expose this candidate's questionable political alliances, she would win. They refused to heed Micaela's advice. Instead, they again implored Micaela to "tone it down" and join them in a "whisper campaign," where they would go to sporting and other events to gently inform people of this candidate's weaknesses. They wanted to use these quiet methods to turn votes rather than engage in confrontational tactics. In the end, the mayor's candidate won. Liberal organizations were left with one vote they hoped to count on instead of two.

Confrontational tactics ultimately worked to remove the superintendent. Given the political context of the town as well as the history of the board's slow response to well-reasoned public comment, these tactics were likely the only way to force him out. However, these methods are hard to sustain without support from a critical mass of people and multiple organizations. The liberal tendency toward politeness at any cost, the immediate calls for civility after the radical group's success, and the disappointing reaction of liberal organizations who tried to steal credit from radicals may mean that most residents will fall back on milder, non-confrontational tactics in the long run.

Lessons Learned:
Liberal White Supremacy and Racism-Evasiveness

This case study provides important lessons on liberal methods that can also be applied to racism-specific cases. First, liberal conflict-aversion prevents progressives from challenging the power structure, and this liberal tendency toward nonconfrontation ultimately leads to racism-evasiveness (see figure 4). In the Essex Town case, no one was saying overtly racist things—at least not publicly—but what decades of research on racism show is that one does not have to be openly racist to sustain white supremacy.[39] Essex Town was racially diverse, but all of the important political positions in the town and the directors of town services were occupied by European Americans (see table 4). The mayor, police chief, fire chief, superintendent, board of education president, town council president, and so on were all European American. While there were certainly people of color on the town council, they were not the presidents or ultimate authorities. Furthermore, placing people of color into positions of authority is not enough to create significant change, especially if these people of color conform to the same liberal ideology and methods as the white power structure. People of color can be used to offer the desired image of diversity without challenging the dominant positions of European Americans. Radical confrontational methods threatened to expose corruption among officials in the town and unseat people in positions of authority, most of whom were European American. The mayor had a political relationship with the superintendent that he likely did not want disrupted. The radical group is currently investigating the mayor precisely for his political and financial connections, which they believe he uses to maintain his position and to secure positions for his friends and family. The radical group has also been informed by police officers that the mayor makes racist comments about African Americans in private. Liberal methods will be insufficient in confronting this white power structure, especially if the ultimate goal of liberals is to be a part of it.

Second, likely because liberals wanted to be part of that power structure, and because they had an elitist attitude toward radicals, they developed tactics to marginalize and discredit the radical group. The liberal tactics of focusing on proper procedure, civility, and threatening and shaming radicals were employed by the power structure to delay and prevent the goal of exposing social injustice and corruption. These standard liberal tactics can be used against people who attempt to expose racism in their institutions. Racism scholars have argued that people who

TABLE 4
Who Benefits from the Image of a Friendly and Diverse Town?
"Race" and Gender of Politicians and Directors of Essex Town Services

Position	"Race" and gender
Mayor	European American man
Police chief	European American man
Fire chief	European American man
Town attorney	European American man
Superintendent	European American man
Board of education president	European American man
Town council president	European American woman
Town clerk	European American woman
Director of parks and recreation	European American man

address racism explicitly are labeled as too confrontational, divisive, and uncivil.[40] Scholars and activists who openly voice their concerns about racism have been attacked during protests, have been harassed at work, and have lost their jobs. Recently, Cornel West was denied tenure at Harvard University, though the university reconsidered after public outcry, and Nikole Hannah-Jones, the Pulitzer Prize–winning journalist who worked on the racism-centered 1619 Project, was denied tenure at Princeton University.[41] There have been many cases like this where faculty of color who speak out on racism are targeted, harassed, threatened, and fired, using the same liberal tactics found in this case study.

Third, liberals appropriate the success of radical movements but do not adopt radical methods to continue that success toward creating significant change. In this case, appropriation occurred when liberals portrayed the success of the radical group as their own and then implored the community to return to "civil discourse" and electoral politics as key social change tactics. This same pattern occurs in racism-specific cases. The Black Panthers had a more radical approach than other progressive organizations and made significant changes as a result. There are initiatives today, such as the free breakfast program for school children that the Black Panthers started and that liberals support without crediting the more radical groups and methods that developed them.[42] The radical, confrontational methods of the Movement for Black Lives has forced racism, white supremacy, and anti-blackness into the national discourse. We now see corporations and universities championing the movement through statements on antiracism, yet these are followed up with liberal approaches. The racism-focused agenda of the Movement for Black Lives gets transformed by liberals into issues of diversity, equity, and inclusion that then benefits liberals who will be hired to support these initiatives or will receive credit for serving on diversity committees. Diversity, then, becomes a selling point that props up the white power structure. There is profit in maintaining a "diverse" image and claiming to support diversity. As funding for diversity-based initiatives rolls into institutions based on the success of the Movement for Black Lives, European American liberal faculty will be quick to show that their work is "diverse" (whether or not it has anything to do with racism) and eager to serve on committees to prove their commitment to stakeholders. They may be praised for their work while faculty of color, who have been doing racism-centered work their entire careers, go unrecognized and unpromoted.

Past research has found that European American progressives celebrate "diversity" to feel good about themselves, to appear sophisticated, and to gain legitimacy as antiracists.[43] In one study of progressive communities, a self-identified white antiracist expressed excitement for living as an "Oreo cookie," sandwiched between two people of color on his street.[44] In such communities, real estate agents and politicians benefit from new commitments to "diversity," which they use as a selling point to attract progressive buyers.[45] In Essex Town, the image of a friendly and diverse town supported the white power structure, which profited off of it. This power structure did not have to self-identify as liberal to benefit from liberal ideology. After all, political conservatives welcomed the liberal focus on civil rights and diversity in the late 1940s so long as it did not pose a challenge to the (white) capitalistic status quo.[46]

Fourth, this case study offers insight into liberal superiority and how it maintains racism-evasiveness. I argue that European American liberals view themselves as superior to other European American progressives. In this case, they viewed themselves as more professional and civil than their radical counterparts, whom they portrayed as "mean-spirited" and "unstable." They also viewed themselves as superior to other European American liberals because they lived in a diverse town. Past research has found that individual liberals point to more conservative and extreme racists to ignore their own racism.[47] Likewise, when a racist incident occurred in a neighboring progressive town, Essex Town liberals were quick to point it out on social media along with praise of their friendlier, less racist town. This becomes a problem, especially when European American liberals are the ones in power, and they dedicate their time to identifying villains on which to place blame rather than taking concrete actions to promote effective antiracist solutions.

In the next chapter, I examine an organization in which the majority of members were radical. They prided themselves on direct action and more confrontational approaches. However, this case illustrates other problems common in

progressive organizing, and that is a focus on class solidarity at the expense of discussions on racism. I analyze how this practical action-centered and racism-evasive
approach is informed both by internal organizational culture and by external liberal discourse on civility. Together, these case studies reveal the contours of a problem in liberal organizing; one that must be confronted if progressives are to move
a social justice agenda on the national level.

CHAPTER 4

Walk the Walk but Don't Talk the Talk

Liberal Discourse, Radical Action, and Racism-Evasion

> When white people acknowledge racism, they often tend to intellectualize the issues and spend too much time talking about them rather than experiencing the emotional impact of racism and taking anti-racist action.
>
> —Illana Shapiro,
> *Training for Racial Equity & Inclusion*, 2002

> People of color don't get to orchestrate the terms of civility; instead we are always responding to what civility is supposed to be so it's inherently undemocratic, and unequal, and racist.
>
> —Gaye Theresa Johnson,
> "When Civility Is Used as a Cudgel," 2019

This chapter addresses my second case study, which focuses on racism-evasiveness in a progressive, grassroots, interracial organization, Center for Economic Democracy, and its coalition, Community-Labor Alliance. For the purposes of brevity, I sometimes refer to these groups as "the organization" and "the coalition," respectively. Both groups are located in a northeastern city that I call Union City and are near a university that I call Elite U.[1] I spent three years with these groups, documenting their struggle to achieve a community benefits agreement from their opponent, Elite University Hospital, which I sometimes refer to as "the hospital." The hospital had a history of pursuing redevelopment in the Valley, a mostly working-class, African American and Latine neighborhood. Unlike in Essex Town, the organization and coalition worked more directly to combat racist policies, and yet it was still silenced as an issue. This case also differed from Essex Town in that radical activists were part of an established organization, which may have contributed to the silencing of racism as an issue that should be addressed internally. Activists in the coalition who wanted more discussion on racism and other issues felt that the culture of the organization stifled it. This case and the Essex Town case were similar in that progressive groups were posed against a political machine that used divisive tactics to demonize radical progressives. In both cases, groups used alliances with and pressured sympathetic board members—the Union City Board of Alderpersons and the Essex Town Board of Education.

I characterize the organization's and coalition's direct action approach as "walking the walk but not talking the talk." Activists saw themselves as walking the walk literally through marches, rallies, and political walks that lasted well into the night, even during their scheduled work vacations. They filled city hall during board of alderperson meetings and testified against University Hospital's construction, held press conferences, conducted house meetings, and regularly canvassed the Valley neighborhood to recruit members. They were willing to speak back loudly to the hospital administration and not let their opponents get the upper hand. This action-centered approach justified their decision to not "talk the talk" on controversial issues, such as racism. They recognized fighting racial injustice as part of their agenda but thought addressing it explicitly, especially internally, would threaten solidarity. My analysis of this case illustrates the class over racism perspective and action-centered approach of radicals compared to liberals. Action-centered labor unions, and radicals in general, have a history of privileging class solidarity over discussions on racism.[2] I show that this action-centered, racism-evasive strategy is partially a response to poor experiences with liberal, talk-centered methods. While this organization uses radical, confrontational methods, they operate within a dominant liberal discourse of civility that limits the way activists address racism, sexism, and other intersecting forms of oppression. This organizational culture and history interacts with external color-blind ideology, which is tied to liberal discourse (see figure 5). In addition to contrasting radical with liberal politics, this case complicates past work on color-blind racism. Before discussing these findings, I first detail the history of Union City, the Center for Economic Democracy, and the Community-Labor Alliance.

Background and Political Context of Union City

Union City has been described by some as an academic company town due to the economic and political dominance of Elite U, a predominantly white institution with well-connected alumni. Since the 1920s and 1930s, mayors and other political elites connected to Elite U assisted the university in receiving land taken from small businesses and poor residents. Graduates of Elite U also sat on the city's urban renewal committee and wrote reports about the university's needs, which assisted Elite U in acquiring land for its development. Through urban renewal, Elite

U accumulated much wealth off residential areas, such as the Valley. The amount of tax-exempt land owned by Elite U more than doubled from 1950 to 1990. The Valley remained an increasingly impoverished neighborhood, and staff members at the university continued to make poverty wages, despite the university's increasing wealth.

When I joined the Center for Economic Democracy (the organization) and the Community-Labor Alliance (the coalition) in 2004, members had recently completed a project on redlining and had developed a social contract. The Community-Labor Alliance was formed as a means to get Elite U's hospital to sign onto a community benefits agreement (CBA) with the Valley, when Elite U announced plans to build a state-of-the-art cancer center right next to the Valley. Organizers in the Center for Economic Democracy knew this would be a sore point with Valley residents given Elite U's long and problematic relationship with the community. Members of the coalition often argued that the public schools and other institutions University Hospital built as part of its community relations efforts did little to benefit Union City residents. The schools were largely built in impoverished areas and offered poor-quality education, which residents thought contributed to school violence and high dropout rates. What also concerned Union City residents was that these institutions did not create good jobs for them, and more than 60 percent of Elite U's employees lived outside of the city. Furthermore, the hospital's development produced pollution, which coalition members linked to the Valley's high asthma rate in children. This pollution was exacerbated by the parking problems that had occurred in the Valley, because University Hospital employees were forced to park along residential streets and in front of residents' homes. This long history of Elite U and University Hospital's relationship to Union City's communities, such as the Valley, informed the issues developed as part of the CBA. Those issues included good jobs, parking, affordable housing, environment, and access to health care.

The Center for Economic Democracy focuses on economic and racial issues. Its mission is to influence policies in and around working-class communities, immigrant communities, and communities of color affected most by social and economic inequality. It is a nonprofit organization built through the successful interracial leadership of Adrianna Stone, a white woman from South Africa, and Michael Cross, an African American pastor. Their relationship was often evoked by activists as a powerful catalyst for building interracial membership and inspiring trust within the membership. Both leaders had committed their adult lives to social justice activism and were able to draw on their resources to create an organization where European Americans were as actively engaged as African American and Latine members. Some of the key leaders and members of the organization and coalition were actively involved in the 1960s civil rights movement and often drew on the memories and words of Malcolm X and Martin Luther King Jr. during speeches at public meetings and rallies. Both the organization and coalition were unique in their diverse interracial, interfaith, and interclass membership. All these factors provided for a more nuanced investigation of color-blind ideology and organizational strategies than has previously been attempted. Rather than examining the expressions of color-blind ideology by individual European Americans versus people of color, I was able to study how this ideology and racism-evasiveness operated within a racially diverse organizational setting. The organization and coalition clearly dealt with racist practices by their opponent. The history of urban renewal in Union City and elsewhere targeted people of color, as did discrimination in education, employment, and redlining. I studied how the organization addressed these issues in a political climate of racism-evasiveness that emphasized liberal color-blindness and what they tell us about radical versus liberal methods.

Methods of Capturing Silence

Scholars of color-blind ideology and racism-evasiveness face a unique challenge, because we are investigating the seeming absence of a phenomenon rather than the presence of it. We have to navigate the "slippery, apparently contradictory, and often subtle . . . rhetorical maze" of this phenomenon.[3] To my advantage, I studied people working together on the same projects in the same organization. This gave me some direction and control in analyzing any contradictions in what respondents said. Triangulating data from participant observation, in-depth interviews, media coverage, organizational materials, reports, and so forth allowed me to compare what I observed to what respondents volunteered in interviews. Using these methods, I developed a case study of the Center for Economic Democracy and Community-Labor Alliance during the years 2004–2007. Although this was over ten years ago, I believe the racial and class dynamics I documented within this progressive group were a harbinger of divides we are now witnessing on the national scene.

Because the coalition, Community-Labor Alliance, formed from the organization, Center for Economic Democracy, and was the main focus of the organization during the time of my study, I investigated both of these groups in tandem. Observations of meetings and other organizational activities allowed me to assess the kind of organizational culture the Center for Economic Democracy and the Community-Labor Alliance had. This revealed how and if members discussed racism in public and private settings and provided insight into how strategies were developed. Interviews allowed me to understand why members used different kinds of strategies and how they felt about discussing racism within the organization. These data also enabled me to assess the extent to which the organization allowed for critical discussion of racial differences and racism or if it focused on commonalities. My observations guided my interviews, which lasted two hours on average. During my participant observation, I found that activists consistently emphasized racial unity and rarely talked explicitly about racism. Therefore, I asked activists why interracial unity was emphasized during public meetings, whether they saw problems with this emphasis, and whether the organization should explicitly address racism as part of its agenda. I also asked activists about their personal experiences with racism or other forms of discrimination both within and outside of the organization. Furthermore, I asked how the organization managed to recruit a diverse membership and whether projects became divided along racial lines.

After two months of participant observation, I began approaching members for interviews. By this time I had identified the key leaders and active members of the organization and had developed rapport with a few of the members, who became my main contacts. I conducted the first interviews with these contacts and active members. At the end of each interview, I asked participants if they could recommend other members for interviews until I reached most of the respondents recommended. To ensure confidentiality, I disguised the names of the respondents, the organization, the coalition, the organization's opponent, local politicians, the city, and the neighborhoods within the city. Table 5 shows the ethnicity and gender of the respondents. Of the twenty-five interviews conducted, five were with African American women, and six were with African American men. One interviewee identified as a Jamaican woman. There were four European American men, six European American women, two Latino men, and one Latina woman in the sample. Eighteen were members of the coalition. Six of these members held the position of "cochair" in the coalition, four were also members of the Service Employees International Union, and three were members of a local neighborhood

TABLE 5
Ethnicity and Gender of Respondents Interviewed by Author

Ethnicity	Women	Men	Total
African American	5	6	11
European American	6	4	10
Latine	1	2	3
Jamaican	1	0	1
TOTAL	13	12	25

group that was predominantly white. Two other members were part of the Socialist Party in Union City and three respondents were community residents with no other title. Seven of the members interviewed were paid staff of the Center for Economic Democracy.

Although the organization states that it has a membership of over six hundred individuals, much of that membership is not regularly involved in organization meetings. This membership is tapped when the organization is planning rallies or marches. During the early meetings of the coalition, fifty to sixty members were present at public meetings. As time went on, twenty-five to thirty members were present. Although my interviews were initially with these more visible and active members, their recommendations for potential interviewees allowed me to access other less visible members. During their speeches and meetings I was able to observe members who could not be reached for interviews. I also had informal conversations with them before and after meetings. Interviews were semi-structured, transcribed verbatim, and conducted in activists' homes, local restaurants of the interviewee's choosing, or at the organization's office. The format of the interviews allowed members to speak freely. Activists provided rich details about their personal lives and shared documents about the history of the organization and coalition. I started the interviews with simple questions on how the activists became involved with the organization and then led up to the more difficult questions about racism, starting with personal experiences before addressing their views of the organization. Similar to what Jennifer Pierce found in her study of law firms and affirmative action,[4] respondents answered questions easily until it came to racism. Unlike Pierce's experience, no one asked me to leave. Instead, they would take a breath, sit back, and offer a thoughtful response. At this point in the interview, a few respondents stated that they were now glad that I was disguising their names. Initially, they were puzzled that I had given them a form on confidentiality, because the organization had nothing to hide. This at least provides some assurance that respondents felt safe discussing racism with me.

Many studies have considered the impact interviewer ethnicity has on respondents' willingness to discuss racism.[5] Deirdre Royster navigated the boundaries of Black and white, sometimes presenting herself as an "ordinary white" graduate student and other times as a "sister struggling to get a degree from Hopkins."[6] Like Royster, I am also racially ambiguous, and my ethnicity often comes up for debate among people who think I belong to this or that racial group. I have been called a multitude of racial slurs and classified a number of ways including "mulatto," indigenous, Native American, Nepalese, Vietnamese, and most often Latine. When I visited stores in and around the research setting, people would often speak to me in Spanish and were puzzled when I answered back in English. However, activists rarely questioned my ethnicity. What most interested them was my accountability to the organization, an important factor for acceptance.[7] I showed up for meetings, rallies, and press conferences, went door to door, and participated in political walks. One activist said that he would use me as an example to get other members to show up because I was there even in the later stages of my pregnancy. My family's class background also played a role in the openness of these conversations. Activists were interested in the fact that my father worked in coal mines at the age of twelve. For example, Joseph, a retired African American cochair in the coalition laughed with me over my father's stories about the conditions of mines in his day versus today. Joseph shared his theories with me that coal-mining jobs were "coming back."

The ease with which respondents spoke about their personal lives, their experiences with racism and other forms of discrimination, the length at which they spoke, and the details they offered led me to believe that they were comfortable giving their honest assessment of the organization. Most respondents, regardless of their ethnicity, did not think the organization should address racism. It was not that African Americans told me a different story than Latines or European Americans, which would indicate that my ethnicity played a strong role. Of those who felt that the organization should address racism, one was Latino, one African American, and one European American. In addition, what interviewees told me seemed to match what was said at public events, where I was largely invisible. Members did not address racism explicitly in those settings. I easily disappeared among the excitement of the meetings. The only time I participated was during smaller meetings, where I would volunteer for "turnouts" (a commitment to bring a certain number of people to the next rally or event). I took copious field notes before and after meetings, jotting down important references, quotes, and situations. It was fairly easy to take notes during meetings, because many of the residents would jot down notes or read. I would also record my thoughts and quotes from the meetings on my drive home immediately after the meetings. I recorded other public events, such as rallies, press conferences, and aldermanic hearings and compared what happened to what was reported in news coverage.

I recorded 282 single-spaced pages (532,030 words) of field notes on public events alone, coding for words or discussions related to "race," racism, diversity, and racial disparities. I paid close attention to when, how, and why racism was discussed or not discussed and noted any conversations related to inequality. I was also interested in the metaphors activists used to discuss their work on oppression.[8] Activists sometimes made reference to slavery and "plantation mentality" when talking about Elite U. In fact, it was these early references that showed activists had an awareness of racism yet at the same time strategically downplayed racial differences.

The organization had more of a top-down structure with a clear board of directors compared to the coalition. Both the coalition and organization meetings were usually led by the founders of the organization, but occasionally the Community-Labor Alliance meetings were led by cochairs. Each of these cochairs represented an issue from the community benefits agreement. Their job was to educate the community about these issues and speak on them at public events, such as hearings and rallies. They also represented the coalition when they met with Elite University Hospital administration. I learned much about the structure of this organization during my first meeting.

A Typical Meeting of the Community-Labor Alliance

I met Adrianna at a university book talk that included community organizations and well-known scholars, such as Frances Fox Piven. After several weeks of phone calls, Adrianna invited me to the next public meeting of the coalition happening on October 6, 2004. The meeting took place in the library of a public school. Michael Cross led the meeting. He was friendly but also had a commanding presence. He was a bit over six feet tall, and his voice filled the room when he spoke. He asked everyone to go around the room and quickly state their names. After introductions, Michael went straight to business, asking the cochairs to share reports.

The first issue addressed was parking. The cochair, Evelyn, was a young African American woman in her early twenties. She spoke about living in the Valley district all her life—over twenty years. She spoke passionately about the parking problems in her community. She stated that renters in the surrounding community were having their parking spaces taken up by University Hospital workers and that renters had to pay for a sticker to park in their own spaces. When they did not have stickers, their cars were towed. An audience member raised her hand and stated that visitors should also be able to park for free at the hospital. She shared her story about how she had to pay to park when she took her relative for an outpatient procedure. Adrianna asked the audience member if she wanted this to be added to the list of demands. The audience member replied "Yeah" in an uncertain way, as if she hadn't thought about this when she started telling her story, but since it was offered to be on the agenda, she agreed to it. Evelyn replied firmly, "That won't keep them off our streets." Michael and Adrianna chimed in, stating that the issue of visitor parking could be tackled after Evelyn met with University Hospital staff and found out how responsive they would be to getting their cars off the streets. Michael did not jump quickly from one issue to the next. However, it was clear that the organizers wanted to adhere to the agenda and managed public comments, stories, and complaints so that they would remain on task.

The next issue report was from Trinity, an African American woman. She was standing in the audience rather than sitting at the table with the other cochairs. She began her report on "Environment and Open Space" by stating that the Valley had high asthma rates due to pollution from trucks and the hospital's medical and hazardous waste. She stated that studies of the Valley showed the rates were high and this could be an even worse problem if Elite U continued its construction. She raised her voice for emphasis, advising that the coalition demand free medical coverage for the children in the Valley. While Trinity was going over her report, the audience cheered "Amen" and "C'mon now," showing their support for Trinity's proposal. Michael commended Trinity on her report. He said he wanted to hear from the residents in the audience. A resident proposed that the group keep getting more environmental studies. Michael stated that they already knew asthma was a problem for the kids in the Valley, and more studies would not help them. He asserted that consistent care should be their focus because "the asthma doesn't go away with construction." He reminisced about a time when there were asthma clinics and asthma vans. The audience responded to this with "That's right" and "Uh-huh." Adrianna was concerned about the wording of the demand and suggested that they state that the health care for Valley residents begin *before* construction. The audience agreed and voted in favor of the motion following *Robert's Rules of Order*.

The meeting continued in this manner. Leaders wanted to promote a democratic process, listening to residents, opening up discussion on agenda items, and revising with input from everyone. Public meetings were quite lively with residents and cochairs sharing stories of their experiences, cheering each other on, and giving rousing commentary to emphasize the importance of the issues. Call and response, testifying, prayer, gospel songs, and other elements of Christian church culture were often a part of the coalition and organization meetings. Mary Patillo-McCoy argues that organizations like this use the church as a cultural toolkit from which they draw to energize their members.[9] Pastors were particularly powerful during public meetings. They would make passionate statements on the issues or offer their perspective on strategies. In one instance, a member insisted that a well-known pastor in the community be provided a translator because he wanted to hear "that fire and brimstone" in the pastor's native language of Spanish. At another particularly lively meeting, Michael Cross exclaimed, "I feel like I'm in church!" In my interviews with union organizers, some members who were not Christian and not particularly religious claimed that their most spiritual moments were during coalition meetings.[10] At the same time, the leaders rarely strayed too far from the agenda. They had staff meetings prior to public meetings, where they could discuss their vision for moving forward and develop an agenda that would support this vision. In my time with the group, there was only one instance when leaders allowed a long discursion from the agenda. This case involved sexual harassment.

This issue was brought to the attention of coalition members by a local pastor, Jorge, who was a member of the organization's board of directors at the time. The women affected were members of his congregation. At the meeting, women shared their stories of being sexually harassed by their employers. They recounted incidents where their employers fondled them and left them sexually explicit notes. Members of the coalition reacted most strongly to the women's statements that they were fired without adequate explanation. One woman stated that after she was laid off with the explanation that production was slow, her employer hired five more people. And another explained that her employer stated that because she was a "minority," she did not have any rights. The woman also spoke about undocumented workers at the factory who were vulnerable to this harassment. After the women spoke, Jorge explained why he brought this issue to the meeting: "This situation is in our neighborhood. I think we have residents here who need to know about this situation, because I live in [the Valley]. I don't want my wife going to work in a factory where she doesn't have the liberty, the freedom to work because a man wants to harass her and touch her."[11]

Other members at the meeting stated that the women should file complaints and go to the unemployment office to collect. One man cried, telling the women that he had seen them in his neighborhood, and if he had known about the situation, he would have called the police. It was not long before Michael concluded the discussion, indicating that the leaders had already decided on a course of action. He stated that he and a group of other pastors had already visited the factory and that they were going again that Friday. The members at the meeting applauded loudly, and Michael moved onto the next agenda item.

At the next coalition meeting, the pastors who went to the factory on behalf of the women discussed the outcome of the meeting with the employers. Miguel, a union organizer and one of the pastors present at the meeting, explained that they asked the owners for the manuals at the factory. Miguel stated that none of these manuals were translated into Spanish, even though the owner had bragged about having eight Spanish countries in the factory, meaning that he hired people from countries where Spanish was the dominant language. The owner also stated that the factory was a family. To this, Miguel stated, "they were a dysfunctional family, because there are those who do not know that someone is being sexually harassed by one of the family."[12] He also stated that the owners were trying to turn the coalition's own against them. By this he meant that the assistants at the factory, who denied any evidence of sexual harassment, were from the African American church. Adrianna also indicated that the organization was speaking to an immigration rights lawyer about the possibility of getting the undocumented workers visas to stay in the country. After this brief update on the factory, the leaders moved onto hearing reports from coalition cochairs on issues in the community benefits agreement.

Although this incident involved some discussion, it was an illustration of the coalition's and organization's action-centered focus. The case of sexual harassment at the factories involved multiple identities of the workers as documented or undocumented, Spanish-speaking women and people of color. These identities were noted, but there was no extensive discussion of them, nor was there explicit discussion of sexism in the workplace as a persistent problem for women workers that should be addressed by the groups.[13] Leaders of the organization focused on the actions they were going to take to handle the problem and involved the coalition only by giving members infrequent updates on the case. It was clear that the parent organization, Center for Economic Democracy, had already made a plan on how to address this issue *before* it was brought to the coalition for discussion. It was not developed as an issue or project for the community coalition, which remained focused on the struggle for a community benefits agreement. The reason the group acted on this specifically was likely because a well-respected member of the board of directors and pastor in the organization brought it to the group. The pastors acting to protect these women were men. In many ways, the organization's response to these cases of sexual harassment were reinforced by patriarchal ideologies.

In general, the organization avoided talk-centered approaches to controversial issues, such as racism and sexism, that were silenced in favor of seemingly less time-consuming issues, such as class. The sexual harassment of these women was an issue for the organization and coalition because of their class positions as workers in a factory. However, something other than organizational culture influenced decisions over what issues were worthy of the organization's time. In what follows, I share interviews with activists that illustrate the interaction of several internal and external factors ultimately resulting in racism-evasive action. First, activists had negative experiences with liberal organizations that claimed to care about injustice but did very little to address it directly. They responded to these experiences by doing the exact opposite—"walking" instead of "talking." Second, leftist organizations, such as labor unions, have a history of subsuming racism to class. This history certainly impacted the action-centered organizational culture that the coalition had adopted simply by being parented by a union organization within the

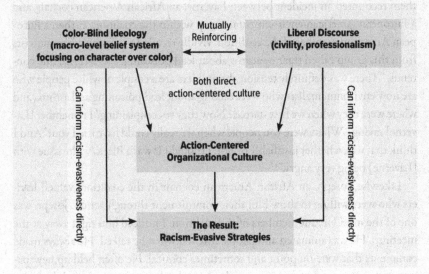

FIGURE 5
The Interaction of Racial Ideologies and Organizational Culture,
Producing Racism-Evasiveness

larger labor movement. One coalition member stated that this coalition inherited the "tunnel vision" of the union, which prevented any critical discussion on controversial issues. All of this is shaped by societal-level ideologies of denial and color-blindness as well as a dominant liberal discourse that glorifies civility (see figure 5). These factors inform the issues organizers choose to minimize. Thus, organizational culture is not the only culprit influencing the result of racism-evasiveness in more radical groups—external racial ideologies act on these internal dynamics.

The Effect of Liberal White Supremacy and Discourse

ACTION-CENTERED RACISM-EVASIVENESS
AS A RESPONSE TO TALK-CENTERED LIBERALS

Some of my earliest conversations with organizers referenced problems with professional, liberal organizations. Rob, a Latino union organizer with the Service Employees International Union (SEIU), stated that liberal groups such as Green Peace look nice but are out of touch with the lives of everyday people. These liberal organizations, he argued, had no clue about the environmental racism impacting poor people of color. For Rob, the organization and coalition were different because they worked directly with people living in communities affected by injustice. When I asked members about any racial tensions within the coalition, a few of them recounted an incident between Laverne, an African American cochair, and a European American environmental group within the coalition. Esther, a European American member of the coalition, vividly recalled a meeting where activists from this group raised their concerns about lead poisoning and asthma. She contends, "There was definitely tension about 'Here are a couple of white people who are now environmentalists who were talking about lead poisoning and asthma and where were they when we first started? Now they're complaining.' I remember [Laverne] saying, 'Where were you people when we really could have used you?' And I think that was, whether justifiably or not, I thought it was a Black/white issue with [Laverne] being very angry."[14]

Likewise, Joseph, an African American cochair in the coalition, valued leaders who were willing to show him their commitment through action. Joseph was one of the most vibrant members of the coalition. I noticed him right away at the meetings. He was animated and people listened when he talked. He always made comments that were on point and sometimes comical. He often held up newspapers to point out stories and connect them to what he was saying. Joseph had a lot of negative experiences with people who said they would help the community and never did. He was recruited by Jen, a European American woman organizer with the organization. He was impressed by her focus on direct action. Comparing his experiences with other organizations to what he saw in the coalition, Joseph stated, "[The coalition] are people who are real," not like those who "tell you one thing and do something else."[15] Adding to this, Joseph's daughter stated, "Jen and the girls, they not only came in here to talk with people, they got in the trenches and they got dirty right along with the people . . . and whatever she said, she not only said, she did it as well."[16]

Adrianna, the cofounder of the organization, shared her disappointment with liberal groups, including the union. In my interview with her, she explained why she developed the Center for Economic Democracy: "The union had for many years done what unions do everywhere, which is to wait until there was a crisis moment and they were allowed to go on strike, and the union would then run out and get community support just for that crisis moment, and then once everything was settled and back to normal, then all the ties would be gone, and everybody would go back to business as usual."[17] She further stated, "We can't just sit and talk about color. We have to be prepared to take on real power and to be prepared to fight the fight where we've got common ground."[18]

The organization had other reasons to be suspicious of liberal groups in the community. One way Elite U attempted to divide the coalition and delegitimize their demands for a community benefits agreement was by claiming they gave money to another neighborhood organization, Valley Development Association, that allegedly helped people acquire housing through homeownership counseling and building or rehabilitating housing. This community group partnered with the hospital on a number of projects, and hospital managers sat on Valley Development's board of directors. The coalition invited Valley Development to join their movement to no avail, and coalition members thought Valley Development had been bought out by Elite U. As one coalition member put it, "Clearly the hospital is using [Valley Development]. It's sad that they settled for peanuts and bread crumbs."[19]

Valley Development Association was also a group composed predominantly of African American and Latine people. According to coalition members, the hospital argued that Valley Development represented the Valley's interests, and their partnership with Valley Development took the place of a community benefits agreement. I see this kind of "partnering" as a capitalistic, liberal tactic for gaining power and influence in communities. This partnership between Valley Development and Elite U was not unlike the relationship between liberal organizations and the board of education in Essex Town (see chapter 3). The point of such liberal partnerships is not to fundamentally alter unequal power relationships in a way that gives the most marginalized people a voice, but for liberals to become part of the power establishment. People of color are just as capable of contributing to this liberal agenda as liberal European Americans and can be used by the latter in powerful positions to legitimize their goals.

The organization often noted Elite U's tactic of discrediting their movement through the use of people of color as figure heads. Julie, a union organizer, stated:

> The same way that the Bush administration does with Condoleezza Rice ... [Elite U] would sort of put these figureheads of color out in front of them to legitimize their agenda. They have a minister named [William Bose] who ... is supposed to somehow represent Black clergy in [Union City] ... [Elite U] would put a newsletter out with [William Bose] on the front page saying how [Elite U] is great, and they shouldn't have to be responsible to anybody, and 'I'm from this neighborhood and I love [Elite U].' They've used that race card many times to try to delegitimize the goals of what [Center for Economic Democracy] and other organizations have done.[20]

This respondent pointed out that William Bose was a strategic choice for Elite U, because the coalition "had over sixty churches on board, many of whom were led by African American leaders."[21] Miguel, a Latino organization member, explained that the use of figureheads was particularly dangerous to relationships between African Americans and Latine people in the community.

Miguel recounted a time when an African American pastor in the city publicly spoke out against workers who were on strike. Latine pastors involved in the organization's social contract movement, which later became a part of the coalition's movement for a community benefits agreement, took this to mean that African Americans were speaking out against the movement. During their next meeting, Latine pastors confronted African American pastors. Miguel explained, "They said, 'No, that's not us. That's another group.' And that's the first time we noticed, about the black African culture, that they're divided."[22]

Miguel also recognized potential divisions among people of color and progressive European Americans: "We noticed that Anglos have a way of doing things, being so conniving... They are not in the fight, in the trenches. But if the publicity is there and the newspapers are there... they'll show up and the colored people hate that... We don't talk about it, because if you talk about it and you say racism and all that, then you can jeopardize the whole movement."[23] Organizers did not deny the significance of racism but wanted to avoid the mistakes of liberal talk-centered organizations, so they opted for action-centered, class-based politics that they thought supported unification and got results. In fact, activists claimed their organization accomplished more on racism by *not* having time-consuming discussions on it. These decisions were also influenced by organizational culture. I find that activists who had significant experiences with racism or a racism-centered perspective in other parts of their lives transformed that analysis to a class-centered one within the confines of the organization. Some members were more aware than others of a strategic racism-evasiveness within the organization. Miguel openly stated that the organization avoided racism to prevent division. Others seemed to unknowingly privilege class over racism (see the interview with Carol below).

ORGANIZATIONAL CULTURE AND LIBERAL DISCOURSE

Many of the European Americans in the organization and coalition witnessed racism against people of color in their youth, and this shaped their desire to address racism as adults. Alex, a European American Lutheran pastor, spoke about his deep commitment to antiracism, his parents' influences, and his experiences in racially diverse public schools in the 1960s. His parents were both Republicans who taught him liberal ideologies of fairness and equality. They did not tolerate any racist or vulgar language in their home and were "very political and very social justice oriented."[24] In middle school, he and his African American friends insisted on breaking down racial barriers. They would engage in acts that Alex characterized as "radical" for the time—organizing and attending interracial parties. Alex states, "That was a big deal in the sixties in a city. It was a big deal that Black kids came to a party at the home of a white kid and that white kids went to a party at the home of a Black kid."[25] One of Alex's most memorable moments in high school was when he took his close friend, an African American woman, to homecoming. According to Alex, she was the first African American woman to be chosen for homecoming court in his city. Her boyfriend had graduated from high school and thought the event was silly, so he refused to attend. Alex explained, "So I took her to homecoming. I mean this was a big deal, a Black girl and a white guy ... and there was a price to be paid for it ... I had an encounter with a group of Black boys who were like, you know, 'Keep your hands off ours,' you know [laughs], and I was like, 'Hey none of you guys asked her' [laughing] ... We decided to get active and decided to break these racial barriers ... It was our idea that we would bring forth a generation that would get past this."[26] Alex was willing to use radical methods, to put himself in uncomfortable situations, and to be confrontational.

Throughout my interview with Alex, he spoke repeatedly about how "destructive," "artificial," and "ridiculous" racial barriers were. This was what drew him to the coalition. He stated that he did not see any racial tensions in the coalition but admitted that perhaps, after a lifetime of antiracist activism, he did not *want* to see them. In his 1960s organizing, he saw a lot of patronizing attitudes by European Americans toward African Americans and the notion that European Americans had to teach African Americans how to lead. He argued that this kind of paternalism has decreased and was less of a problem for the coalition. Alex's liberal ideology certainly influenced his interpretation of racial differences within the coalition. He attributed differences to culture. For example, he recounted a story of when he attended a dinner at an African American pastor's home. All of the women served the food and did not join the male pastors for the discussion. He subscribed to a cultural understanding of these differences, which scholars have long critiqued.[27] At the same time, Alex was one of the few respondents who stated enthusiastically that the coalition should address racism explicitly. He went into great detail about how Republicans use code words to demonize Mexicans as illegal immigrants and how they are forced to do "slave labor." This is all tied to racism. However, he concluded that the coalition addresses racism through a focus on economic issues. So while Alex's personal liberal perspective influenced his views, the action-centered organizational culture also encouraged him to analyze racism largely in terms of class solidarity.

Like Alex, Jen, a younger European American organizer in her late twenties, embodied what Becky Thompson called the principles of white antiracist culture.[28] This involves a lifelong commitment to unlearning racist behavior and never being completely self-assured in one's own antiracism. Unlike antiracist European Americans in past studies, Jen did not take the usual position as white savior or claim color capital by having Black friends.[29] She did not personally deny the existence of racism and in fact seemed to have a sophisticated understanding of structural racism and white privilege. In my interview with her, Jen recounted her first memories of learning about racism. It was around third grade when she noticed that she and other European American children were placed into educational tracks that were separate from African American and Latine children. She noticed that her friends were no longer in classes with her and how the teachers talked more positively to students in her class, which was a higher track with mostly European American children. She stated, "That early experience ... just how young people are when they get sort of characterized and classified and separated. It really made me think we needed to, you know, pull together like a broad movement to address it."[30] Jen learned that educational tracking was supposed to be based on intelligence tests but thought they were really based on both race and class. Yet within the organization, Jen emphasized the class over racism-centered perspective. She argued that talking directly about racism in the organization could "take a huge nose dive." Outside of the organization, Jen participated in antiracist trainings and workshops that centered discussions on racism, but she hesitated to bring that focus into the organization or coalition.

Jen was known for her ability to recruit across racial lines. She was praised by African American respondents for her honesty and commitment to the organization. Fred, an African American teacher, was one of Jen's recruits. In my interview with him, Fred called Jen "my good friend and my good sister."[31] Jen and another European American organizer had a few breakfast meetings with Fred to convince him to join the coalition. Fred was upfront with them about his initial suspicions of organizations led by liberal European Americans. Fred stated, "Well, first I asked, I said, 'Well how many blacks are in this group?' She said, 'Oh, a lot!' ... I said, [laughing] 'I might as well be straight with you ... how many white folks are in this group?' ... Jen said, 'Look, I'm a lifetime resident of [Union City]. I went to college and I came back, and we saw what was being done and we didn't like it.'"[32] Jen told Fred that the white people in the organization were not in it for publicity. They were against the gentrification they saw happening and were committed to stopping it. Fred also explained how Jen found him. They had been in the same marches together protesting redlining in Union City, the Martin Luther King Jr. march, walking "in the freezing cold." According to Fred, Jen "sought me out, and she said I like your energy, I like your drive, I like what you're about, I think you could represent us."[33] Fred was suspicious of liberal European Americans who tried to recruit people of color for their organizations. Jen addressed these issues honestly in her responses to Fred's questions, and like some of the other African American respondents, he saw something different in her. He admired that Jen "walked the walk."

Throughout his interview, Fred named racism as a key problem in Union City, even arguing that the organization should address racism explicitly, recognizing that people, in general, were afraid to discuss it. He stated, "Like Dr. Cornel West said. Race matters in this country.[34] Most people shy away from it. They don't want to address it. They think it will go away like fog."[35] However, I asked Fred repeatedly about his thoughts on how the organization actually addressed racism, and each time I did, he went into a disconnected discussion of *societal* racism. For example, he stated:

> Several of the organizers and staff members have talked about that [racism] and ... it's been expressed, um, not in a covert way. It's been very out front, without hesitancy, because we know that that plays a factor in some of the things that gets done around here ... You got a president, when you have a president of the United States that says, 'Oh, I didn't know that there was racism.' I think that was either Nixon or Reagan. Something's wrong with them ... Because their mindset is that everything is all hunky dory. Everything ain't hunky dory. We have 40 million something people in this country with no health insurance.[36]

He also addressed institutional racism in the media and how African Americans were portrayed as "rapists" and "murderers." However, when it came to the internal functioning of the organization, Fred took a liberal color-blind and class-centered perspective emphasizing the need for different ethnic groups to interact and accept one another in their common struggles. He advised his students to "know how to interact with someone other than who you see in your neighborhood ... now we have with the influx of Asians, Pakistan[is], Indians, Arabs, there's more than Black and white ... but I have never ... let those color barriers keep me from interacting."[37] During public meetings, Fred often stood up and emphasized that Elite U tried to divide the community and that the coalition must communicate that they are unified across racial lines.

Yet, I had been on door-to-door recruitment drives with Fred, and he did discuss racial discrimination with residents, not just commonalities across class. Fred had not worked out how racial and class discrimination mattered in the organization's goals. Personally, Fred had a racism-centered worldview, but within the confines of the organization, he seemed to focus on acceptance, interracial solidarity, and class exploitation. Fred's confusion around these issues illustrates some of the disadvantages of a racism-evasive organizational approach (see chapter 5). Part of the racism-evasiveness in the organization had to do with the group's desire to appear "professional." Fred stated that Elite U did not take the organization seriously at first, and that alderpersons saw them as a "renegade group" that lacked professionalism and could easily be dismissed. My interview with Laverne shows how this image of liberal professionalism was connected to the organization's racism-evasive strategy.

Laverne was an African American organizer with the Center for Economic Democracy, who worked in Elite U's dining hall for twelve years. During a leave of absence from the dining hall, she volunteered in the community and worked with the union. Adrianna was impressed by Laverne and recruited her. Throughout my time with the organization and coalition, Adrianna and Michael gave Laverne more and more responsibilities, grooming her as a leader for the organization. It was clear in my interview with Laverne that she recognized racist practices carried out by Elite U, but she thought the organization had to keep such issues "under their hat" in public settings. She stated:

> They are clearly um, let me see, they are clearly, um, I don't know if the right word is "racist" or just very insensitive to poor folk. You know, they have no regard for human life, for people, I guess, less fortunate than they are. So I mean when you get around them, you don't want to call them an asshole straight to their face ... But you know what it is ... because there's a lot of things I want to say to them, but you just can't say it, you know, in public or I guess in a professional setting.[38]

Following this statement, I asked Laverne, "So you wouldn't want to say that [Elite U's] policies are racist because that's a strong word even though they are?" and she replied, "Yeah. Right. Right ... and there's a way that you can bring that out without actually saying, you know just organizing. Everything will speak for itself. It will eventually come to the forefront."[39] Laverne's statement is not simply an expression of her opinion. Her perspective is influenced by a dominant liberal discourse that portrays any discussions of racism as uncivil and disruptive.[40] Thus, to call someone racist, or to name a corporation's practices as racist, is akin to calling someone an "asshole."

Dawn, an African American cochair in the coalition similarly stated, "If we start to address the racist, then that's only going to draw negative attention to our group, which we don't need."[41] Why would addressing "the racist" or naming Elite U's practices as racist draw negative attention to the group? The answer has to do with the impact of external racial ideologies and liberal discourse on the organizational culture. In this context talking about racism is viewed negatively because to do so is to recognize color, which by itself is seen as racist.[42] To deal with racism in this color-blind environment, activists in the organization and coalition used racism-evasive strategies by subsuming racism under less controversial class issues and avoiding internal discussions, which they feared would be divisive. Further, radical leftists do not control the societal discourse that is focused on a liberal sense of civility.[43] A focus on liberal "civil discourse" can shut down discussions of racism that are viewed as uncomfortable and unprofessional. People of color, in particular, who call out racism are often viewed as angry individuals playing the race card.[44] Activists may individually feel that Elite U's practices are racist and want to challenge them as such, but if they do, they run the risk of being labeled too radical in the public sphere.

The organizational strategy of silencing racism was so strong that one respondent realized, seemingly for the first time, that Elite U's practices were as racist as they were classist. Carol, an African American member of the coalition, witnessed significant changes to her community over the years. She talked about a highway developed near her neighborhood, which "nobody knew about until it was done." She wanted to have a voice in the changes affecting her neighborhood, and she thought the coalition gave her that voice. During our interview Carol also recounted experiences with racism at work. She explained the differences between what she called southern prejudice and northern prejudice. She stated, "Don't grin in my face and act like you like me, but you're prejudiced; you really don't care for Black people," as she described various racist incidents, where her manager would consistently give her unfavorable work schedules in comparison to European American coworkers.[45] I asked Carol if the coalition should address racism explicitly, and she stated that the organization had nothing to do with racism. When I pointed to examples where the organization did talk about Elite U as having a plantation mentality and that its policies target people of color, she engaged in thoughtful reflection on the question: "Yeah! ... I guess you could say that they targeted the poorer areas. I never looked at it like that. That, you know, it was a racial thing. I just know that [Elite U] moves in on ... the poor areas ... I guess that is a racial thing, because [Elite U] hasn't moved up in the [Westview] area ... Never thought of it like that ... That's the truth I never thought of it like that."[46] After a pause, I attempted to move onto the next question, but Carol again listed off the neighborhoods that Elite U targets and asked "*Is it racism*? ... See, you made me really think on that one, because I never thought of it that way."[47]

Ileana M. Rodríguez-Silva argues that racial oppression can be revealed when silences are disrupted.[48] By pointing out some of the racialized issues with which the coalition deals, I was inadvertently disrupting the silence for Carol, and this made her question whether the coalition was up against racial or class oppression. Carol recognized that her experiences at work had everything to do with racism, and she confronted her manager about the incidents. Yet, the analysis of racism she applied in her personal life was somehow transformed in her work with the coalition to one that was more centered on class than racism.

There were times when the organization was more centered on talk rather than action, but not on the issue of racism. A member recalled an incident where the coalition did not follow a strict agenda. This incident involved the suicide of a young man in [the Valley]. Laverne was leading the meeting. Rachel, a member of the coalition stated, "She couldn't even go on with the meeting, and no one would've let the meeting go on. It was a very emotional issue. They broke up into groups to talk about how they were feeling about the suicide. That was the first time I've ever seen them stop the meeting and go off the agenda."[49]

Here, open and honest discussion of members' feelings on a topic that was totally unrelated to the coalition's agenda was permitted, and that discussion was valued over action-centered talk about strategies and tactics. Indeed, during interviews, members indicated that open and honest discussion was the coalition's strength. However, such discussions were not often centered on the issue of racism, differences in racialized identities, or racialized experiences. The kinds of discussions that most often did occur included focused remarks on strategies and tactics, not long-winded comments on experiences or feelings, unless a key leader of the organization or coalition brought them up. In the rare times when racism was brought up in meetings, it was mentioned briefly as an external issue—not something to be discussed at length internally. Most organization staff and coalition members indicated that addressing racism as an issue would be detrimental to the success of the organization. Cultures of common interest politics that foster action over talk are not likely to lead to racism-centered discussions, especially when operating within a larger racist culture that promotes racism-evasiveness.[50] The fact that the organization did spend time talking about some issues and not others shows that the action-centered culture was influenced by external racial ideologies.[51]

Rodríguez-Silva contends that silence is not a total absence of discussion but is manifest in attempts to shape or prevent talk.[52] The organization and coalition referenced a plantation mentality, slavery, and even racism here and there, but they never named racism as part of their campaign against Elite U. Activists justified these racism-evasive strategies by emphasizing action over talk. For example, John, an African American union organizer, argued, "What we project as an organization and the way that our organization looks automatically says it for itself."[53] Phillip, a European American union organizer, shared this perspective: "You know, I think that the [coalition], I think that the [organization] does address that [racism] . . . We live in a city here that's 60% African American and Latino . . . disproportionately members of those communities are poor . . . I think [the organization] makes the point without . . . using the labels."[54] Hence, working on projects that disproportionately affect people of color is understood as walking the walk on racism and given as a reason for why the organization did not need to discuss it.

European American, Latine, and African American activists had nearly equal responses to the question of whether the organization should address racism explicitly (see table 6). However, in personal interviews, European Americans tended to emphasize racial unity more often than did people of color. People of color, in

TABLE 6
Responses to Whether the Organization Should Address Racism Explicitly

Respondents by ethnicity	Yes	No	Not sure	Total
African American	2	8	1	11
European American	2	7	1	10
Latine	1	2	0	3
Jamaican	0	1	0	1
TOTAL	5	18	2	25

particular, feared divisions between Latines and African Americans, while European Americans emphasized success in overcoming those divisions. The main success story told by European Americans concerned the strike of 2003 after Latine temporary workers marched across a largely African American picket line directed at Elite U. Due to the organization's efforts, thirteen of those temporary workers quit their jobs a few weeks into the strike and joined African Americans. However, people of color in the organization did not feel those divisions were settled. One issue had to do with different job outcomes. African Americans faced problems in getting promoted whereas Latine workers had problems getting any job at all. Miguel, one of the few activists who discussed racism within the organization, also argued that Latines "have this mentality of . . . what the hell are they [African Americans] so angry about? . . . You don't see us [Latinos] asking for retribution or whatever the hell they're asking for."[55] For this and other reasons, Travis, an African American activist, concluded that it would be dangerous to address racism internally:

> For instance, to have an African American try to help a Hispanic with a racist situation that he's dealing with or understanding how his racism is affecting his attitude toward the organization itself or different members in the organization [pauses] it is something we really have never talked about . . . Should we? I want to say yes, but until . . . we have a stronger connection to each other, I don't think we should . . . because we're not cohesive enough as a group yet to deal with that very touchy situation, and I think some of us really fear that would separate the group.[56]

The organization seems to have adopted this strategy without any explicit discussion on it.

The word "racism" was barely uttered at public meetings of the organization. In my 282 pages of single-spaced field notes on public events, it was spoken only two times. Both times it was mentioned briefly as an external issue—not something to be discussed at length internally—and was framed to show the significance of unity around a particular issue. Ironically, when racism was discussed, it was in response to Elite U's attempts to divide the organization, such as when Elite U claimed the coalition was a front group for the union. This contradicts the organization's stance that talking about racism threatens solidarity. In fact, honestly naming racism may have been necessary to *prevent* division in this situation, since there was suspicion among residents about the union using people of color.

As Quiet as It's Kept:
Intersecting Silences of Racial Ideologies, Liberal
Discourse, and Organizational Culture

Radical progressive European Americans in the organization and coalition did not deny the significance of racism the way that many closet racists do or engage in the typical liberal racism-evasive strategies of pointing to more extreme racists to feel better about themselves. The racism-evasiveness they engaged in was more strategic and less cosmetic.[57] The organization and coalition were racially diverse not only in terms of the membership but also in terms of leadership. They were aware of and seemed to avoid typical mistakes of white paternalism and denial. When compared to most interracial organizations, past and present, the Center for Economic Democracy and the Community-Labor Alliance were probably best prepared to combat racist practices head on. So why were they cautiously quiet on racism when they knew it was a central part of their work in Union City? Racism-evasiveness was influenced, not only by internal organizational culture, but also by dominant liberal racial ideologies external to the group.

Many activists in the organization and coalition witnessed the hypocritical behavior of liberal European Americans who claimed to care about racism. In discussions on racism, European Americans may act paternalistically toward people of color or feel entitled and expect people of color to do much of the work in teaching them about oppression.[58] They may become overly concerned with their image as good, nonracist people, refuse to address their individual role in perpetuating racism, or become hostile and defensive.[59] The report *Training for Racial Equity and Inclusion* stresses that European Americans talk too much about racism instead of taking action.[60] Perhaps the organization and coalition evaded discussions on racism to avoid common mistakes of more liberal organizations. As Jen stated, talking about racism "can get so muddled so fast," and the group could get a lot accomplished without making racism a central issue.[61]

In chapter 1, I conceptualized Carter Wilson's theory on the evolution of racism. Here, I elaborate specifically on the racist culture that was created historically through the decisions of political and economic elites in an effort to maintain oppressive economic arrangements that benefited them. As I stated in chapter 1, color-blind ideology is a significant part of contemporary racist culture that upholds the racial and economic status quo. This racial ideology interacts, in a mutually reinforcing relationship, with dominant liberal discourse that emphasizes civility. Both of these external, macro-level ideologies influence meso-level organizational culture. Activists within such organizations make decisions about the issues they are going to discuss explicitly or evade. Thus, action-centered organizational cultures inform the strategies activists use, but that culture is shaped specifically toward racism-evasiveness by the pressures of liberal color-blind ideology in larger society (see figure 5). Liberal white supremacy impacted this more radical group because they were responding to external pressures to remain silent on racism and liberal notions of "civility" and "professionalism." Thus, while they used radical, confrontational methods, they operated within a limiting dominant liberal discourse and organizational culture that constrained their ability to address racism explicitly.

CHAPTER 5

Challenging Liberal White Supremacy

Not everything that is faced can be changed, but nothing can be changed until it is faced.

—James Baldwin, *The New York Times Book Review*,
January 14, 1962

I don't think there will ever be a time when people will stop wanting to bring about change.

—Yuri Kochiyama, quoted in Maria Iu, letter

In this book, I have laid out what I see as the fundamental differences between liberals and radicals to show the limits of liberal ideology and how this perpetuates liberal white supremacy and racism. What I witnessed during my study of the labor organization Center for Economic Democracy and the Community-Labor Alliance between the years 2004 and 2007 was a burgeoning of these liberal/radical conflicts that were about to burst onto the national scene. My case study of Essex Town from 2018 to 2020 captured the conflict between radicals and liberals, ultimately revealing the effectiveness of radical methods. In both case studies, liberal ideology and discourse was a limiting force. In Union City, the organization and coalition worked within liberal notions of civility and color-blind ideology, thus preventing a racism-centered focus, even while they used more radical, confrontational methods. In Essex Town, liberals unwilling to use confrontational methods attempted to demonize a small radical group, even though they agreed with this group's goals. Both radicals and liberals claim to care about progressive social change. Any progressive organization can use the model I develop on liberal versus radical approaches to assess where their strengths and weaknesses are.

Liberal ideology has infiltrated and compromised the ability of most organizations to address racism explicitly, because liberals work to maintain the racial and economic status quo that benefits them. For there to be systemic change, radicals must be willing to organize outside of the confines of liberal ideologies and allow for both class *and* racism-centered perspectives. Liberals must be willing to join and support radicals, even when it is unpopular to do so. Individual liberals who truly want to dismantle systemic racism must do more than just talk about it; they must seriously examine their superiority complex and take actions. As I conclude, I examine how liberal ideology continues to limit current movements, allyship, and politics, as well as how we can challenge liberal white supremacy through action-oriented and racism-centered intersectional approaches.

Perceived Advantages and Disadvantages of Racism-Centered versus Racism-Evasive Approaches

In chapter 4, I argue that the organization and coalition employed racism-evasiveness as a strategic response to societal liberal discourse on racism and to maintain interracial solidarity. Ironically, these racism-evasive approaches can actually cause the internal tensions activists were trying to avoid. In table 7, I address these and other perceived advantages and disadvantages to racism-centered versus racism-evasive approaches. Because the organization and coalition did not discuss racism openly, they did not have a clear strategy for dealing with potential complaints. Some members discussed their dissatisfaction with the organization's action-centered focus and wanted more discussion on controversial issues. For example, Rachel, a European American woman and member of the coalition, stated that the rigid structure of the organization "does not allow people to become critical thinkers," and she felt this was important for residents "so that they can sit in a meeting with people like [Ben Patterson, spokesperson for University Hospital] and challenge what he says."[1] An African American member of the coalition agreed, stating that the organization underestimated the people in the community, who he believed were perfectly capable of having "taboo conversations" on racism. He stated, "They do too much overstrategizing, overthinking at [the organization]. You know, it's almost like, 'We wannna ruffle the feathers, but we only wanna ruffle them to a certain point.' No! Let's ruffle the feathers until that chicken is bald, naked."[2] This member did ultimately leave the organization because he was dissatisfied with this overly cautious approach to racism. Therefore, taking a racism-evasive approach may help avoid offending some current members, but it can also cause a loss in membership and prevent organizations from building a broader base.

TABLE 7

Advantages and Disadvantages to Racism-Evasive versus Racism-Centered Approaches

Type of approach	Advantages	Disadvantages
Racism-Evasive	Efficient, promotes solidarity, unified front.	Unprepared to deal with complaints of racism, limits goals, internal conflict, less able to confront racist practices of opponent.
Racism-Centered	Retention and expansion of membership, increased trust, greater justice.	Time-consuming, members fear divisions.

Organizers in the Center for Economic Democracy argued that they avoided discussions of racism because everyone had a different understanding of what racism was. In my view, that fact actually warrants the need for racism-centered discussions.[3] Without such discussions, how will they know exactly what the racial injustice component of their struggle is and how to combat it? As revealed in chapter 4, some members struggled to understand the intersections of class and racial oppression in the organization's work. Recall the example of Carol, who pondered whether Elite U's practices were racist as well as classist. If members only understand issues through the lens of class solidarity, how are they to justify their demands for greater representation of people of color on the job and in access to health care and to education, all racialized issues? If labor unions, such as police unions, only organize based on the class interests of their membership, when will they ever address the potential racist culture of their departments? This is an issue the Movement for Black Lives continues to raise. Therefore, racism-evasive approaches limit organizational goals and prevent activists from effectively challenging the racist practices of their opponents (see table 7).

While racism-centered perspectives have their own set of limitations, I believe the potential advantages they offer are worth the risks. Racism-centered approaches move racism out of the secondary position and put it up front with other forms of oppression, allowing organizations to expand goals, build trust, and increase membership by bringing in more allies.[4] I recommend organizations adopt an *action-oriented* and *racism-centered intersectional approach* that rejects the additive perspective, which results in privileging gender or class over other forms of oppression. Non-racism-centered approaches to intersectionality recenter European American women (in the case of gender) and European American men (in the case of class). A racism-centered intersectional approach walks the walk and talks the talk in a way that gives space to marginalized voices. At least two organizations exemplify a racism-centered intersectional approach: Black Lives Matter and Red-neck Revolt.[5]

Effective Models of Racism-Centered Intersectionality

BLACK LIVES MATTER

In response to the murder of Trayvon Martin in 2013, three African American women, Alicia Garza, Patrisse Cullors, and Opal Tometi, created #BlackLivesMatter.[6] Protests sprang up around the country and continued in response to the murders of Eric Garner, Michael Brown, Tamir Rice, Philando Castile, Sandra Bland, Ahmaud Arbery, Breonna Taylor, Tony McDade, and many others.[7] I see the Movement for Black Lives as a racism-centered, intersectional, and radically oriented movement that developed, in part, due to the ineffectiveness of liberal methods and policies. This movement has shifted the liberal discourse on racism, such that liberal Democratic presidential candidates must use the language of systemic racism. Racism is being centered in political discourse to expand potential candidates' constituencies. Joe Biden had to recant some of his previous statements on integration and address his support of the Police Officers Bill of Rights that protected officers during internal investigations.[8] While some elements of this may only be performative, it shows the power of the Movement for Black Lives in shifting the nation toward progressive change. More liberals in the Democratic Party and in suburbs, towns, and cites are now supporting the movement.

Activists in the Movement for Black Lives use a mixture of methods but center confrontation in their actions and their language. They use explicitly racism-centered language and openly criticize capitalism as a root cause of the continued oppression African Americans face. In this way, they continue in the tradition of radical movements, such as the Black Panther Party, the Student Nonviolent Coordinating Committee (SNCC), and Students for a Democratic Society (SDS). Noel A. Cazenave argues that this movement differs from the "old Civil Rights Movement of the 1950s and 1960s" in that their leadership is not prototypically male and heteronormative.[9] Indeed, of the three women who created #BlackLivesMatter, two identify as queer, Patrisse Cullors and Alicia Garza. Cullors argues that focusing only on one part of Black identity is a harmful and ineffective way to create greater social justice.[10] She and other activists in the Black Lives Matter movement have accomplished a practical application of intersectional theory that has been lost on many academics and other organizations. When intersectional theory became popular in the social sciences, for example, it often whitewashed some of the most controversial issues on racism and heterosexism, focusing instead on gender as a color-blind sisterhood. Rather than centering the lives of women of color, intersectionality was criticized as taking an "add and stir" approach that recentered the voices of European American women.[11] The Movement for Black Lives adopts intersectionality the right way by centering the most marginalized and silenced voices, trans and working-class Black people and other people of color. This is why the Movement for Black Lives is a movement that benefits us all. It addresses the authoritarianism and fascism within institutions and organizations, such as police departments, that are fueled by racist beliefs but can harm anyone.

In fact, the bullying and harassment of children that Micaela and Tom recorded in Essex Town was the result of the authoritarian control that teachers, staff, and other school officials felt free to exert over African American and Latine children (see chapter 3). Micaela's and Tom's children attended schools that were 45 and 51 percent Black and Latine, respectively. The European American children in these racially diverse schools are also impacted by overly authoritarian behaviors. Kenneth Neubeck and Noel Cazenave were among the first to make this argument in their work on welfare racism.[12] They showed that abusive welfare policies were fueled by racist beliefs about Mexican and African American recipients. These racist policies, in turn, affected European American welfare recipients. Therefore, when we address racism and anti-blackness explicitly, everyone can benefit. This is why Redneck Revolt argues that racism must first be tackled if we are to make any economic changes that benefit the working class in general.

REDNECK REVOLT (AND LIBERAL CLASS BIAS)

Redneck Revolt is radical in its members' perspectives on capitalism, approach to racism, approach to social class, and social movement tactics. They have supported the Movement for Black Lives from its inception, at a time when many middle-class European American liberals did not. The latter have yet to begin explicitly addressing their class prejudice against the working class, both those they pejoratively call "rednecks" and working-class people of color. As I argue in this book, many European American liberals use both groups to assert their supremacy. They hold paternalistic attitudes toward people of color and scapegoat the white working class as the problem, taking attention away from their own racist behavior.

Women of color in the reproductive rights and other movements have noted the inability of European American middle-class women to empathize with their working-class comrades.[13] Connecting with movements such as Redneck Revolt is a good place to start. Like the Movement for Black Lives, Redneck Revolt both talks the talk and walks the walk on racism. Members have pride in their revolutionary working-class identity but also require their membership to recognize that working-class European Americans benefit from the system of racism. Among their core organizing principles, Redneck Revolt states:

> In the periods before widespread adoption of white supremacist ideals, the white working class occasionally openly rebelled and found common cause alongside slaves, natives, and other people being attacked and exploited. In recognition of such bonds and cross-race unity amongst the lower classes, the rich created laws to favor white workers and servants, at the expense of workers and servants of color, to drive divisions between us. The relative privileges that white working poor have been afforded since that time have kept them protecting the rich while also keeping our communities impoverished and unstable. The entire working class will only see real political, economic, and social stability once we all abolish any allegiance to white supremacy, and stand for the same liberation for all people.[14]

This organization also "recognizes that women, femme, queer, and trans folks are disproportionately deprived of their liberty and threatened with violence." It calls on its members to address how men continue to benefit from patriarchy and argues that "true liberation includes the freedom to live authentically and safely, regardless of our gender or sexual identity."[15]

How many European American professional middle-class liberals know about organizations such as Redneck Revolt? How many respectfully engage with the white working-class population, and how many continue to blame them for a Trump presidency? While more ethnographic research should be conducted on these organizations to examine how their members experience these principles on the ground, both the Movement for Black Lives and Redneck Revolt offer racism-centered intersectional approaches in their language and confrontational methods.

The Liberal Response to the Movement for Black Lives and the Murder of George Floyd

Although liberals seem to be oblivious to organizations such as Redneck Revolt, they are quite familiar with the Movement for Black Lives and use it as an opportunity to express their level of "wokeness." When George Floyd was murdered in May 2020, the movement was already well known and covered in national news. It was uncommon for me to see neighbors with Black Lives Matter T-shirts or signs in their yards after the murder of Eric Garner, but by 2016, as the movement became popularized and in response to the election of Trump, these signs were springing up everywhere. The movement had also become commercialized. In my local Supercuts, the predominantly African American hairdressers wore T-shirts presumably required by their company that read "Hair Lines Matter." Likewise, while visiting Massachusetts in 2018, I saw an advertisement for engagement rings encouraging viewers to "take a knee," a blatant commercialization of Colin Kaepernick's stance against saluting the flag during the Black Lives Matter protests.[16]

George Floyd was murdered during a time when many states were under quarantine due to the COVID-19 pandemic. Large groups of people were unemployed, working from home, or stuck at home. African Americans were being affected by the pandemic at disproportionate rates compared to other racial groups. At the same time, they were being disproportionately targeted and brutalized by police officers for allegedly failing to maintain social distance. The conditions of the pandemic coalesced with the murder of George Floyd and threw the Movement for Black Lives onto the national scene once more. Protests continued across the country as gruesome attacks on African Americans and protesters from all walks of life were televised. In Brooklyn, a police car drove into a crowd of protestors.[17] A twenty-year-old protester, Dounya Zayer, was shoved to the ground by police officers and suffered a concussion.[18] A video surfaced of police officers in Buffalo, New York, shoving Martin Gugino, a seventy-five-year-old European American man, to the ground, causing blood to spill from his head. Police officers claimed the man slipped on his own.[19] In California, a twenty-seven-year-old Black man, Derrick Sanderlin, who helped train San Jose police offers in implicit bias, was shot in the testicles by officers from that same police department. When he was shot with a rubber bullet, he was trying to de-escalate a confrontation between the officers and protesters.[20] This kind of coverage was constant and graphic throughout the summer of 2020. Many questioned the intentions of showcasing this trauma on mostly African American bodies.

The intensity of the violence enacted on African Americans prompted a litany of statements from corporations, academic departments, and other institutions proclaiming support for the movement and calling for a discussion of racism within their organizations. Some of these statements may have been sincere, but many of them were the epitome of liberal white supremacy.[21] I received emails from academic departments scrambling to write statements as fast as they could in response to African American students accusing them of silence. Many of the people most active in these emails were the very people I had witnessed engaging in racial hostility against people of color, while they claimed to be enlightened on racism. I witnessed them disrespectfully and continuously interrupt presentations by African American faculty and faculty of color, with unsubstantiated claims that their work on racism was biased. In discussions of Kimberlé Crenshaw's work that centers the discrimination African American women face, these self-identified European American liberals would engage in typical racism-evasive tactics, arguing that gender was the more important variable, pointing to several unlearning racism workshops they attended, discussing the racial diversity of their families or schools, and so on. They did not listen respectfully to the experiences of their African American colleagues or other colleagues of color. They spent much of their time in departmental discussions on racism dominating the conversation and desperately trying to show that they were not only good white people, but that they were the best white people—superior to other white progressives, white conservatives, uneducated white working-class people, and people of color. By talking over people of color and redirecting the conversation to their own knowledge and good deeds, they reinforced a white racial frame that placed their voices at the center.[22] When I saw statements being provided by these very individuals, I was quite skeptical of their purpose. One of the problems with most of these statements is that they are not tied to any direct, confrontational, or radical actions. Calling for conversations on racism is similar to the responses of corporations to protests by African Americans in earlier periods of American history. Faith Davis Ruffins argues that corporations began injecting funds into museums for African American history after the riots of the 1960s.[23] This is certainly an easier move for liberal, moderate, and conservative European Americans than restructuring the economy and confronting racial capitalism.[24] These statements and experiences in academic conversations on racism speak to the need for *genuine* allyship.

Liberals and Allyship:
Is It Possible to Be Antiracist and Who Can Be an Ally?

At one of my talks on liberal white supremacy, on June 11, 2020, audience members asked two important questions: Is it possible for European Americans to ever be truly antiracist and who can be an ally? In response to the first question, I referenced a list of resources concerning problems in antiracist organizing. Becky Thompson's *A Promise and a Way of Life* offers insightful reflection from European American antiracists who argue that antiracism is a lifetime commitment that they can never truly master. It requires constant self-reflexivity and sacrifice, possibly even cutting ties with long-time friends and relatives. In that sense, it is a promise and a way of life.[25]

Karyn D. McKinney and Joe R. Feagin distinguish this dedicated group of antiracists from a more problematic group of "anti-prejudiced" European Americans. Anti-prejudiced European Americans focus on being nice and raising children to be respectful of difference. Antiracists understand that simply being friendly to one another is not enough. Antiracists are not afraid to raise questions that might make people uncomfortable, and they do not subscribe to color-blind ideology or racism denial.[26] For example, one of McKinney and Feagin's antiracist respondents stated: "When my daughters come home talking about Columbus, I tell them the real story. I ask them—did they teach you that he took the Native people from America and made them slaves? Or did they tell you that there were 20 million Native Americans living here when Columbus came?"[27] This respondent constantly questioned the curriculum her children were receiving on racism. This distinction between anti-prejudiced and antiracist is somewhat similar to Joe Barndt's discussion of nonracists and antiracists: "Nonracists try to deny that the prison exists . . . Anti-racists work for the prison's eventual destruction."[28] There are many people who may identify as antiracist but whose behavior and beliefs are more in line with McKinney and Feagin's anti-prejudiced category, and some may fall in between the categories. I see anti-prejudiced and nonracist European Americans as more liberal and talk centered and antiracists as more radical and action centered. To be genuine allies, I argue that people must align themselves with the behaviors of antiracists as conceptualized by McKinney and Feagin.[29]

Likewise, Jessie Daniels writes about the need for white women, in particular, to engage in critical self-reflection. She argues that white women who focus on gender inequality and fail to see their racial privilege are sensitive to criticism and deal poorly with feelings of shame and guilt. Daniels advocates for a wellness industry that focuses on "a radical collective politics" rather than clean eating, goops, and other potions. She writes, "telling the truth about white supremacy and working to end it are interlaced with my own liberation and yours."[30]

My response to the second question of who can be an ally is simple. Anyone can be an ally. Allyship does not have to depend on skin color, life experiences, or formal education. The more important question is *how* can one be an ally. Ibram Kendi, Crystal Fleming, Tsedale Melaku, Ijeoma Oluo, Karyn McKinney and Joe Feagin, and other scholars provide several answers to this question.[31] The first step in being an ally is to listen. European American allies, in particular, should not dominate the discussion. This is something that men have recognized as a practical tool they can apply in anti-sexist work.[32] Allan Johnson has observed meetings where men dominate and women are often silent.[33] Therefore, he actively remains quiet, giving marginalized voices a chance to come to the center. Based on my own experiences, I would add that European American liberals who purport to care about unlearning racism should not react immediately with disbelief when a person of color shares their experiences. Resist the urge to deny the racism people of color experience by claiming that they perhaps were discriminated against because of sexism, not racism, or because they look young, were not dressed appropriately, did not present themselves appropriately, and so forth. Studies have found that people of color are very good at reading the situation when they experience discrimination, and they have likely already analyzed all the possible options for their mistreatment other than racism.[34] As W. E. B. Du Bois stated of African Americans, they have been "gifted with a second sight."[35] More recently, Rosalind S. Chou and Joe Feagin applied this analysis to Asian Americans.[36]

White people ready to engage in genuine alliances with people of color do not proceed with a list of all their good deeds. Their main goal is not to convince themselves or others that they are antiracist. They understand that this kind of work involves a lifetime commitment and constant self-reflection.[37] A list of good deeds is unnecessary from genuine allies, because they show their allyship through action. As Noel Ignatiev points out, genuine European American allies will show you their position in their behaviors. He states, "The fight against white supremacy is not something to engage in as a favor to anyone. All people who wish to be free have an equal stake . . . in overturning the system of white supremacy."[38]

This brings us to the second step, and that is to show up. As I mentioned in chapter 4, by constantly showing up to rallies, meetings, and community events, I gained the trust of activists in the Community-Labor Alliance, and that trust allowed them to speak openly with me about their experiences. However, "showing up" can be demonstrated in ways that do not only involve one's physical presence at marches. It means supporting radical activists even when it is unpopular or uncomfortable to do so. Radicals have reason to distrust liberals. In this book, I noted a history of liberals helping silence radicals in an effort to secure their own positions within the political establishment. Liberals then claimed radicals' work as their own when the tide turned, and radical perspectives became more acceptable in the popular discourse. In my case study of Essex Town, liberal community members were brazen in their attempt to claim credit for the work of radicals in achieving changes in educational leadership. These same liberals are now voicing their support for the Movement for Black Lives but were silent or opposed to the radical methods when the movement first began. True allies show up in the moment, when the publicity is not there. They show up to support radical people of color, helping center their stories rather than taking the opportunity to showcase their own activities. Allies show up by protecting colleagues, especially people of color, who are brave enough to identify and address racist behaviors and practices in their organizations. Kerry Ann Rockquemore provides an excellent list of questions allies should address:

> Consider the last time you were in the presence of underrepresented faculty members and someone engaged in a microaggression toward that person. What did you do? Did you push back? Did you freeze? Did you stay silent and expect your junior colleague to deal with it? Do you feel skilled and prepared to respond to such situations? And equally important, what do you do when things come up behind closed doors, in

social settings and in contexts where your underrepresented colleagues are not present but are being discussed? How do you respond? Are you proactive or reactive? Do you act as a sponsor or take a backseat? Are you willing to expend some of your political capital on behalf of your junior colleagues? And if you have a tendency toward silence, what skill set do you need to acquire to confidently support your existing underrepresented faculty members?[39]

Rockquemore also states that academic department leaders are often aware of who the toxic people are in their departments, but they choose to ignore them. I have been in many situations like this, where department leaders attempt to empathize with me *after* they witness the so-called microaggressions toward me. They have said to me that they know certain people are problematic, and they know I am being targeted. People of color need more than this recognition; we need action. What I would like to see from leaders in those moments is an immediate confrontation of the racist, toxic behavior, much like we do in our classrooms. When a student is giggling or having a side conversation with a friend because they do not like what someone else has said, good professors will call them out. Ask them to share. Ask, "Is something wrong? I noticed you and Karen rolled your eyes while our colleague was presenting." If they continue in this problematic behavior, call them to a meeting and let them know that their behavior is unprofessional. This removes some of the burden from faculty of color, who are likely exerting a substantial amount of energy managing those behaviors for their own survival.

Finally, read. The burden of learning how to be an ally must ultimately fall to European Americans. They must put in the work. There is plenty of scholarship specifically on how European American antiracists reproduce racism. Read beyond the popular books featured in the *New York Times* or other high-profile places. In academia, a good place to start is by reading the work of racism scholars in your own department. If you develop reading lists, make sure to recognize the work of your colleagues of color. Often scholars of color are called upon to do the work when it is not recognized. In May and June 2020, when departments were rushing to issue statements in support of the Movement for Black Lives, I watched as European American liberal faculty developed lists of resources, never mentioning the work of their own colleagues who were known experts in the field. It does not get any more disrespectful than that. Allies, or better yet accomplices, will recognize this work, read it, and actively apply it to their own lives.

This book provides a list of problematic behaviors I encountered from self-proclaimed progressives. These are behaviors people should avoid if they want to be allies, accomplices, or coconspirators. Genuine allies do not use people of color as color capital; they do not dominate discussions; they do not constantly point to their good deeds but simply act; they do not deny the significance of racism or the experiences of their colleagues of color; they do not use their friends of color when they need expertise on understanding racism; they do not claim to have special knowledge because they have people of color in their families or live in diverse neighborhoods. Some of my strongest European American allies have been those who do not have any people of color in their families, and if they do, I never hear them use this to justify their superior knowledge on racism. On the other hand, some of my worst interactions have been with people who have biracial children or relatives, who talk over me and disrespect my years of experience and knowledge as a racism scholar.

Part of all liberals' self-reflexivity should include an examination of their own class prejudice toward both working-class people of color and European Americans. For European American professional-class liberals, the white working class often becomes a tool to support their own moral superiority. When they caricature working-class people as uneducated "rednecks" or buffoons, they are usually doing so to intentionally distract from their own racist behavior. When they do this, they are dehumanizing and stereotyping an entire group of people, which is the exact opposite of the humanism they purport to uphold. As I argue in this book, liberal approaches to racism and class oppression work in tandem to reinforce white supremacy. Their approaches to both maintain the racial and economic status quo, allowing them to keep their dominant positions. This leaves us with a persistent silence on both racial and class oppression.

A Crucial Need for Rainbow Warriors

Focusing on white allyship is important, but it also bears the risk of recentering whiteness and white dominance. It is crucial to build alliances between people of color. In 1998, Elizabeth Martinez wrote on the need for "rainbow warriors."[40] She argued that when Vincent Chin was beaten to death by a European American man who thought he was Japanese, all people of color should have protested, not just people of Asian descent. The same can be said about the Movement for Black Lives. All people of color must be united against anti-blackness. In 2016, Asian American coalitions issued a statement against police violence and the Asian American officer, Peter Liang, who shot Acai Gurley, an African American man. These and other organizations such as Asian Americans for Black Lives and activists such as Grace Lee Boggs and Yuri Kochiyama, who were highly respected activists in the civil rights and Black Panther movements, set examples for rainbow warriors. White supremacy has impeded these alliances for centuries. Radical scholars of color allying together is frightening to European American liberals and conservatives. Such alliances have the potential to challenge the capitalistic bedrock on which many institutions are founded and that support the careers of both liberals and conservatives. Perhaps this is why the Federal Bureau of Investigation took note of Du Bois's travels to Asia and feared that he wanted to "unite the yellow and black races in opposition to the white race."[41]

People of color must struggle to create and maintain these alliances, and European American allies must resist the urge to interfere with, interrupt, or retaliate against them. This retaliation takes many forms. When I developed a faculty of color affinity group with Black faculty, white faculty reacted with anger and verbal attacks and by spreading harmful rumors about members of the group. It was clear to us that we had disrupted the space that European American faculty felt *belonged* to them. Our meetings would often be interrupted by a knock on the door with some excuse of needing to share something with us. One European American faculty member accused us of racial hostility, even though she claimed to support the need for faculty of color to have an organizational space. These reactions and accusations toward affinity groups, caucuses, and cultural centers meant to provide a safe space for people of color have been documented in research on the transparency phenomenon and predominantly white institutions.[42] Genuine allyship from European Americans allows space for people of color to organize without interruption and without viewing such alliances as a racist attack on them. People of color have experienced centuries of internalized racism, violence, and trauma that we must deal with together. We have our own divisions to address, and we must be given the same voice and space as European American allies.

Challenging Systemic Liberal White Supremacy

In chapter 1, I argued that liberal white supremacy and liberal color-blind ideology compose the ideological core that sustains systemic racism. I placed this ideological component within Carter Wilson's analysis of racist culture, which developed out of an interaction between oppressive economic arrangements and political elites. Political elites historically have produced and used racist culture to support their economic positions. For example, the U.S. slave-owning elite developed laws and racist images to justify the enslavement of African Americans for their own enrichment. Political conservatives have used liberal color-blind ideology to argue against affirmative action and other progressive platforms.[43] Liberal political elites are just as culpable in perpetuating a system that helps them stay relevant and maintain their powerful positions.

In the 2020 election, liberals were left with one viable choice for president of the United States, Joe Biden. As with Hillary Clinton's run, liberals spent numerous hours debating who Biden's vice president should be. This is a familiar pattern among liberals that should be broken. They should spend more time discussing how they are going to push the president, Democrat or Republican, to fight for greater equality. Noel A. Cazenave states that we need a radical antiracism movement that is "nothing less than the *destruction of systemic racism*—not just persuasion of the order to be more diverse and accepting of 'minorities.'"[44] What methods are we willing to use? How can we coordinate multiple methods and adopt racism-centered intersectional and confrontational approaches to bring forth real change? Moving forward, progressives cannot sit back, the way many of us did with the election of President Obama, because he spoke in a respectable way. Joe Biden is not a serious threat to the capitalist power structure, so we must question how much the Democratic political candidates we are continually asked to support actually differ from Republican candidates. Few, if any, politicians will do anything without pressure, without people in the streets. This is true of our most revered liberal Democrats, such as John F. Kennedy. The civil rights movement led by Martin Luther King Jr., now embraced by liberals, used radical-confrontational methods. Liberals have yet to reckon with that history and the fact that many of the policies they claim as their own were moved forward by the radical, confrontational methods they often chastise. Liberals must join the radical progressives on the ground or support them in other ways.

Although class-privileged European Americans benefit the most from systems of oppression, people of color can uphold liberal white supremacy by engaging in the same behaviors: embracing a liberal politics of respectability that silences racism, talking openly about racism while engaging in class prejudice, and uncritically embracing capitalism. In my Essex Town case study, people of color who supported and received favors from the white political machine openly attacked radical activists, referring to one progressive European American woman as a "Karen" (see the epilogue). Institutions and politicians will embrace people of color who are accommodating and do not challenge the racial and economic status quo. Recall from chapter 2 that the political establishment of the 1950s began accepting racial diversity as long as it was not insurgent.

What progressives must do now is act in whatever capacity we can, wherever we can—in our workplaces, our communities, our writing, and our teaching and by confronting mayors and local politicians. We have to recognize when rhetoric is only rhetoric and demand more. When politicians, school officials, administrators, and others tell you they will respond to your demands, ask, "When?" "What is your next step?" "What can you do right now?" Those truly committed to social justice are not concerned with maintaining friendships with corrupt people in positions of power or managing the impressions of their racist institutions or neighborhoods. Radical progressives burn a lot of bridges, but we will also build new ones that are based on a more solid foundation. Robin D. G. Kelley reminds us, "Progressive social movements do not simply produce statistics and narratives of oppression; rather the best ones do what great poetry always does: transport us to another place, compel us to relive horrors, and, more importantly, enable us to imagine a new society."[45]

There are multiple ways to support radical movements that go beyond putting a sign in your yard. As Astead W. Herndon argued in a *New York Times* article, "Not being Trump is not enough."[46] Herndon states: "Progressive black leaders are extremely critical of Mr. Trump, as are many black voters. But they also believe that Democrats have sometimes been their greatest obstacle in addressing police brutality and racial inequality." If we are to dismantle racism and other forms of oppression, we need confrontational language and action.[47] Be vocal. Do not let white supremacy silence you, particularly if you are in a position of power. In academia, if you are tenured, you have a voice. Use it. Hold your colleagues accountable for what they do and say. Build a racism-centered intersectional perspective in your community organizations. Recognize the rhetoric of liberal white supremacy and stop it in the moment. By conceptualizing the differences between liberals and radicals, I illustrate how both groups can improve and what our errors are in talking and acting on racism and class oppression. If we are to move forward, it is important to understand these differences and how progressives sustain racial and class oppression through acts of liberal white supremacy. Otherwise, we will never achieve the humanism we purport to uphold.

The Many Faces of Racism-Evasiveness and Liberal White Supremacy

There are at least two problematic groups of progressives that perpetuate racism-evasiveness and liberal white supremacy: *elitist racism-evasive and class-evasive liberals* and *racism-evasive, class-centered radicals*. In this epilogue, I offer an update on the case studies, showing how these patterns have continued to persist in the organizations. Throughout this book, I have addressed racism and class-evasive liberals as the talk-centered self-identified antiracists who engage in book clubs or similar sessions where they explicitly discuss racism but do not follow through with actions and ultimately reproduce the behaviors of liberal white supremacy. In this update, I show how liberals in Essex Town, both European Americans and people of color, contributed to racism and class evasion, as the radical group moved on to target other sites of injustice and corruption. Furthermore, I discuss how the pattern of racism-evasion through a class-centered focus persisted in the Center for Economic Democracy after I left the study site.

Update on the Center for Economic Democracy and Community-Labor Alliance

In December 2004, the Center for Economic Democracy and the Community-Labor Alliance formally announced and voted on the community benefits agreement at a public event attended by over six hundred people. After years of struggling with Elite University Hospital, the CBA was reached in 2006. After the hospital agreed to sign on to the demands in the agreement, the coalition faced a new battle. The agreement allotted a time limit for negotiation of each of the benefits. The most important goal to achieve was unionization of university employees, because without the union, the community would have less power to hold the corporation of Elite U and University Hospital responsible for other issues in the agreement. The agreement did not guarantee university employees a union; it only stated that the coalition and organization would be allowed to speak with employees about unionizing. The least amount of time was allotted to unionization. Furthermore, University Hospital did everything in its power to prevent unionization. In December 2006, the hospital was found to have violated their agreement by engaging in union intimidation. According to the ruling, University Hospital management threatened to fire workers or to curb their benefits and pay if they talked with union organizers. Hospital management also held mandatory anti-union meetings with their employees and lied to workers about union dues and activities. Nevertheless, the organization and coalition continued to work on the demands of the community benefits agreement and their hospital debt and social contract projects. Much of their efforts were focused on electoral politics throughout the early 2000s. They supported Barak Obama's campaign and canvassed neighborhoods, promoting supportive members of the board of alderpersons and mayoral candidates.

RACISM-EVASIVE, CLASS-CENTERED RADICALS

After the agreement was won, many of my key informants moved to other states or other projects. The Center for Economic Democracy branched out to other cities, and the major unions they worked with, such as SEIU, pursued other projects. The organization is now an affiliate of Partnership for Working Families. Their website consists only of links to articles and economic reports. In 2017, I spoke with a former member of the organization's board of directors, who shared his disappointment with how the group had changed over the years. He stated that the new branch of the organization in a neighboring city wanted to address racism explicitly, especially in the leadership of public schools. They could not secure funding from the teacher's union or other labor organizations, such as UNITE HERE and SEIU, for their work. Like Rachel, who disliked the tunnel vision of the union, he argued that these labor unions limited the topics the organization could address. According to this former director, the unions would tell them their racism-centered projects were "a really great idea, but we can't fund it right now."[1] Consequently, the *racism-evasive, class-centered radicals* in this case continued to keep racism off the organization's main agenda.

UPDATE ON ESSEX TOWN

The radical group in Essex Town is still investigating the political corruption that is connected to decisions involving their schools. They are now focused on what they see as corrupt practices by the mayor, other politicians, and both liberal and conservative loyalists to the political machine. The radical group discovered text messages between the mayor and the superintendent that showed how the mayor influenced personnel decisions to secure jobs in the school system for his friends and family, who were less qualified than other candidates. They also found evidence implicating the mayor in acts of bribery that helped direct business to his companies as well as orchestrating straw donor donations.[2] The evidence they accumulated prompted the county prosecutor to get involved, launching a separate investigation of the mayor. As the radical group shared their evidence on social media, friends and family of the mayor retaliated against the radical group. Micaela's son reported that a person associated with the mayor yelled the N-word at him while he walked their family dog (see chapter 3). The town increased Micaela's property taxes without justification, a fact that alarmed the county prosecutor.

ELITIST RACISM-EVASIVE AND CLASS-EVASIVE LIBERALS

A particularly interesting kind of retaliation developed after the radical group began investigating the mayor's public relations consultant, who is an African American woman. This woman, whom I call Deborah, and her family attacked Micaela on social media, calling her a "Karen."[3] While she was working with the mayor on public relations, Deborah was permitted to run a local performing arts organization that was supposed to be a charity. However, according to the documents the radical group discovered, she and her family used the organization as a vehicle to enrich themselves. The evidence showed that Deborah would sell alcohol at events, without a liquor license, and set up the credit card machines to funnel payment into her family's for-profit companies. In addition, they would make event organizers submit payment to these private companies instead of to the performing arts charity. Their nonprofit charity status was revoked by the IRS in the summer of 2018, yet they continued to hold events, claiming they were for charity. Due to her company's unlawful activities, Deborah was charged with third-degree theft in 2021. Deborah accused Micaela and Barry of being racists after they shared this evidence on social media. Because Deborah tagged Barry's workplace in one of these accusatory tweets, Barry felt pressured to step down from administering his town social media page. In her retaliation, Deborah used language that centered racism, but she did so to keep the focus away from the corruption in which she and political elites were engaged. One of these political elites was the mayor. Police officers in Essex Town informed the radical group that the mayor used racist language in private settings. At the same time, the mayor would use people of color, such as Deborah and other important town officials, to support his agenda. After the murder of George Floyd, Essex Town had a vigil at the town hall. The mayor took advantage of this vigil, posing for a photo opportunity beside his daugh-

ter, who held a Black Lives Matter sign. Both the European American mayor and
Deborah, an African American woman, contributed to the agenda of *elitist racism-
evasive and class-evasive liberals.*

Liberal organizations in Essex Town fail to understand the complexities of how
liberal people of color can be used to support white supremacy, and as a result
they are ineffective in challenging corruption and racist practices. There are two
very visible liberal organizations in Essex Town—one organized around education
and the other around development. The liberal organization on development opposed most of the mayor's decisions on development in Essex Town and saw him
as a barrier to the change they wanted. This organization worked to elect a progressive candidate of color, who portrayed herself as someone who would fight corruption and counter the mayor. In February 2019, after a month of serving on the
town council, this individual secured a position with the State Department of Education. Shortly after she received this position, she began voting for the programs
that the mayor supported. The most important vote was in favor of a pilot (payment in lieu of taxes) program to redevelop property. This program gave develop-
ers a $100 million tax cut over thirty years. The radical group began openly ques-
tioning this candidate's alliances with the mayor and her commitment to stamping
out corruption in Essex Town. The radical group believed that this candidate received the state job as a payment for voting with the power structure that she orig-
inally opposed. The liberal organizations continued to support this candidate regardless of her sudden shift. In a social media exchange between the liberal and
radical groups, Micaela noted that the liberal organization was now parroting the
mayor's arguments. This is another example of how elitist racism-evasive and class-
evasive liberals are ultimately concerned with staying relevant and being aligned
with power. This prevents them from effectively confronting injustice.

The kind of political theater I witnessed among liberals in Essex Town is insid-
ious. By calling Micaela a "Karen" and accusing Barry of racism, liberal people of
color used the language of radical, antiracist movements to uphold white supremacy in Essex Town. In my view, Deborah's ultimate purpose in making these claims
was not to further social justice, but to condemn a group of people who threatened a white political machine that helped her benefit financially. These kinds of
practices occur in our workplaces, in local communities, and in national organizations and politics. Progressives must be wary of them and know how to challenge
the many ways that liberal white supremacy maintains systemic racism, even when
people of color are involved in corrupt practices or are used by European American political actors to conceal their reproduction of the racial status quo.

NOTES

INTRODUCTION. A Divided Left

1. See Stolberg, "For Democrats, Ilhan Omar."

2. See Beeman, "Liberal White Supremacy."

3. In an article in *The Atlantic* ("Anti-Trump 'Resistance'"), Clare Foran discusses the anger and dismay over Trump that led to protests even in red states. Another list of such organizations is provided in a blog by Jordan James-Harvil, "19 Resistance Organizations."

4. The term "woke" has become so popular that it is now included in the *Merriam-Webster's Unabridged Dictionary*, where it is defined as "aware of and actively attentive to important facts and issues (especially issues of racial and social justice)" (see https://www.merriam-webster .com/dictionary/woke). Although this term has been around for some time, it was repopularized during the Black Lives Matter movement. It became used, some would argue overused, by "white" liberals (see Sanders, "It's Time to Put 'Woke' to Sleep").

5. R. Bush, *End of White World Supremacy*, 154.

6. Ray, "Race-Conscious Racism."

7. Cazenave, *Conceptualizing Racism*, 9.

8. Bonilla-Silva, *Racism without Racists*, 3.

9. A. J. Cooper, *Voice from the South*.

10. See Terborg-Penn, *African American Women*; Simien, *Black Feminist Voices in Politics*; Jones, *Vanguard*.

11. Ladner, *Tomorrow's Tomorrow*.

12. See Taylor, *How We Get Free*, 15.

13. Crenshaw's analysis was informed by several important works, including the 1977 "Combahee River Collective Statement"; Angela Davis, *Women, Race and Class*; and bell hooks, *Ain't I a Woman*. In my teaching, I trace this intersectional perspective to Sojourner Truth's 1851 speech, "Ain't I a Woman," which she delivered at the Women's Convention in Akron, Ohio.

14. See D. E. Smith, *Conceptual Practices of Power*; Essed, *Understanding Everyday Racism*; Espiritu, *Asian American Women and Men*; Collins, *Black Feminist Thought*; Brewer, "Black Radical Theory and Practice"; Harding, *Feminist Standpoint Theory Reader*; Simien, *Black Feminist Voices in Politics*; Branch, *Opportunity Denied*; Durr and Wingfield, "Keep Your 'N' in Check"; Wingfield, *Flatlining Race, Work, and Health Care*; Wingfield, "Systemic Racism Persists"; Melaku, *You Don't Look Like a Lawyer*.

15. From Marx and Engels, *Manifesto of the Communist Party*, chapter 1.

16. From Marx, "Economic and Philosophic Manuscripts," first written in 1844 and published posthumously in 1932, 36.

17. From Marx and Engels, *German Ideology*, first written in 1845–1846 and first published posthumously in 1932. See especially Marx and Engels's thoughts on labor in Part 1: *Feuerbach: Opposition of the Materialist and Idealist Outlook*.

18. From Marx, "Economic and Philosophic Manuscripts," first written in 1844 and published posthumously in 1932. See especially 30–32.

19. See Weber, *Economy and Society.*.

20. Cox, *Caste, Class, and Race*, 104.

21. As quoted in Laslett, *John Locke*, 341–342.

22. Charles W. Mills, *Racial Contract*, 27.

23. Parker, Minkin, and Bennett, "Methodology."

24. Charles W. Mills, *Racial Contract*, 127.

25. In 1916 Madison Grant wrote *The Passing of the Great Race*, which argued that there existed a pure "Nordic race," superior to other people of European descent.

26. For a detailed discussion of this history, see Bashi Treitler, *Ethnic Project*; Roediger, *Wages of Whiteness*.

27. See "Note on Terminology" at the end of the introduction for an explanation of why I problematize the term "white."

28. See Wilson, *Racism*.

29. See Smedley, *Race in North America*.

30. See Thompson, *Promise and a Way of Life*; Morgen, *Into Our Own Hands*; Walsh, *Talking about Race*; Ernst, *Price of Progressive Politics*; Melaku and Beeman, *Academia Isn't a Safe Haven*.

31. See Cazenave, *Conceptualizing Racism*.

32. See Yancy, "Should I Give Up?"

33. Thompson, *Promise and a Way of Life*.

34. See Sullivan, *Good White People*.

35. Nancy Coleman explains why the *New York Times* began capitalizing the word "Black" in her piece "Why We're Capitalizing Black"; John Eligon interviews scholars and activists to address this issue in his article "Debate over Identity and Race."

36. See Ewing, "I'm a Black Scholar."

37. See Smedley, *Race in North America*; Allen, *Invention of the White Race*.

38. See Du Bois, *Black Reconstruction in America*; Smedley, *Race in North America*; Allen, *Invention of the White Race*.

39. See Smedley, *Race in North America*.

40. See Roediger, *Wages of Whiteness.*

41. See Waters, "Optional Ethnicities."

42. Cazenave, "Conceptualizing 'Race' and Beyond," 5.

43. J. E. Williams, *Decoding Racial Ideology in Genomics.*

44. Ramamurthy, "Politics of Britain's Asian Youth Movements."

45. Ignatiev and Garvey, *Race Traitor,* 289.

46. M. E. L. Bush, *Everyday Forms of Whiteness,* 8.

47. Noe-Bustamante, Mora, and Hugo Lopez, "About One-in-Four U.S. Hispanics."

48. See Del Real, "'Latinx' Hasn't Even Caught On among Latinos."

CHAPTER 1. Racism, Class, and Liberal White Supremacy

1. See Bonilla-Silva, "Rethinking Racism"; Bonilla-Silva, *Racism without Racists;* Beeman, "Liberal White Supremacy"; Beeman, "Walk the Walk"; Fields, *Racecraft;* Golash-Boza, *Race and Racisms.*

2. See Steinberg, *Race Relations;* Cazenave, *Conceptualizing Racism.*

3. See Embrick, "Discontents Within the Discipline."

4. See Cazenave, *Conceptualizing Racism.*

5. Ibid.

6. Smedley, *Race in North America;* Allen, *Invention of the White Race;* Bashi Treitler, *Ethnic Project.*

7. Smedley, *Race in North America.*

8. Ibid.

9. Ibid.

10. I borrow this phrase from Winthrop Jordan's 1968 book *White over Black.* Smedley distinguishes her work from Jordan's, which focuses on American attitudes toward African Americans. Smedley focuses on the "ideological ingredients of which the idea of race was itself was composed." See Smedley, *Race in North America,* 15.

11. Smedley, *Race in North America.*

12. Allen, *Invention of the White Race.*

13. Ibid., 251.

14. Ibid.

15. Du Bois, *Black Reconstruction in America.*

16. Allen, *Invention of the White Race,* 241.

17. Ibid.

18. "America and West Indies," 16–31.

19. Ibid.

20. Smedley, *Race in North America.*

21. Jefferson, *Notes on the State of Virginia.*

22. Wilson, *Racism.*

23. Ibid., 73.

24. Ibid., 74.

25. Ibid., 70.

26. Haldeman, *Haldeman Diaries*, 66.

27. As quoted in Steinberg, "Role of Race."

28. Wilson, *Racism*.

29. Harlan, as quoted in Carr, *"Color-Blind" Racism*, ix.

30. Ibid., x.

31. Carr, *"Color-Blind" Racism*, x.

32. See also R. C. Smith, *Racism in the Post–Civil Rights Era*.

33. Bonilla-Silva, *White Supremacy & Racism*.

34. Ibid.

35. See Hughey, *White Bound*.

36. Bonilla-Silva, *Racism without Racists*, 104.

37. Bobo and Smith, "From Jim Crow to Laissez-Faire Racism."

38. See studies addressing racism against middle-class African Americans: Feagin and Sikes, *Living with Racism*; Feagin and McKinney, *Many Costs of Racism*. See also Pager, Western, and Bonikoswki, "Discrimination in a Low-Wage Labor Market." This study addresses racial discrimination against African American and Latino men on the job market despite education, income, residence, physical appearance, self-presentation, etc. Among other findings, the authors note that European American men *with* a criminal record have as good or slightly better chances of getting a job callback as African American and Latino men *without* a criminal record.

39. Bonilla-Silva, *White Supremacy & Racism*, 150.

40. Melanie E. L. Bush finds similar themes expressed among highly educated college students, who she argues parrot what they learn from their families, education, and media institutions. See Bush, *Everyday Forms of Whiteness*.

41. For works that define systemic racism this way, see Cazenave, *Urban Racial State*; Cazenave, *Conceptualizing Racism*; Feagin, Hernan, and Batur, *White Racism*.

42. Carmichael and Hamilton, *Black Power*.

43. Wise, "Motive and Opportunity."

44. Oliver and Shapiro, *Black Wealth/White Wealth*.

45. Pollock, *Colormute*.

46. Pierce, *Racing for Innocence*.

47. Risman and Bannerjee, *"Kids Talking about Race."*

48. Cazenave, *Conceptualizing Racism*.

49. See Fields, *Racecraft*.

50. Cazenave, *Conceptualizing Racism*.

51. See also Dowd, "Public and Academic Questions."

52. Frankenberg, *White Women, Race Matters*, 268.

53. Cazenave, *Conceptualizing Racism*, 23.

54. Ibid.

55. Ibid. Cazenave states that "racism denial can be viewed as a racism evasive process backed by numerous racism denial practices" (23). He also refers to several of the racism-denial practices he lists on pages 24–25 as racism-evasive on page 91. For example, on page 91, he refers to "conceptual misdirection" as both a racism denial and racism-evasive practice.

56. Beeman, "Walk the Walk."

57. Cazenave, *Conceptualizing Racism*.

58. Melaku, *You Don't Look like a Lawyer*, ii.

59. For conceptualization of "race-talk" see Bonilla-Silva, *White Supremacy & Racism*. For conceptualization of "racecraft" see Fields, *Racecraft*. For conceptualization of linguistic racial accommodation see Cazenave, *Conceptualizing Racism*.

60. See Feagin, *White Racial Frame*; Melaku, *You Don't Look like a Lawyer*.

61. Feagin, *White Racial Frame*.

62. In *A Voice from the South*, Anna Julia Cooper stated, "Only the Black Woman can say, when and where I enter . . . then and there the whole Negro race enters with me" (31).

63. See Embrick, "Discontents within the Discipline"; Melaku and Beeman, "Academia Isn't a Safe Haven."

64. For further discussion of Clinton's racial and class-biased policies, see Cazenave, *Conceptualizing Racism*.

65. See Schwartz, "Nina Turner vs. Hilary Rosen."

66. While this was the perception status quo liberals had of Sanders, I would not type Sanders as a radical socialist. In fact, David Wagner argues Sanders offered vague comments on socialism and often avoided questions about it. See Wagner, *Progressives in America*.

CHAPTER 2. Liberals and Radicals, a Conceptual Model

1. Rossinow, *Visions of Progress*.

2. Ibid., 195.

3. Ibid., 9.

4. Interestingly, David Wagner, in *Progressives in America*, states that the Communist Party (CP) of the Popular Front era was not so radical, as they attempted to align with the Democratic Party. He also criticizes the CP for their top-down approach.

5. Hedges, *Death of the Liberal Class*. See also R. Bush, *End of White World Supremacy*.

6. Rossinow, *Visions of Progress*.

7. Hedges, *Death of the Liberal Class*.

8. See Hedges, *Death of the Liberal Class*; Morgan, *Reds*; Sandbrook, *Eugene McCarthy*.

9. Hedges, *Death of the Liberal Class*.

10. Ibid., 65.

11. Ibid.

12. For further discussion of this controversy, see Ceplair, "Shedding Light." See also Rampbell, "High Noon."

13. Rossinow, *Visions of Progress*.

14. Ibid., 198. Rossinow and I differ on our perspective on liberals versus radicals. Rossinow argues that they are more alike than they are different. In his view, their long history of collaboration and conflict ultimately led to important progressive changes. My work is more concerned with liberal actions, behaviors, and tactics. Liberals and radicals both say they want equality, but, in my view, the way they go about achieving that equality and their approaches to issues differ.

15. Kutulas, *American Civil Liberties Union.*

16. Rossinow, *Visions of Progress,* 165.

17. See Fairclough, *Better Day Coming;* Hedges, *Death of the Liberal Class;* D. Smith and Hanley, "Anger Games."

18. Hedges, *Death of the Liberal Class,* 107.

19. Rossinow, *Visions of Progress.*

20. Delton, *Rethinking the 1950s.*

21. Rossinow, *Visions of Progress.*

22. Ibid..

23. See R. Bush, *End of White World Supremacy,* especially chapter 5.

24. Rossinow, *Visions of Progress.*

25. See R. Bush, *End of White World Supremacy,* 156.

26. See Digital SNCC Gateway, "Red-Baiting."

27. Rossinow, *Visions of Progress.*

28. Ibid., 2.

29. Ibid., 241–242.

30. David Wagner, in *Progressives in America,* offers a "crib sheet" that lists differences between liberals, progressives, and radicals on capitalism, socialism, and reform; environmental issues; foreign policy and war; immigration issues; income, egalitarianism, and social welfare; libertarian issues; public and private ownership; and race, gender, and sexual minorities. His perspective regarding liberal support of capitalism is consistent with mine. However, I further examine how liberal and radical approaches to social class intersect with beliefs and practices that affect people of color, working-class people, and the issue of racism. Wagner argues that radicals have embraced the "identity movements" of people of color, women, and sexual minorities, but I argue that radicals have not adequately addressed these movements and face problems in explicitly addressing racism. I link these weaknesses in radical movements to societal-level liberal discourse and color-blind ideology.

31. I borrow this phrase from the 2018 documentary *Shift Change,* directed by Dworkin and Young.

32. Cazenave, *Conceptualizing Racism,* 17. Here Cazenave is speaking about the ignorance of socially dominant groups. I apply this syndrome to liberals' unwillingness or lack of motivation to learn about alternatives to capitalism. The IPA syndrome also applies to liberals' ignorance of working-class issues and attitudes toward working-class people.

33. See Gabriel, Resnick, and Wolff, "State Capitalism versus Communism."

34. See ibid.; Mulder, *Transcending Capitalism.*

35. See Ball, *Imagining America;* Curtis, *Pandora's Box.*

36. Piketty and Saez, "Income Inequality in the United States"; Piketty, *Capital in the Twenty-First Century;* see also Hembree, "CEO Pay Skyrockets"; Mishel and Davis, "Top CEOs Make 300 Times More."

37. Mulder, *Transcending Capitalism.* See also Kelley, *Freedom Dreams.*

38. Flanders, "Talking with Chomsky."

39. Hedges, *Death of the Liberal Class,* 36.

40. Ibid., 8.

41. Rossinow, *Visions of Progress*.

42. Ibid., 155.

43. Lewis, as quoted in Rossinow, *Visions of Progress*, 229.

44. Activist, as quoted in ibid.

45. See Student Nonviolent Coordinating Committee, "Black Power."

46. Baldwin, *Fire Next Time*, 94.

47. Ibid., 95.

48. See ibid., 58.

49. See Melaku and Beeman, "Academia Isn't a Safe Haven."

50. DiAngelo, *White Fragility*.

51. See Wellman, *Portraits of White Racism*; R. C. Smith, *Racism in the Post–Civil Rights Era*; Bonilla-Silva, *White Supremacy & Racism*; Bonilla-Silva, *Racism without Racists*; M. K. Brown et al., *White-Washing Race*; Doane and Bonilla-Silva, *White Out*; Korgen and O'Brien, "Black/White Friendships"; Hughey, *White Bound*; Beeman, "Teaching to Convince."

52. Benwell, "Common-Sense Anti-Racism."

53. Beeman, "Liberal White Supremacy."

54. See Hughey, *White Bound*.

55. O'Brien, *Whites Confront Racism*.

56. Ibid., 109.

57. Ibid., 115.

58. See Hughey, *White Bound*.

59. See ibid., 122.

60. See ibid., chapter 7.

61. See ibid., 154–155.

62. See Underhill, "Diversity Is Important to Me."

63. DiAngelo, *White Fragility*, 77–78.

64. Beeman, "Emotional Segregation"; Beeman, "Legacy of Emotional Segregation."

65. Alexander, *New Jim Crow*; see also Embrick, "Two Nations Revisited."

66. X, "Malcolm X Speech."

67. See Sue, *Race Talk*; Feagin and Sikes, *Living with Racism*; Feagin and McKinney, *Many Costs of Racism*.

68. Beeman, "Liberal White Supremacy."

69. See Frank, *Listen, Liberal*.

70. Jessie Jackson is often credited with coining the term "Rainbow Coalition," but, in fact, this was a movement developed by the Black Panther Party. See Jakobi Williams, *From the Bullet to the Ballot*.

71. See ibid.

72. Frank, *Listen, Liberal*.

73. Ibid., 30.

74. Reilly, "Read Hillary Clinton's 'Basket of Deplorables' Remarks.'"

75. In her "deplorables" speech, HRC also stated that the other half of Trump's voters were not deplorable but just felt abandoned by the government. It was this half, she argued, that needed empathy. However, liberals ran with the deplorables comment, offering little empathy

or sympathy for the abandoned people HRC referenced. The "basket of deplorables" fit with the liberal imagination of the working-class Trump voter they hated.

76. See Beeman, "Why Doesn't Middle America Trust Hillary?"

77. Ibid.

78. See ibid.

79. Manza and Crowley, "Working Class Hero?"

80. In fact, Arlie Hochschild interviewed a highly educated, wealthy Tea Partyer from Louisiana, who took offense at the term "redneck." He likely looked down on the lower-class people in his community. By contrast, many low-income, working-class people take pride in the term "redneck." For example, Redneck Revolt tries to reclaim the historical significance of the term.

81. See Carr, *"Color-Blind" Racism*; Brown et al. *White-Washing Race*.

82. Williamson, "Chaos in the Family." A precursor to this opinion can be found in the Democratic Leadership Council founded in 1985. In *Listen, Liberal* Thomas Frank notes that by the 1990s, the DLC abandoned the working class and, indeed, reveled in their downfall. As the Democratic Party began to cater to the professional "learning class" and valorize education and skill as the answer to everything, the DLC condescendingly likened the uneducated classes to "illiterate peasants in the Age of Steam" (59).

83. Carnes and Lupu, "It's Time to Bust the Myth."

84. Ibid. These numbers are consistent with the findings of the 2016 American National Election Study.

85. Hochschild, *Strangers in Their Own Land*.

86. Plumer, "What a Liberal Sociologist Learned."

87. Kurtzleben, "Here's How Many Bernie Sanders Supporters."

88. Geier, "Inequality among Women."

89. Ibid.

90. See Featherstone, "Elite, White Feminism."

91. See Bourdieu, *Distinction*.

92. Rossinow, *Visions of Progress*.

93. Ibid.

94. Myrdal, *American Dilemma*.

95. See Carmichael and Hamilton, *Black Power*; Wellman, *Portraits of White Racism*; Bonilla-Silva, "Rethinking Racism"; Bonilla-Silva, *Racism without Racists*; Cazenave and Maddern, "Defending the White Race"; Cazenave, *Conceptualizing Racism*; Doane and Bonilla-Silva, *White Out*; Beeman, "Emotional Segregation"; DiTomaso, *American Non-Dilemma*.

96. DiTomaso, *American Non-Dilemma*.

97. See Wellman, *Portraits of White Racism*; Doane and Bonilla-Silva, *White Out*; Houts Picca and Feagin, *Two-Faced Racism*; Bonilla-Silva, *White Supremacy & Racism*; Bonilla-Silva, *Racism without Racists*; M. E. L. Bush, *Everyday Forms of Whiteness*.

98. Hartigan, "Who are These White People?," 97.

99. Just because there is white privilege does not mean there are no racist stereotypes of white people. Poor Appalachian white people do face discrimination. They have high rates of unemployment, have low graduation rates, and face employment as well as housing discrimination due to their accents and lifestyles. I have met people in academia who, like me, came from various parts of Appalachia. Among other things, they share a common story of how they

unlearned their accents and had to be careful, after visiting their homes and returning to academia, that their accents did not come back with them. People of color and European Americans can stereotype them as a separate racial group. However, just because there are racist stereotypes against white rednecks does not mean that the entire system of racism has been reversed to now benefit people of color or that white privilege disappears. For more on the differences between racial bigotry and systemic racism and the situations that can allow for people of color to discriminate on an individual level, see Cazenave, *Conceptualizing Racism*; Davis, "White Racism Black Bigotry." For data on how people of color may participate in color-blind ideology, see Bonilla-Silva, *White Supremacy & Racism*; Bonilla-Silva and Embrick, "Are Blacks Color Blind Too?"

100. Warfield, "Why Redneck Revolt."

101. Jakobi Williams, *From the Bullet to the Ballot*.

102. Lee, as quoted in ibid., 133.

103. Fesperman, as quoted in ibid., 142.

104. Lee, as quoted in ibid., 134.

105. Hartigan, "Who are These White People?," 111.

106. Warfield, "Why Redneck Revolt."

107. Embrick, "Diversity Ideology."

108. Beeman, "Liberal White Supremacy."

109. Hartigan, "Who are These White People?"

110. See Wilkins, "Not Out to Start a Revolution"; Chou and Feagin, *Myth of the Model Minority*.

111. See D. Smith and Hanley, "Anger Games."

112. See Hedges, *Death of the Liberal Class*; Frank, *Listen, Liberal*.

113. Cameron, *Radicals of the Worst Sort*.

114. Ibid., 1.

115. See Desmond and Emirbayer, *Racial Domination, Racial Progress*; Jakobi Williams, *From the Bullet to the Ballot*. See also R. Bush, *End of White World Supremacy*; R. Bush, "Introductory Comment."

116. Zinn and Arnove, *Voices of a People's History*, 361.

117. See Fujino, *Heartbeat of Struggle*.

118. Foley Library, Gonzaga University, "Internment and Service."

119. See Digital SNCC Gateway, "Inside SNCC."

120. Hale, "Forgotten Story."

121. See Digital SNCC Gateway, "SNCC Culture Clips."

122. See Digital SNCC Gateway, "Red-Baiting."

123. Oglesby, "Let Us Shape the Future."

124. Students for a Democratic Society, "America and the New Era," 13.

125. See Cone, *Martin & Malcolm & America*; R. Bush, *End of White World Supremacy*.

126. King, "Give Us the Ballot."

127. Martin Luther King, Jr., letter to Bishop C. C. J. Carpenter et al., April 16, 1963. This letter is often referred to as the "Letter from Birmingham Jail."

128. Frank, *Listen, Liberal*, 41.

129. Ibid., 24.

130. Ibid.

131. Beeman, "Post–Civil Rights Racism and OWS."

132. See Jakobi Williams, *From the Bullet to the Ballot*.

133. Lee, as quoted in Jakobi Williams, *From the Bullet to the Ballot*, 140.

134. Merton, *Sociological Ambivalence and Other Essays*.

135. See Hughey, *White Bound*.

136. Hayden and Wittman, "Interracial Movement of the Poor?", 6.

CHAPTER 3. The Friendliest Town

1. United States Census Bureau, "Profile of General Population and Housing Characteristics" (website redacted to preserve anonymity of town).

2. These are the racial categories used by the United States Census.

3. These are the categories used by the school statistics.

4. Tom, personal conversation, November 12, 2018.

5. C. A. Brown, "Discipline Disproportionality among American Indian Students"; Whitford, "School Discipline Disproportionality"; United States Government Accountability Office, "K-12 Education"; see also Shedd, *Unequal City*.

6. Ksinan et al., "National Ethnic and Racial Disparities."

7. Gilens, *Why Americans Hate Welfare*.

8. Neubeck and Cazenave, *Welfare Racism*.

9. Micaela's post to community social media page, February 20, 2018.

10. Ibid.

11. Ibid.

12. Barry, interview, December 3, 2018.

13. Tom, interview, October 2018.

14. Ibid.

15. Micaela, interview, January 2020.

16. Superintendent's email sent to faculty, December 14, 2016.

17. Tom, interview, October 10, 2018.

18. Tom contacted a number of certified fraud examiners, who suggested that the superintendent should have implemented several safeguarding measures after the incident: (1) remove the person who made the transfer from check-signing authority and give her no access to blank checks; (2) change passwords for online banking immediately; (3) prohibit electronic funds transfers on the accounts; (4) ensure blank checks have a statement indicating the check is void if two signatures are not presented; (5) place a new person without check-signing authority in control of storage and issuing of checks; (6) send a bank statement to the district office for review by someone with appropriate training and skill. None of these measures were taken.

19. Micaela's post to community social media page, May 22, 2018.

20. Ibid.

21. Ibid.

22. Ibid.

23. Superintendent's statement at BOE meeting, June 4, 2018.

24. Vice president's statement at BOE meeting, June 4, 2018.

25. Ibid.

26. Board member's statement at BOE meeting, June 4, 2018.

27. Feagin and O'Brien, *White Men on Race*.

28. Statement issued by the BOE, May 25, 2018.

29. Micaela's post to community social media page, August 2, 2018.

30. See also Hedges, *Death of the Liberal Class*.

31. Tom, public comment at BOE Meeting, October 19, 2018.

32. Ibid.

33. Micaela, public comment at BOE Meeting, October 19, 2018.

34. Clark and Remo, "Will N.J.'s Teacher Sexual Misconduct."

35. Davidson, "Toward a Student Syndicalist Movement," 3.

36. Achbar and Wintonick, *Manufacturing Consent*.

37. Merton, *Sociological Ambivalence and Other Essays*.

38. Lichterman, "Piecing Together Multicultural Community"; Bernstein, "Celebration and Suppression"; Lichterman, "Talking Identity in the Public Sphere."

39. Carmichael and Hamilton, *Black Power*; Feagin and Feagin, *Discrimination American Style*; Wellman, *Portraits of White Racism*; Feagin, Vera, and Batur, *White Racism*; Bonilla-Silva, "Rethinking Racism"; Cazenave and Maddern, "Defending the White Race"; Bonilla-Silva, *White Supremacy & Racism*; Bonilla-Silva, *Racism without Racists*; Trepagnier, *Silent Racism*; Coates, *Covert Racism*; Cazenave, *Conceptualizing Racism*.

40. See Feagin and O'Brien, *White Men on Race*; Beeman, "Walk the Walk"; Sue, *Race Talk*; Cazenave, *Conceptualizing Racism*; Melaku and Beeman, "Academia Isn't a Safe Haven."

41. Lieblich, "Harvard's History"; Robertson, "Nikole Hannah-Jones Denied Tenure."

42. Williams, *From the Bullet to the Ballot*.

43. Bell and Hartmann, "Diversity in Everyday Discourse"; Burke, *Racial Ambivalence in Diverse Communities*; Hughey, *White Bound*; Underhill, "Diversity Is Important to Me."

44. Hughey, *White Bound*.

45. Aptekar and Cieslik, "Astoria, New York"; Rai, *Democracy's Lot*.

46. Rossinow, *Visions of Progress*.

47. Bonilla-Silva, *White Supremacy & Racism*; Bonilla-Silva, *Racism without Racists*; DiTomaso, *American Non-Dilemma*; DiAngelo, *White Fragility*.

CHAPTER 4. Walk the Walk but Don't Talk the Talk

1. Names of the city and the university are disguised.

2. Geschwender, *Class, Race, and Worker Insurgency*; Surkin and Georgakas, *Detroit*; Taylor, *From #Blacklivesmatter to Black Liberation*; Taylor, *How We Get Free*.

3. Bonilla-Silva, *Racism without Racists*, 53.

4. See Pierce, *Racing for Innocence*.

5. Wellman, *Portraits of White Racism*; Royster, *Race and the Invisible Hand*; Walsh, *Talking about Race*.

6. Royster, *Race and the Invisible Hand*, 3.

7. O'Brien, "Political Is Personal"; Walsh, *Talking about Race.*

8. Shapiro, *Training for Racial Equity.*

9. Patillo-McCoy, "Church Culture as a Strategy."

10. European Americans stated that the Christian church culture and ideology used during public meetings was important to rousing the residents, a large group of whom were African American. Interestingly, when I asked Latine and African American pastors about the use of prayers and church culture, they stated that it meant nothing to them and that some of them disliked doing it. They also argued it was necessary for the membership. Yet, some of this membership, including an African American cochair, stated that the church was hypocritical, and they did not care for the use of church culture in the meetings. Thus, organizers may have been making false assumptions about their African American and Latine membership. A few organizers and members also shared that there was some discontent among Jewish members with the use of these prayers and sermon-like speeches.

11. Quoted from observation of a coalition meeting, November 17, 2004.

12. Observation of public meeting, November 17, 2004.

13. See Milkman, *On Gender, Labor, and Inequality,* for a discussion of unions' failure to address gender inequality.

14. Esther, personal interview, June 15, 2006.

15. Joseph, personal interview, October 20, 2005.

16. Joseph's daughter, personal interview, October 20, 2005.

17. Adrianna, personal interview, July 6, 2007.

18. Ibid.

19. Quoted from observation of a coalition meeting, March 30, 2005.

20. Julie, personal interview, July 18, 2007.

21. Ibid.

22. Miguel, personal interview, May 17, 2006.

23. Ibid.

24. Alex, personal interview, May 15, 2007.

25. Ibid.

26. Ibid.

27. Neubeck and Cazenave, *Welfare Racism*; Steinberg, *Ethnic Myth*; Pierre, "Black Immigrants"; Bashi Treitler, *Ethnic Project.*

28. Thompson, *Promise and a Way of Life.*

29. See Hughey, *White Bound.*

30. Jen, personal interview, November 16, 2005.

31. Fred, personal interview, November 5, 2005.

32. Ibid.

33. Ibid.

34. This respondent is referring to Dr. Cornel West's important book, *Race Matters.*

35. Fred, personal interview, November 5, 2005.

36. Ibid.

37. Ibid.

38. Laverne, personal interview, August 5, 2005.

39. Ibid.

40. See B. Cooper, *Eloquent Rage*; Bates, "When Civility Is Used."

41. Dawn, personal interview, May 24, 2007.

42. R. C. Smith, *Racism in the Post–Civil Rights Era*.

43. See Cazenave, *Conceptualizing Racism*.

44. Feagin and O'Brien, *White Men on Race*; Sue, *Race Talk*.

45. Carol, personal interview, May 15, 2006.

46. Ibid.

47. Ibid.

48. Rodríguez-Silva, *Silencing Race*.

49. Rachel, personal interview, June 15, 2006.

50. See Lichterman, "Piecing Together Multicultural Community"; Lichterman, "Talking Identity in the Public Sphere."

51. Pollock, *Colormute*, finds that sometimes the culture of an organization can be so profound that it even affects outsiders. She noted that when an outside speaker came to her schools, he tempered his emphasis on racial differences in response to an uncomfortable silence from the audience. I argue that societal ideologies of racism denial prompt organizations to develop cultures of silence on specific issues.

52. Rodríguez-Silva, *Silencing Race*.

53. John, personal interview, June 2, 2006.

54. Phillip, personal interview, June 1, 2006.

55. Miguel, personal interview, May 17, 2006.

56. Travis, personal interview, May 17, 2006.

57. See Ernst, *Price of Progressive Politics*.

58. Thompson, *Promise and a Way of Life*; O'Brien, "Political Is Personal"; Hughey, *White Bound*; Beeman, "Teaching to Convince."

59. Feagin, Vera, and Batur, *White Racism*; Rodriquez Silva, *Silencing Race*; Sullivan, *Good White People*; DiAngelo, *White Fragility*; Melaku and Beeman, "Academia Isn't a Safe Haven."

60. Shapiro, *Training for Racial Equity*.

61. Jen, personal interview, November 16, 2005.

CHAPTER 5. Challenging Liberal White Supremacy

1. Rachel, personal interview, June 15, 2006.

2. Member of the coalition, personal interview, June 13, 2007.

3. See also Shapiro, *Training for Racial Equity & Inclusion*.

4. See also Clawson, *Next Upsurge*.

5. Several other organizations may also exemplify a racism-centered intersectional approach, including the Poor People's Campaign organized by Dr. Martin Luther King Jr., later taken over by Ralph Abernathy, and currently cochaired by Reverend William Barber and Reverend Dr. Liz Theoharis.

6. See Cazenave, *Killing African Americans*, 262.

7. O'Kane, "Say Their Names."

8. McDermott and Steck, "Biden Repeatedly Pushed Bill."

9. Cazenave, *Killing African Americans*, 265.

10. See Pennello, "Left for Dead."

11. Crenshaw, "Mapping the Margins"; Simien, *Black Feminist Voices in Politics*.

12. Neubeck and Cazenave, *Welfare Racism*.

13. Morgen, *Into Our Own Hands*.

14. Redneck Revolt, "Redneck Revolt Organizing Principles."

15. Ibid.

16. Paul, "Jewelers Made a 'Take a Knee' Pun."

17. Cohen, "Video Shows NYPD Vehicles."

18. Gioino and Goldberg, "George Floyd Protestor Shoved."

19. Vigdor, Victor, and Hauser, "Buffalo Police Officers Suspended."

20. Koran, "Activist Gave Police Anti-Bias Training."

21. Melaku and Beeman, "Academia Isn't a Safe Haven."

22. Feagin, *White Racial Frame*; see also Wingfield and Feagin, *Yes We Can?*

23. Ruffins, "Faithful Witness."

24. Robinson, *Black Marxism*; see also Beeman, "Royall Must Fall."

25. Thompson, *A Promise and a Way of Life*; see also Melaku et al., "Be a Better Ally."

26. McKinney and Feagin, "Diverse Perspectives on Doing Anti-Racism."

27. Ibid., 246.

28. Barndt, *Dismantling Racism*, 65.

29. McKinney and Feagin, "Diverse Perspectives on Doing Anti-Racism."

30. Daniels, *Nice White Ladies*, 3.

31. Kendi, *How to Be an Antiracist*; Fleming, *How to Be Less Stupid about Race*; Melaku, *You Don't Look like a Lawyer*; Oluo, *So You Want to Talk*; McKinney and Feagin, "Diverse Perspectives on Doing Anti-Racism."

32. Smith and Johnson, *Good Guys*.

33. Johnson, *Privilege, Power, and Difference*.

34. Feagin and McKinney, *Many Costs of Racism*.

35. Du Bois, *Souls of Black Folk*, 3.

36. Chou and Feagin, *Myth of the Model Minority*.

37. Thompson, *Promise and a Way of Life*; McKinney and Feagin, "Diverse Perspectives on Doing Anti-Racism"; Desmond and Emirbayer, *Racial Domination, Racial Progress*.

38. Ignatiev, "Treason to Whiteness," 610.

39. Rockquemore, "For a Diverse Faculty."

40. Martinez, *De Colores Means All of Us*.

41. Federal Bureau of Investigation, "William E. B. Dubois."

42. Gallagher, "Miscounting Race."

43. See M. K. Brown et al., *Whitewashing Race*.

44. Cazenave, *Killing African Americans*, 178, emphasis in original.

45. Kelley, *Freedom Dreams*, 9.

46. Herndon, "Black Americans Have a Message."

47. See Cazenave, *Conceptualizing Racism*.

EPILOGUE. The Many Faces of Racism-Evasiveness
and Liberal White Supremacy

1. Former director, personal interview, November 2017.

2. Straw donor donations refer to the practice of someone, Person A, giving a donation to someone else, Person B, with the direction that they donate that money to the political candidate of Person A's choice. This disguises the amount of money any one person gives to a political candidate, allowing them to circumvent campaign contribution limits.

3. Karen is a name used to refer to European American women who call the police on African Americans for ridiculous reasons. It became more popular during the Movement for Black Lives protests over the summer of 2020 and following news reports of Amy Cooper, who called the police on Christian Cooper, an African American man, because he asked her to leash her dog in Central Park.

BIBLIOGRAPHY

Achbar, Mark, and Peter Wintonick. *Manufacturing Consent*. New York: Zeitgeist Films, 1992.

Alexander, Michelle. *The New Jim Crow: Mass Incarceration in the Age of Colorblindness*. New York: New Press, 2012.

Allen, Theodore. *The Invention of the White Race*. Vol. 2, *Racial Oppression and Social Control*. New York: Verso, 1997.

"America and West Indies: May 1736, 16–31." In *Calendar of State Papers, Colonial Series: America and West Indies*. Vol. 42, *1735–1736*, 207–220. London: Her Majesty's Stationery Office, 1953. British History Online. Accessed August 24, 2020. http://www.british-history.ac.uk/cal-state-papers/colonial/america-west-indies/vol42/pp207-220.

Aptekar, Sofya, and Anna Cieslik. "Astoria, New York." In *Diversities Old and New: Migration and Socio-Spatial Patterns in New York, Singapore and Johannesburg*, edited by Steven Vertovec, 23–44. Basingstoke UK: Palgrave Macmillan, 2015.

Baldwin, James. "As Much Truth as One Can Bear: To Speak Out about the World as It Is, Says James Baldwin, Is the Writer's Job." *New York Times Book Review*, January 14, 1962.

———. *The Fire Next Time*. New York: Vintage Books, 1962.

Ball, Alan M. *Imagining America: Influence and Images in Twentieth-Century Russia*. Lanham, MD: Rowman & Littlefield, 2003.

Barndt, Joseph. *Dismantling Racism: The Continuing Challenge to White America*. Minneapolis: Augsburg Books, 1991.

Bashi Treitler, Vilna. *The Ethnic Project: Transforming Racial Fictions into Ethnic Factions*. Stanford, CA: Stanford University Press, 2013.

Bates, Karen Grigsby, host. "When Civility Is Used as a Cudgel against People of Color." *All Things Considered* (podcast), NPR, March 14, 2019. Accessed July 12, 2021. https://www.npr.org/sections/codeswitch/2019/03/14/700897826/when-civility-is-used-as-a-cudgel-against-people-of-color.

Beeman, Angie. "Emotional Segregation: A Content Analysis of Institutional Racism in US Films, 1980–2001." *Ethnic and Racial Studies* 30, no. 5 (August 2007): 687–712. https://doi.org/10.1080/01419870701491648.

———. "The Legacy of Emotional Segregation: Barriers to an Integrated Society." Paper presented at the Annual Meeting of the American Sociological Association, Philadelphia, August 20, 2018.

———. "Liberal White Supremacy: Charlottesville and a Conversation with Justice." *Racism Review: Scholarship and Activism Towards Racial Justice* (blog), August 2017. http://www.racismreview.com/blog/author/angie-beeman/.

———. "Post–Civil Rights Racism and OWS: Dealing with Color-Blind Ideology." *Socialism & Democracy* 26, no. 2 (June 2012): 51–54. https://doi.org/10.1080/08854300.2012.686268.

———. "Royall Must Fall: Old and New Battles on the Memory of Slavery in New England." *Sociology of Race and Ethnicity* 5, no. 3 (July 2019): 326–339. https://doi.org/10.1177/2332649218784731.

———. "Teaching to Convince, Teaching to Empower: Reflections on Student Resistance and Self-Defeat at Predominantly White vs. Racially Diverse Campuses." *Understanding & Dismantling Privilege* 5, no. 1 (February 2015): 13–33.

———. "Walk the Walk but Don't Talk the Talk: The Strategic Use of Color-Blind Ideology in an Interracial Social Movement Organization." *Sociological Forum* 30, no. 1 (March 2015): 127–147. https://doi.org/10.1111/socf.12148.

———. "Why Doesn't Middle America Trust Hillary? She Thinks She's Better Than Us and We Know It." *Counterpunch*, July 26, 2016. https://www.counterpunch.org/2016/07/26/why-doesnt-middle-america-trust-hillary-she-thinks-shes-better-than-us-and-we-know-it/.

Bell, Joyce M., and Douglas Hartmann. "Diversity in Everyday Discourse: The Cultural Ambiguities and Consequences of 'Happy Talk.'" *American Sociological Review* 72, no. 6 (December 2007): 895–914. https://doi.org/10.1177/000312240707200603.

Benwell, Bethan. "Common-Sense Anti-Racism in Book Group Talk: The Role of Reported Speech." *Discourse & Society* 23, no. 4 (July 2012): 359–376. https://doi.org/10.1177/0957926512441106.

Bernstein, Mary. "Celebration and Suppression: The Strategic Uses of Identity by the Lesbian and Gay Movement." *American Journal of Sociology* 103, no. 3 (November 1997): 531–565. https://doi.org/10.1086/231250.

Bobo, Lawrence, and Ryan Smith. "From Jim Crow to Laissez-Faire Racism: The Transformation of Racial Attitudes." In *Beyond Pluralism: The Conception of Groups and Group Identities in America*, edited by Wendy F. Katkin, Ned Landsman, and Andrea Tyree, 182–220. Urbana: University of Illinois Press, 1998.

Bonilla-Silva, Eduardo. *Racism without Racists: Color-Blind Racism and the Persistence of Racial Inequality in the United States*. Lanham, MD: Rowman & Littlefield, 2003.

———. "Rethinking Racism: Toward a Structural Interpretation." *American Sociological Review* 62, no. 3 (June 1997): 465–480. https://doi.org/10.2307/2657316.

———. *White Supremacy & Racism in the Post–Civil Rights Era*. Boulder, CO: Lynne Rienner, 2001.

Bonilla-Silva, Eduardo, and David Embrick. "Are Blacks Color Blind Too? An Interview-Based Analysis of Black Detroiters' Racial Views." *Race & Society* 4, no. 1 (January 2001): 47–67. https://doi.org/10.1016/S1090-9524(02)00034-7.

Bourdieu, Pierre. *Distinction: A Social Critique of the Judgement of Taste*. Paris: Les Editions de Minuit, 1979.

Branch, Enobong Hannah. *Opportunity Denied: Limiting Black Women to Devalued Work*. New Brunswick, NJ: Rutgers University Press, 2011.

Brewer, Rose. "Black Radical Theory and Practice: Gender, Race, and Class." *Socialism and Democracy* 17, no. 1 (2003): 109–122. https://doi.org/10.1080/08854300308428344.

Brown, Carolyn A. "Discipline Disproportionality among American Indian Students: Expanding the Discourse." *Journal of American Indian Education* 53, no. 2 (2014): 29–247.

Brown, Michael K., Martin Carnoy, Elliot Currie, Troy Duster, David B. Oppenheimer, Marjorie M. Shultz, and David Wellman. *White-Washing Race: The Myth of a Color-Blind Society*. Berkeley: University of California Press, 2003.

Burke, Meghan A. *Racial Ambivalence in Diverse Communities: Whiteness and the Power of Color-Blind Ideologies*. Lanham, MD: Lexington Books, 2012.

Bush, Melanie E. L. *Everyday Forms of Whiteness: Understanding Race in a "Post-Racial" World*. New York: Rowman % Littlefield, 2011.

Bush, Roderick. *The End of White World Supremacy: Black Internationalism and the Problem of the Color-Line*. Philadelphia: Temple University Press, 2009.

———. "Introductory Comment: The Panthers and the Question of Violence." In *In Search of the Black Panther Party: New Perspectives on a Revolutionary Movement*, edited by Jama Lazerow and Yohuru Williams, 59–66. Durham, NC: Duke University Press, 2006.

Cameron, Ardis. *Radicals of the Worst Sort: Laboring Women in Lawrence, Massachusetts, 1860–1912*. Urbana: University of Illinois Press, 1983.

Carmichael, Stokely, and Charles V. Hamilton. *Black Power: The Politics of Liberation in America*. New York: Random House, 1967.

Carnes, Nicholas, and Noam Lupu. "It's Time to Bust the Myth: Most Trump Voters Were Not Working Class." *Washington Post*, June 5, 2017. https://www.washingtonpost.com /news/monkey-cage/wp/2017/06/05/its-time-to-bust-the-myth-most-trump-voters -were-not-working-class/.

Carr, Leslie G. *"Color-Blind" Racism*. Thousand Oaks, CA: Sage, 1997.

Cazenave, Noel A. "Conceptualizing 'Race' and Beyond." *Association of Black Sociologists Newsletter* (February 2004): 4–6.

———. *Conceptualizing Racism: Breaking the Chains of Racially Accommodative Language*. Lanham, MD: Rowman & Littlefield, 2016.

———. *Killing African Americans: Police and Vigilante Violence as a Racial Control Mechanism*. New York: Routledge. 2018.

———. *The Urban Racial State: Managing Race Relations in American Cities*. Lanham, MD: Rowman & Littlefield, 2011.

Cazenave, Noel A., and Darlene A. Maddern. "Defending the White Race: White Male Faculty Opposition to a 'White Racism Course.'" *Race and Society* 2, no. 1 (1999): 25–50. https://doi.org/10.1016/S1090-9524(00)00003-6.

Ceplair, Larry. "Shedding Light on 'Darkness at High Noon.'" *Cineaste* 27, no. 4 (Fall 2002): 20–23. https://www.jstor.org/stable/41689518.

Chou, Rosalind S., and Joe R. Feagin. *The Myth of the Model Minority: Asian Americans Facing Racism*. New York: Routledge, 2016.

Clark, Adam, and Jessica Remo. "Will N.J.'s Teacher Sexual Misconduct Law Work? It's up to Administrators." *NJ Advance Media*, April 16, 2018. https://www.nj.com/education/2018/04/will_njs_teacher_sexual_misconduct_law_work_its_up.html.

Clawson, Dan. *The Next Upsurge: Labor and the New Social Movements*. Ithaca, NY: Cornell University Press, 2003.

Coates, Rodney. *Covert Racism: Theories, Institutions, and Experiences*. Chicago: Haymarket, 2012.

Cohen, Li. "Video Shows NYPD Vehicles Driving into Protesters in Brooklyn." *CBS News*, May 31, 2020. https://www.cbsnews.com/news/video-shows-nypd-vehicles-driving-into-protesters-in-brooklyn-2020-05-31/.

Coleman, Nancy. "Why We're Capitalizing Black." *New York Times*, July 5, 2020. https://www.nytimes.com/2020/07/05/insider/capitalized-black.html.

Collins, Patricia Hill. *Black Feminist Thought: Knowledge, Consciousness, and the Politics of Empowerment*. New York: Routledge, 2000.

———. *Intersectionality as Critical Social Theory*. Durham, NC: Duke University Press, 2019.

"The Combahee River Collective Statement." April 1977. Library of Congress Web Archive. https://www.loc.gov/item/lcwaN0028151/.

Cone, James H. *Malcolm & Martin & America: A Dream or a Nightmare*. New York: Orbis, 1991.

Cooper, Anna J. *A Voice from the South*. Xenia, OH: Aldine Printing House, 1892.

Cooper, Brittney. *Eloquent Rage: A Black Feminist Discovers Her Superpower*. New York: St. Martin's Press, 2018.

Cox, Oliver C. *Caste, Class, and Race: A Study in Social Dynamics*. New York: Monthly Review Press, 1948.

———. *Race Relations: Elements and Social Dynamics*. Detroit: Wayne State University Press, 1976.

Crenshaw, Kimberlé. "Demarginalizing the Intersection of Race and Sex: A Black Feminist Critique of Antidiscrimination Doctrine, Feminist Theory and Antiracist Politics." *University of Chicago Legal Forum* 1, no. 8 (1989): 139–167.

———. "Mapping the Margins: Intersectionality, Identity Politics, and Violence against Women of Color." *Stanford Law Review* 43, no. 6 (July 1991): 1241–1299. https://doi.org/10.2307/1229039.

Curtis, Adam. *Pandora's Box: A Fable from the Age of Science*. DVD. London: BBC, 1992.

Daniels, Jessie. *Nice White Ladies: The Truth about White Supremacy, Our Role in It, and How We Can Help Dismantle It*. New York: Seal Press, 2021.

Davidson, Carl. "Toward a Student Syndicalist Movement or University Reform Revisited: A Working Paper Prepared for the National Convention of the Students for a Democratic Society," Clear Lake, Iowa, Students for a Democratic Society, August 1966. https://exhibits.stanford.edu/activism/catalog/yh365wm6981.

Davis, Angela. *Women, Race and Class*. New York: Random House, 1981.

Del Real, Jose A. "'Latinx' Hasn't Even Caught On among Latinos," *Washington Post*, Decem-

ber 18, 2020. https://www.washingtonpost.com/outlook/latinx-latinos-unpopular-gender
-term/2020/12/18/bf177c5c-3b41-11eb-9276-ae0ca72729be_story.html.

Delton, Jennifer A. *Rethinking the 1950s: How Anticommunism and the Cold War Made America Liberal.* New York: Columbia University Press, 2013.

Desmond, Matthew, and Mustafa Emirbayer. *Racial Domination, Racial Progress: The Sociology of Race in America.* New York: McGraw Hill, 2009.

DiAngelo, Robin. *White Fragility: Why It's So Hard for White People to Talk about Racism.* Boston: Beacon Press, 2018.

Digital SNCC Gateway. "Inside SNCC: Establishing SNCC." Accessed June 15, 2019. https://snccdigital.org/inside-sncc/establishing-sncc/.

———. "Red-Baiting." Accessed June 15, 2019. https://snccdigital.org/inside-sncc/international-connections/red-baiting/).

———. "SNCC Culture Clips." Accessed June 15, 2019. https://snccdigital.org/inside-sncc/sncc-culture/sncc-culture-clips/.

DiTomaso, Nancy. *The American Non-Dilemma: Racial Inequality without Racism.* New York: Russell Sage, 2013.

Doane, Ashley W., and Eduardo Bonilla-Silva, eds. *White Out: The Continuing Significance of Racism.* New York: Routledge, 2003.

Dowd, Jeffrey. "Public and Academic Questions on Race: The Problem with Racial Controversies." *Sociological Forum* 29, no. 2 (June 2014): 496–502. https://doi.org/10.1111/socf.12094.

Du Bois, W. E. B. *Black Reconstruction in America, 1860–1880.* New York: Free Press, 1935.

———. *The Souls of Black Folk: Essays and Sketches.* Chicago: A.C. McClurg, 1903.

Durr, Marlese, and Adia Harvey Wingfield. "Keep Your 'N' in Check: African American Women and the Interactive Effects of Etiquette and Emotional Labor." *Critical Sociology* 37, no. 5 (September 2011): 557–571. https://doi.org/10.1177/0896920510380074.

Dworkin, Mark, and Melissa Young. *Shift Change: Putting Democracy to Work.* Oley, PA: Bulldog Films, 2018.

Eligon, John. "A Debate over Identity and Race Asks, Are African Americans 'Black' or 'black'?" *New York Times*, June 26, 2020. https://www.nytimes.com/2020/06/26/us/black-african-american-style-debate.html.

Embrick, David G. "Discontents within the Discipline: Sociological Hypnagogia, Negligence, and Denial." *Social Problems* 64, no. 2 (May 2017): 188–193. https://doi.org/10.1093/socpro/spx007.

———. "The Diversity Ideology in the Business World: A New Oppression for a New Age," *Critical Sociology* 37. no. 5 (July 2011): 541–556. https://doi.org/10.1177/0896920510380076.

———. "Two Nations Revisited: The Lynching of Black and Brown Bodies, Police Brutality, and Racial Control in 'Post-Racial' Amerikkka," *Critical Sociology* 41, no. 6 (June 2015): 835–843. https://doi.org/10.1177/0896920515591950.

Ernst, Rose. *The Price of Progressive Politics: The Welfare Rights Movement in an Era of Color-Blind Racism.* New York: NYU Press, 2012.

Espiritu, Yen Le. *Asian American Women and Men: Labor, Laws, and Love.* 2nd ed. Lanham, MD: Rowman & Littlefield, 2007.

Essed, Philomena. *Understanding Everyday Racism: An Interdisciplinary Theory.* New York: Sage, 1991.

Ewing, Eve. "I'm a Black Scholar Who Studies Race: Here's Why I Capitalize 'White.'" *Medium*, July 2, 2020. https://zora.medium.com/im-a-black-scholar-who-studies-race-here -s-why-i-capitalize-white-f94883aa2dd3.

Fairclough, Adam. *Better Day Coming: Blacks and Equality, 1890–2000.* New York: Penguin Books, 2002.

Feagin, Joe R. *Racist America: Roots, Current Realities, and Future Reparations.* New York: Routledge, 2000.

——. *Systemic Racism: A Theory of Oppression.* New York: Routledge, 2006.

——. *The White Racial Frame: Centuries of Racial Framing and Counter-Framing.* New York: Routledge, 2009.

Feagin, Joe R., and Clairece Booher Feagin. *Discrimination American Style: Institutional Racism and Sexism.* Malabar, FL: Krieger, 1978.

Feagin, Joe. R., Vera Hernan, and Pinar Batur. *White Racism: The Basics.* New York: Routledge, 2001.

Feagin, Joe R., and Karyn D. McKinney. *The Many Costs of Racism.* Lanham, MD: Rowman & Littlefield, 2005.

Feagin, Joe R., and Eileen O'Brien. *White Men on Race: Power, Privilege, and the Shaping of Cultural Consciousness.* Boston: Beacon, 2003.

Feagin, Joe R., and Melvin P. Sikes. *Living with Racism: The Black Middle Class Experience.* Boston: Beacon, 1994.

Featherstone, Liza. "Elite, White Feminism Gave Us Trump: It Needs to Die." *Versobooks.com* (blog), November 2016. https://www.versobooks.com/blogs/2936-elite-white-feminism -gave-us-trump-it-needs-to-die).

Federal Bureau of Investigation. "William E. B. Dubois." Part 1 of 5. Document no. 100–99729. Report made in New York, 1942. Accessed June 8, 2020. https://vault.fbi.gov/E.%20B. %20%28William%29%20Dubois/E.%20B.%20%28William%29%20Dubois%20Part %201%20of%205.

Fields, Barbara J. *Racecraft: The Soul of Inequality in American Life.* New York: Verso, 2014.

Flanders, Laura. "Talking with Chomsky." *Counterpunch*, April 30, 2012. https://www .counterpunch.org/2012/04/30/talking-with-chomsky/.

Fleming, Crystal M. *How to Be Less Stupid about Race: On Racism, White Supremacy, and the Racial Divide.* New York: Penguin Random House, 2019.

Foley Library, Gonzaga University. "Internment and Service: Japanese Americans from the Inland Empire: Patriotism through Protest." Accessed August 1, 2019. https:// researchguides.gonzaga.edu/c.php?g=67732&p=436799.

Foran, Clare. "The Anti-Trump 'Resistance' in Red States: Protests against the Administration Have Spread to Republican Strongholds, but It Remains Unclear if They Will Sway GOP Members of Congress." *The Atlantic*, February 17, 2017. https://www.theatlantic.com /politics/archive/2017/02/trump-resistance-liberal-tea-party-protest/517023/.

Frank, Thomas. *Listen, Liberal: Or, What Ever Happened to the Party of the People?* New York: Henry Holt, 2016.

Frankenberg, Ruth. *White Women, Race Matters: The Social Construction of Whiteness*. Minneapolis: University of Minnesota Press, 1993.

Fujino, Diane. *Heartbeat of Struggle: The Revolutionary Life of Yuri Kochiyama*. Minneapolis: University of Minnesota Press, 2005.

Gabriel, Satya, Stephen A. Resnick, and Richard D. Wolff. "State Capitalism versus Communism: What Happened in the USSR and the PRC." *Critical Sociology* 34, no. 4 (July 2008): 539–556. https://doi.org/10.1177/0896920508090851.

Gallagher, Charles. "Miscounting Race: Explaining Whites' Misperceptions of Racial Group Size." *Sociological Perspectives* 46, no. 3 (September 2003): 381–396. https://doi.org/10.1525/sop.2003.46.3.381.

Geier, Kathleen. "Inequality among Women Is Crucial to Understanding Hillary's Loss." *The Nation*, November 11, 2016. https://www.thenation.com/article/archive/inequality-between-women-is-crucial-to-understanding-hillarys-loss/.

Geschwender, James A. *Class, Race, and Worker Insurgency: The League of Revolutionary Black Workers*. Cambridge: Cambridge University Press, 1977.

Gilens, Martin. *Why Americans Hate Welfare: Race, Media, and the Politics of Antipoverty Policy*. Chicago: University of Chicago Press, 1999.

Gioino, Catherina, and Noah Goldberg. "George Floyd Protestor Shoved to the Ground by NYPD Says She's Still Traumatized by Ugly Run-In." *NY Daily News*, June 2, 2020. https://www.nydailynews.com/new-york/ny-dounya-zayer-nypd-shove-video-20200602-gz05swsrurby7aazr6bfmug5zu-story.html.

Golash-Boza, Tanya Marie. *Race and Racisms: A Critical Approach*. Oxford: Oxford University Press, 2018.

Grant, Madison. *The Passing of the Great Race; or, The Racial Basis of European History*. New York: Charles Scribner's Sons, 1916.

Haldeman, H. R. *The Haldeman Diaries: Inside the Nixon White House*. New York: G. P. Putnam's Sons, 1994.

Hale, John N. "The Forgotten Story of the Freedom Schools." *The Atlantic*, June, 26, 2014. https://www.theatlantic.com/education/archive/2014/06/the-depressing-legacy-of-freedom-schools/373490/.

Harding, Sandra, ed. *The Feminist Standpoint Theory Reader: Intellectual and Political Controversies*. New York: Routledge, 2004.

Hartigan, John, Jr. "Who Are These White People? 'Rednecks,' 'Hillbillies,' and 'White Trash' as Marked Racial Subjects." In Doane and Bonilla-Silva, *White Out*, 253–270.

Hayden, Tom, and Carl Wittman. "An Interracial Movement of the Poor?" Working notes distributed by Students for a Democratic Society and related groups and activities, room 302, 119 Fifth Avenue, New York, 1963. Accessed March 5, 2018. http://www.sds-1960s.org/Interracial-Movement-Poor.pdf.

Hedges, Chris. *Death of the Liberal Class*. New York: Nation Books, 2010.

Hembree, Diana. "CEO Pay Skyrockets to 361 Times That of the Average Worker." *Forbes*, May 22, 2018. https://www.forbes.com/sites/dianahembree/2018/05/22/ceo-pay-skyrockets-to-361-times-that-of-the-average-worker/#223dc664776d.

Herndon, Astead W. "Black Americans Have a Message for Democrats: Not Being Trump Is

Not Enough." *New York Times*, May 31, 2020. https://www.nytimes.com/2020/05/31/us
/politics/black-americans-democrats-trump.html.

Higginbotham, Evelyn Brooks. *Righteous Discontent: The Women's Movement in the Black Bap-
tist Church, 1880–1920*. Cambridge, MA: Harvard University Press, 1994.

Hochschild, Arlie. *Strangers in Their Own Land*. New York: New Press, 2016.

hooks, bell. *Ain't I a Woman: Black Women and Feminism*. Boston: South End Press, 1981.

Houts Picca, Leslie, and Joe R. Feagin. *Two-Faced Racism: Whites in the Backstage and Front-
stage*. New York: Routledge, 2007.

Hughey, Matthew. *White Bound: Nationalists, Antiracists, and the Shared Meanings of Race*.
Stanford, CA: Stanford University Press, 2012.

Ignatiev, Noel. "Treason to Whiteness Is Loyalty to Humanity: An Interview with Noel
Ignatiev of *Race Traitor* Magazine." In *Critical White Studies: Looking behind the Mirror*,
edited by Jean Stefancic and Richard Delgado, 607–612. Philadelphia: Temple University
Press, 1997.

Ignatiev, Noel, and John Garvey, eds. *Race Traitor*. New York, NY: Routledge, 1996.

James-Harvill, Jordan. "19 Resistance Organizations on the Forefront of the Anti-Trump
Movement." *Organizer* (blog, July 2017. https://blog.organizer.com/19-resistance
-organizations-on-the-forefront-of-the-anti-trump-movement.

Jefferson, Thomas. 1998. *Notes on the State of Virginia*. Penguin Classics. London: Penguin
Books.

Johnson, Allan G. *Privilege, Power, and Difference*. New York: McGraw-Hill, 2006.

Jones, Martha S. *Vanguard: How Black Women Broke Barriers, Won the Vote, and Insisted on
Equality for All*. New York: Basic Books, 2020.

Jordan, Winthrop D. *White over Black: American Attitudes toward the Negro, 1550–1812*.
Chapel Hill: University of North Carolina Press, 1968.

Kelley, Robin D. G. *Freedom Dreams: The Black Radical Imagination*. Boston: Beacon Press,
2002.

Kendi, Ibram X. *How to Be an Antiracist*. New York: Penguin Random House, 2019.

Kimeldorf, Howard. *Reds or Rackets? The Making of Radical and Conservative Unions on the
Waterfront*. Berkeley: University of California Press, 1988.

King, Martin Luther, Jr. "'Give Us the Ballot,' Address Delivered at the Prayer Pilgrimage for
Freedom." Washington, D.C., May 17, 1957. Martin Luther King, Jr. Research and Education Institute, Stanford University. https://kinginstitute.stanford.edu/king-papers
/documents/give-us-ballot-address-delivered-prayer-pilgrimage-freedom.

———. "Letter from Birmingham Jail." Letter to Bishop C. C. J. Carpenter, Bishop Joseph A.
Durick, Rabbi Milton L. Grafman, Bishop Nolan B. Harmon, the Rev. George H. Mur-
ray, the Rev. Edward V. Ramage, and The Rev. Earl Stallings, April 16, 1963. Martin Luther
King, Jr. Research and Education Institute, Stanford University. http://okra.stanford.edu
/transcription/document_images/undecided/630416-019.pdf.

Koran, Mario. "An Activist Gave Police Anti-Bias Training. Officers Still Brutalized Him at a
Protest." *The Guardian*, June 8, 2020. https://www.theguardian.com/us-news/2020/jun
/08/san-jose-police-shooting-implicit-bias.

Korgen, Kathleen, and Eileen O'Brien. "Black/White Friendships in a Color-Blind Society."

In *Mixed Messages: Multiracial Identities in the "Color-Blind" Era*, edited by David L. Brunsma, 253–270. Boulder, CO: Lynne Rienner, 2006.

Ksinan, Albert J., Alexander Y. Vazsonyi, Gabriela Ksinan Jiskrova, and James L. Peugh. "National Ethnic and Racial Disparities in Disciplinary Practices: A Contextual Analysis in American Secondary Schools." *Journal of School Psychology* 74 (June 2019): 106–125. DOI: 10.1016/j.jsp.2019.05.003.

Kurtzleben, Daniella. "Here's How Many Bernie Sanders Supporters Ultimately Voted For Trump." *National Public Radio*, August 24, 2017. https://www.npr.org/2017/08/24 /545812242/1-in-10-sanders-primary-voters-ended-up-supporting-trump-survey-finds.

Kutulas, Judy. *The American Civil Liberties Union and the Making of Modern Liberalism, 1930–1960*. Chapel Hill: University of North Carolina Press, 2014.

Ladner, Joyce A. *Tomorrow's Tomorrow: The Black Woman*. New York: Doubleday, 1971.

Laslett, Peter. *John Locke: Two Treatises of Government*. 2nd ed. Cambridge: Cambridge University Press, 1988.

Lichterman, Paul. "Piecing Together Multicultural Community: Cultural Differences in Community Building among Grass-Roots Environmentalists." *Social Problems* 42, no. 4 (November 1995): 513–534. https://doi.org/10.2307/3097044.

———. "Talking Identity in the Public Sphere: Broad Visions and Small Spaces in Sexual Identity Politics." *Theory and Society* 28 (February 1999): 101–141. https://doi.org/10.1023 /A:1006954611027.

Lieblich, Julia. "Harvard's History of Inscrutable Tenure Denials: Cornel West Is Only the Latest Scholar of Color the Ultra-Elite Institution Has Failed to Hold On To." *The Nation*, March 9, 2021. https://www.thenation.com/article/society/harvard-tenure-cornel-west/.

Manza, Jeff, and Ned Crowley. "Working Class Hero? Interrogating the Social Bases of the Rise of Donald Trump." *The Forum* 15, no. 1 (July 2017): 3–28. DOI 10.1515/for-2017-0002.

Martinez, Elizabeth. *De Colores Means All of Us: Latina Views for a Multi-Colored Society*. Boston: Southend Press, 1998.

Marx, Karl. "Economic and Philosophic Manuscripts of 1844." Marx-Engels Archive. Accessed June 7, 2021. https://www.marxists.org/archive/marx/works/download/pdf/Economic -Philosophic-Manuscripts-1844.pdf.

Marx, Karl, and Friedrich Engels. *The German Ideology*. Marx-Engels Archive. Accessed December 3, 2021. https://www.marxists.org/archive/marx/works/1845/german-ideology/

Marx, Karl, and Friedrich Engels. *Manifesto of the Communist Party*. Marx-Engels Archive. Accessed June 5, 2021. https://www.marxists.org/archive/marx/works/1848/communist -manifesto/ch01.htm.

McDermott, Nathan, and Em Steck. "Biden Repeatedly Pushed Bill in Senate That Critics Said Would Have Made Investigating Police Officers for Misconduct More Difficult." *CNN Politics*, June 10, 2020. https://www.cnn.com/2020/06/10/politics/biden-senate-police -officers-kfile/index.html.

McKinney, Karyn D., and Joe R. Feagin. "Diverse Perspectives on Doing Anti-Racism: The Younger Generation." In Doane and Bonilla-Silva, *White Out*, 253–270.

Melaku, Tsedale M. *You Don't Look Like a Lawyer: Black Women and Systemic Gendered Racism*. Lanham, MD: Rowman & Littlefield, 2019.

Melaku, Tsedale M., and Angie Beeman 2020. "Academia Isn't a Safe Haven for Conversations about Race and Racism." *Harvard Business Review*, June 25, 2020. https://hbr.org/2020 /06/academia-isnt-a-safe-haven-for-conversations-about-race-and-racism.

Melaku, Tsedale M., Angie Beeman, David G. Smith, and W. Brad Johnson. "Be a Better Ally: How White Men Can Help Their Marginalized Colleagues Advance." *Harvard Business Review* 98, no. 6 (November 2020): 135–139. https://hbr.org/2020/11/be-a-better-ally.

Merriam-Webster. "Woke." Accessed January 27, 2022. https://www.merriam-webster.com /dictionary/woke.

Merton, Robert K. *Sociological Ambivalence and Other Essays*. New York: Free Press, 1976.

Milkman, Ruth. *On Gender, Labor, and Inequality*. Chicago: University of Illinois Press, 2016.

Mills, Charles W. *The Racial Contract*. Ithaca, NY: Cornell University Press, 1997.

Mills, C. Wright. *The Power Elite*. New York: Oxford University Press, 1963.

Mishel, Lawrence, and Alyssa Davis. "Top CEOs Make 300 Times More Than Typical Workers." *Economic Policy Institute*, June 21, 2015. https://www.epi.org/publication/top-ceos -make-300-times-more-than-workers-pay-growth-surpasses-market-gains-and-the-rest-of -the-0-1-percent/.

Morgan, Ted. *Reds: McCarthyism in Twentieth-Century America*. New York: Random House, 2004.

Morgen, Sandra. *Into Our Own Hands: The Women's Health Movement in the United States, 1969–1990*. New Brunswick, NJ: Rutgers University Press, 2002.

Mulder, Catherine. *Transcending Capitalism through Cooperative Practices*. Basingstoke, UK: Palgrave Macmillan, 2015.

Myrdal, Gunnar. *An American Dilemma: The Negro Problem and Modern Democracy*. New York: Harper & Brothers, 1944.

Neubeck, Kenneth, and Noel A. Cazenave. *Welfare Racism: Playing the Race Card against America's Poor*. New York: Routledge, 2001.

Noe-Bustamante, Luis, Lauren Mora, and Mark Hugo Lopez. "About One-in-Four U.S. Hispanics Have Heard of Latinx, but Just 3% Use It." *Pew Research Center*, August 11, 2020. https://www.pewresearch.org/hispanic/2020/08/11/about-one-in-four-u-s-hispanics-have -heard-of-latinx-but-just-3-use-it/.

O'Brien, Eileen. "The Political Is Personal: The Influence of White Supremacy on White Antiracists' Personal Relationships." In Doane and Bonilla-Silva, *White Out*, 253–270.

———. *Whites Confront Racism: Antiracists and Their Paths to Action*. Lanham, MD: Rowman & Littlefield, 2001.

Oglesby, Carl. "Let Us Shape the Future." Speech, Washington, D.C., November 27, 1965. New Left Notes Document Archives. https://www.sds-1960s.org/sds_wuo/sds_documents /oglesby_future.html.

O'Kane, Caitlin. "'Say Their Names': The List of People Injured or Killed in Officer-Involved Incidents Is Still Growing." *CBS News*, June 8, 2020. https://www.cbsnews.com/news/say -their-names-list-people-injured-killed-police-officer-involved-incidents/.

Oliver, Melvin, and Thomas M. Shapiro. *Black Wealth/White Wealth: A New Perspective on Racial Inequality*. 2nd ed. New York: Routledge, 2006.

Oluo, Ijeoma. *So You Want to Talk about Race*. New York: Seal Press, 2018.

Pager, Devah, Bart Bonikowski, and Bruce Western. "Discrimination in a Low-Wage Labor Market: A Field Experiment." *American Sociological Review* 74, no. 5 (October 2009): 777–799. https://doi.org/10.1177/000312240907400505.

Parker, Kim, Rachel Minkin, and Jesse Bennett. "Methodology: The American Trends Panel Survey Methodology." *Pew Research Center*, September 24, 2020. https://www.pewresearch.org/social-trends/2020/09/24/covid-19-financial-hardships-methodology/.

Patillo-McCoy, Mary. "Church Culture as a Strategy of Action in the Black Community." *American Sociological Review* 63, no. 6 (December 1998): 767–784. https://doi.org/10.2307/2657500.

Paul, Deanna. "Jewelers Made a 'Take a Knee' Pun on a Billboard. Now They're Getting Death Threats." *Washington Post*, September 7, 2018. https://www.washingtonpost.com/business/2018/09/08/jewelers-made-take-knee-pun-billboard-now-theyre-getting-death-threats/.

Pennello, Áine. "Left for Dead, Rebounding from Attack." *MSNBC News*, February 9, 2017. https://www.msnbc.com/msnbc/watch/shot-left-for-dead-lesbian-teens-slow-recovery-367373379613.

Pierce, Jennifer. *Racing for Innocence: Whiteness, Gender, and the Backlash against Affirmative Action*. Stanford, CA: Stanford University Press, 2012.

Pierre, Jemima. "Black Immigrants in the United States and the 'Cultural Narratives' of Ethnicity." *Identities: Global Studies in Culture and Power* 11 (2004): 141–170. DOI: 10.1080/10702890490451929.

Piketty, Thomas. *Capital in the Twenty-First Century*. Cambridge, MA: Harvard University Press, 2014.

Piketty, Thomas, and Emmanuel Saez. "Income Inequality in the United States, 1913–1998." *Quarterly Journal of Economics* 118, no. 1 (February 2003): 1–41. https://doi.org/10.1162/00335530360535135.

Plumer, Brad. "What a Liberal Sociologist Learned from Spending Five Years in Trump's America." *Vox*, October 25, 2016. https://www.vox.com/2016/9/6/12803636/arlie-hochschild-strangers-land-louisiana-trump.

Pollock, Mica. *Colormute: Race Talk Dilemmas in an American School*. Princeton, NJ: Princeton University Press, 2004.

Rai, Candace. *Democracy's Lot: Rhetoric, Publics, and the Places of Invention*. Tuscaloosa: University of Alabama Press, 2016.

Ramamurthy, Anandi. "The Politics of Britain's Asian Youth Movements." *Race & Class* 48, no. 2 (October 2006): 38–60. https://doi.org/10.1177/0306396806069522.

Rampbell, Ed. "High Noon: The Rewrite." *The Nation*, September 19, 2002. https://www.thenation.com/article/archive/high-noon-rewrite/.

Ray, Ranita. "Race-Conscious Racism." *Social Problems* (forthcoming in 2022).

Redneck Revolt. "Redneck Revolt Organizing Principles." Accessed July 14, 2020. https://www.redneckrevolt.org/principles?fbclid=IwAR0MsuaVItsuXae6ke_uH7EBHpo_BKDV8rQEkjdCoeialYo_ch2C2qeS0DY.

Reilly, Katie. "Read Hillary Clinton's 'Basket of Deplorables' Remarks about Donald Trump Supporters." *Time*, September 10, 2016. https://time.com/4486502/hillary-clinton-basket-of-deplorables-transcript/.

Risman, Barbara J., and Pallavi Banerjee. "Kids Talking about Race: Tween-agers in a Post–
    Civil Rights Era." *Sociological Forum* 28, no. 2 (June 2013): 213–235. https://doi.org/10.1111
    /socf.12016.

Robertson, Katie. "Nikole Hannah-Jones Denied Tenure at University of North Carolina."
    New York Times, May 28, 2021. https://www.nytimes.com/2021/05/19/business/media
    /nikole-hannah-jones-unc.html.

Robinson, Cedric J. *Black Marxism: The Making of the Black Radical Tradition*. Chapel Hill:
    University of North Carolina Press, 1983.

Rockquemore, Kerry Ann. "For a Diverse Faculty, Start with Retention." *Inside Higher Ed*, Jan-
    uary 6, 2016. https://www.insidehighered.com/advice/2016/01/06/how-retain-diverse
    -faculty-essay.

Rodríguez-Silva, Ileana M. *Silencing Race: Disentangling Blackness, Colonialism, and National
    Identities in Puerto Rico*. New York: Palgrave Macmillan, 2012.

Roediger, David. *The Wages of Whiteness: Race and the Making of the American Working Class*.
    New York: Verso, 1991.

Rossinow, Doug. *Visions of Progress: The Left-Liberal Tradition in America*. Philadelphia: Uni-
    versity of Pennsylvania Press, 2008.

Royster, Deirdre. *Race and the Invisible Hand: How White Networks Exclude Black Men from
    Blue-Collar Jobs*. Berkeley: University of California Press, 2003.

Ruffins, Faith Davis. "A Faithful Witness: Afro-American Public History in Historical Per-
    spective, 1828–1984." In *Presenting the Past: Essays on History and the Public*, edited by
    Susan Porter Benson, Stephen Brier, and Roy Rosenzweig, 307–338. Philadelphia: Temple
    University Press, 1986.

Sandbrook, Dominic. *Eugene McCarthy: The Rise and Fall of Postwar American Liberalism*.
    New York: Alfred A. Knopf, 2004.

Sanders, Sam. "It's Time to Put Woke to Sleep." *NPR Weekend Edition*, December 30, 2018.
    https://www.npr.org/2018/12/30/680899262/opinion-its-time-to-put-woke-to-sleep.

Scahill, Jeremy. "Scholar Robin D. G. Kelley on How Today's Abolitionist Movement Can
    Fundamentally Change the Country." *The Intercept*, June 27, 2020. https://theintercept
    .com/2020/06/27/robin-dg-kelley-intercepted/.

Schrecker, Ellen. *Many Are the Crimes: McCarthyism in America*. Boston: Little Brown, 1998.

Schwartz, Ian. "Nina Turner vs. Hilary Rosen: 'How Dare You, as a White Woman' Tell Me
    How to Interpret MLK Jr." *RealClear Politics*, March 6, 2020. https://www.realclear
    politics.com/video/2020/03/06/nina_turner_vs_hilary_rosen_how_dare_you_as_a
    _white_woman_tell_me_how_to_interpret_mlk_jr.html?fbclid=IwAR2UCD0rHrv
    UWHW62rpX90eOMyWtQwfwokhoKRybt_AGpOrFA4VQFbkwJpk.

Shapiro, Illana. *Training for Racial Equity & Inclusion: A Guide to Selected Programs*. Washing-
    ton D.C.: Aspen Institute, 2002.

Shedd, Carla. *Unequal City: Race, Schools, and Perceptions of Injustice*. New York: Russell Sage,
    2015.

Simien, Evelyn. *Black Feminist Voices in Politics*. Albany: State University of New York Press,
    2006.

Smedley, Audrey. *Race in North America: Origin and Evolution of a Worldview*. 4th ed. Boul-
    der, CO: Westview Press, 2012.

Smith, David, and Eric Hanley. "The Anger Games: Who Voted for Donald Trump in the 2016 Election, and Why?" *Critical Sociology* 44, no. 2 (February 2018): 195–212. https://doi.org/10.1177/0896920517740615.

Smith, David, and W. Brad Johnson. *Good Guys: How Men can be Better Allies for Women in the Workplace.* Boston, MA: Harvard Business Review Press, 2020.

Smith, Dorothy E. *The Conceptual Practices of Power: A Feminist Sociology of Knowledge.* Boston: Northeastern University Press, 1990.

Smith, Robert C. *Racism in the Post–Civil Rights Era: Now You See It, Now You Don't.* Albany: State University of New York Press, 1995.

Smith, Sharon. *Subterranean Fire: A History of Working-Class Radicalism in the United States.* Rev. ed. Chicago: Haymarket Books. 2018.

Steinberg, Stephen. *The Ethnic Myth: Race, Ethnicity, and Class in America.* Boston: Beacon Press, 2001.

———. *Race Relations: A Critique.* Stanford, CA: Stanford University Press, 2007.

———. "The Role of Race in the Devolution of the Left." *Logos: A Journal of Modern Society and Culture* 10, no. 2 (2011). http://logosjournal.com/2011/the-role-of-race-in-the-devolution-of-the-left/.

Stolberg, Sheryl Gay. "For Democrats, Ilhan Omar Is a Complicated Figure to Defend." *New York Times,* April 16, 2019. https://www.nytimes.com/2019/04/16/us/politics/ilhan-omar-democrats.html.

Students for a Democratic Society, Archives and Resources. "America and the New Era." Paper for Students for a Democratic Society, 1103 East 63rd Street, New York, 1963. Accessed November 25, 2018. http://archive.lib.msu.edu/DMC/AmRad/americanewera.pdf.

Student Nonviolent Coordinating Committee. "Black Power." Position Paper for the SNCC Vine City Project, 142 Vine Street, Atlanta, 1966. Accessed May 7, 2019. http://freedom archives.org/Documents/Finder/DOC513_scans/SNCC/513.SNCC.black.power .summer.1966.pdf.

Sue, Derald Wing. *Race Talk and the Conspiracy of Silence: Understanding and Facilitating Difficult Dialogues on Race.* Hoboken, NJ: John Wiley & Sons, 2015.

Sullivan, Shannon. *Good White People: The Problem with Middle-Class White Anti-Racism.* Albany: State University of New York Press, 2014.

Surkin, Marvin, and Dan Georgakas. *Detroit: I Do Mind Dying; A Study in Urban Revolution.* Chicago: Haymarket Books, 1998.

Taylor, Keeanga-Yamahtta. *From #Blacklivesmatter to Black Liberation.* Chicago: Haymarket Books, 2016.

———. *How We Get Free: Black Feminism and the Combahee River Collective.* Chicago: University of Illinois Press, 2017.

Terborg-Penn, Rosalyn. *African American Women in the Struggle for the Vote.* Bloomington: Indiana University Press, 1998.

Thompson, Becky. *A Promise and a Way of Life: White Antiracist Activism.* Minneapolis: University of Minnesota Press, 2001.

Trepagnier, Barbara. *Silent Racism: How Well-Meaning White People Perpetuate the Racial Divide.* New York: Paradigm, 2010.

Truth, Sojourner. "Ain't I a Woman?" Speech, Women's Convention, Akron, Ohio, December

1851. Modern History Sourcebook. https://sourcebooks.fordham.edu/mod/sojtruth
-woman.asp.

Underhill, Megan R. "'Diversity Is Important to Me': White Parents and Exposure-to-
Diversity Parenting Practices." *Sociology of Race and Ethnicity* 5, no. 4 (October 2019):
486–499.

United States Census Bureau. "Profile of General Population and Housing Characteristics:
2010 Demographic Profile Data." Accessed January 6, 2020. Website redacted to preserve
anonymity of town name.

United States Government Accountability Office. "K-12 Education: Discipline Disparities for
Black Students, Boys, and Students with Disabilities," March 22, 2018. Accessed July 10,
2019. https://www.gao.gov/products/GAO-18-258.

Vigdor, Niel, Daniel Victor, and Christine Hauser. "Buffalo Police Officers Suspended after
Shoving 75-Year-Old Protester." *New York Times*, June 5, 2020. https://www.nytimes.com
/2020/06/05/us/buffalo-police-shove-protester-unrest.html.

Wagner, David. *Progressives in America, 1900–2020: Liberals with Attitude!* Bloomington, IN:
Author Solutions, 2020.

Walsh, Katherine Cramer. *Talking about Race: Community Dialogues and the Politics of Difference.* Chicago: University of Chicago Press, 2007.

Warfield, Zenobia Jeffries. "Why Redneck Revolt Says Deal with Racism First, Then Economics." *Yes Magazine*, November 29, 2017. https://www.yesmagazine.org/social-justice/2017
/11/29/why-redneck-revolt-says-deal-with-racism-first-then-economics/.

Waters, Mary C. "Optional Ethnicities: For Whites Only?" In *Origins and Destinies: Immigration, Race and Ethnicity in America,* edited by Sylvia Pedraza and Ruben Rumbaut, 444–
454. Belmont, CA: Wadsworth Press, 1996.

Weber, Max. *Economy and Society: An Outline of Interpretive Sociology.* Vol.2. Berkeley: University of California Press, 1978.

Wellman, David T. *Portraits of White Racism.* Cambridge: Cambridge University Press, 1993.

West, Cornel. *Race Matters.* New York: Vintage Press, 1994.

Whitford, Denise K. "School Discipline Disproportionality: American Indian Students in
Special Education." *Urban Review* 49, no. 5 (June 2017): 693–706. https://doi.org/10.1007
/s11256-017-0417-x.

Wilkins, Amy. "'Not Out to Start a Revolution': Race, Gender, and Emotional Restraint
among Black University Men." *Journal of Contemporary Ethnography* 41, no. 1 (February
2012): 34–65. https://doi.org/10.1177/0891241611433053.

Williams, Jakobi. *From the Bullet to the Ballot: The Illinois Chapter of the Black Panther and
Racial Coalition Politics in Chicago.* Chapel Hill: University of North Carolina Press, 2013.

Williams, Johnny E. *Decoding Racial Ideology in Genomics.* Lanham, MD: Lexington Books,
2016.

Williamson, Kevin D. "Chaos in the Family, Chaos in the State: The White Working Class's
Dysfunction." *National Review*, March 17, 2016. https://www.nationalreview.com/2016/03
/donald-trump-white-working-class-dysfunction-real-opportunity-needed-not-trump/.

Wilson, Carter A. *Racism: From Slavery to Advanced Capitalism.* Thousand Oaks, CA: Sage,
1996.

Wingfield, Adia Harvey. *Flatlining Race, Work, and Health Care in the New Economy.* Berkeley: University of California Press, 2019.

———. "Systemic Racism Persists in the Sciences." *Science* 369, no. 6502 (July 2020): 351. DOI: 10.1126/science.abd8825.

Wingfield, Adia Harvey, and Joe R. Feagin. *Yes We Can? White Racial Framing and the Obama Presidency.* 2nd ed. New York: Routledge, 2013.

Wise, Tim. "Motive and Opportunity: The Difference between White and 'Other' Racism." *ZNet*, February 12, 2001. http://www.timwise.org/2001/02/motive-and-opportunity-the -difference-between-white-and-other-racism/.

Wright, Erik Olin. *Approaches to Class Analysis.* Cambridge: Cambridge University Press, 2005.

———. *Class, Crisis, and the State.* New York: Schocken Books, 1978.

———. *Class Counts.* Cambridge: Cambridge University Press, 1997.

———. *Classes.* New York: Verso, 1985.

———. *Class Structure and Income Determination.* New York: Academic Press, 1979.

Wright, Erik Olin, Uwe Becker, Johanna Brenner, Michael Burawoy, Val Burris, Guglielmo Carchedi, Gordon Marshall, Peter F. Meiksins, David Rose, Arthur Stinchcombe, and Philippe Van Parijs. *The Debate on Classes.* New York: Verso, 1989.

X, Malcolm. "Malcolm X Speech, 1963." Digital History: Using Technology to Enhance Teaching and Research. Accessed May 19, 2016. http://www.digitalhistory.uh.edu/disp _textbook.cfm?smtid=3&psid=3619&fbclid=IwAR2a1L95Ks5KjBwolwjNbTeeNe8BXXg 6lRumf6fK-aI1-VX9ZDhK602OIqA.

Yancy, George. "Should I Give Up on White People?" *New York Times*, April 16, 2018. https:// www.nytimes.com/2018/04/16/opinion/white-racism-threats.html.

Zinn, Howard, and Anthony Arnove. *Voices of a People's History of the United States.* 2nd ed. Toronto, ON: Seven Stories Press, 2004.

INDEX

Page numbers in italics indicate figures; those with a *t* indicate tables.

Addams, Jane, 30, 48
AFL-CIO, 31
African Americans, 11, 12, 38, 48, 106–8; church culture and, 140n10; in colonial Virginia, 15–18; during COVID-19 pandemic, 116; interracial marriage with, 16, 49; minstrel shows and, 11; as targets of school discipline, 62; during World War II, 53
Allen, Theodore, 3, 15
allyship, 117–22
American Civil Liberties Union (ACLU), 31
American Indians, 11, 16, 62, 115, 118
Americans for Democratic Action (ADA), 30, 31
antiracists, 3, 37–41, 101, 117–18, 123
appropriation of success, 66t, 80, 83, 100
Arbery, Ahmaud, 113
Asian Americans, 119; internment camps of, 53; violence against, 121
asthma, 88, 94, 98
Atwater, Lee, 18–19
authoritarianism, 52; school discipline as, 61–63, 114

Bacon's Rebellion (1676), 16
Baldwin, James, 38, 41–42, 110
Banerjee, Pallavi, 22
Benwell, Bethan, 39
Biden, Joe, 26–27, 113, 122, 123

biologization of culture, 20
Black feminism, 4–5, 62, 114, 116. *See also* gender equality
Black Lives Matter, 115–16; founding of, 113; Movement for Black Lives and, 13, 56, 115–17; racism-centered intersectionality and, 113–14
Black Panthers, 83, 113, 121; Du Bois and, 53; Kochiyama on, 53; rainbow coalition of, 43, 135n70; white working-class supporters of, 49–51; Young Patriots and, 50–51, 57
Black Power, 21, 38, 62
Bland, Sandra, 113
Bobo, Lawrence, 4
Boggs, Grace Lee, 121
Bonilla-Silva, Eduardo, 4, 19–20
book clubs, 34t, 39, 40, 125
Bourdieu, Pierre, 48
Brown, Michael, 113
bullying, 62, 65t, 66t, 75, 114
Bush, George W., 99
Bush, Melanie E. L., 12
Bush, Roderick, 2–3, 32

capitalism, 33–37, 34t; Marx on, 5, 33, 37; Occupy Wall Street movement and, 55, 56; Redneck Revolt and, 51; slavery and, 3–4, 16–18, 92, 105, 106
Carmichael, Stokely, 21, 53–54; on white liberals, 38
Carnes, Nicholas, 46
Carr, Leslie G., 19
caste systems, 6

9 780820 362281